A WORK OF HEART

HOW JEWISH PRAYER UNITES HEAVEN AND EARTH

–

AUTHORS
Rabbi Yosi Wolf
Rabbi Baruch Shalom Davidson
Rabbi Lazer Gurkow
Rabbi Shmuel Super

EDITOR
Rabbi Mordechai Dinerman

INSTRUCTOR ADVISORY BOARD
Mrs. Malky Bitton
Mrs. Shula Bryski
Mrs. Rochel Holzkenner
Mrs. Shaindy Jacobson
Mrs. Leah Rosenfeld
Mrs. Yehudis Wolvovsky

CURRICULUM COORDINATOR
Mrs. Rivki Mockin

ROSH CHODESH SOCIETY ADMINISTRATOR
Mrs. Chana'le Dechter

Printed in the United States of America
© Published and Copyrighted 2024 by
Rosh Chodesh Society
832 Eastern Parkway, Brooklyn, NY 11213

(888) YOUR-JLI/718-221-6900 ext. 212 or 603
www.myRCSociety.com

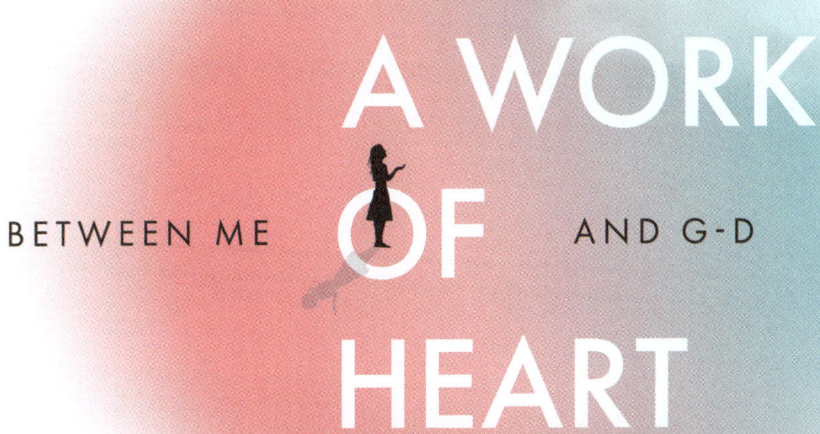

A WORK OF HEART

BETWEEN ME AND G-D

HOW JEWISH PRAYER
UNITES HEAVEN AND EARTH

STUDENT TEXTBOOK

ADVISORY BOARD *of* GOVERNORS

Yaakov and Karen Cohen
Potomac, MD

Yitzchok and Julie Gniwisch
Montreal, QC

Barbara Hines
Aspen, CO

Ellen Marks
S. Diego, CA

David Mintz, OBM
Tenafly, NJ

George Rohr
New York, NY

Dr. Stephen F. Serbin
Columbia, SC

Leonard A. Wien, Jr.
Miami Beach, FL

PARTNERING FOUNDATIONS

Beinoni Foundation

David Samuel Rock Foundation

Diamond Foundation

Estate of Elliot James Belkin

Francine Gani Charitable Fund

Goldstein Family Foundation

The Harvey L. Miller Family Foundation

Kohelet Foundation

Kosins Family Foundation

Leticia and Eduardo Azar Foundation

Lion Heritage Fund at Rose Foundation

Meromim Foundation

Myra Reinhard Family Foundation

Robbins Family Foundation

Ruderman Family Foundation

Schulich Foundation

William Davidson Foundation

World Zionist Organization

Yehuda and Anne Neuberger Philanthropic Fund

Zalik Foundation

PRINCIPAL BENEFACTOR

George Rohr
New York, NY

PILLARS *of* JEWISH LITERACY

Shaya and Sarah Boymelgreen
Miami Beach, FL

Pablo and Sara Briman
Mexico City, Mexico

Zalman and Mimi Fellig
Miami Beach, FL

Edwin and Arlene Goldstein
Cincinnati, OH

Yosef and Chana Malka Gorowitz
Redondo Beach, CA

Shloimy and Mirele Greenwald
Brooklyn, NY

Dr. Vera Koch Groszmann
S. Paulo, Brazil

Carolyn Hessel
New York, NY

Edward and Inna Kholodenko
Toronto, ON

David and Debra Magerman
Gladwyne, PA

Yitzchak Mirilashvili
Herzliya, Israel

David and Harriet Moldau
Longwood, FL

Ben Nash
Sunny Isles Beach, FL

Eyal and Aviva Postelnik
Marietta, GA

Clive and Zoe Rock
Irvine, CA

Michael and Fiona Scharf
Palm Beach, FL

Lee and Patti Schear
Dayton, OH

Isadore and Roberta Schoen
Fairfax, VA

SPONSORS

Moshe and Rebecca Bolinsky
Long Beach, NY

Dr. Stephen and Bella Brenner
New York, NY

Rabbi Meyer and Leah Eichler
Brooklyn, NY

Steve and Esther Feder
Los Angeles, CA

Yoel Gabay
Brooklyn, NY

Dr. Gerald Gilbert Glass
Sunrise, FL

Shmuel and Sharone Goodman
Chicago, IL

Marc Kulick
New York, NY

Michael and Andrea Leven
Atlanta, GA

Joe and Shira Lipsey
Aspen, CO

Josef Michelashvili
Glendale, NY

Rachelle Nedow
El Paso, TX

Peter and Hazel Pflaum
Newport Beach, CA

Abraham Podolak
Princeton Junction, NJ

Dr. Ze'ev and Varda Rav-Noy
Los Angeles, CA

Arthur Isaac Resetschnig
Vienna, Austria

Zvi Ryzman
Los Angeles, CA

Larry Sifen
Virginia Beach, VA

Myrna Zisman
Cedarhurst, NY

Janice and Ivan Zuckerman
Coral Gables, FL

The Rohr Jewish Learning Institute
gratefully acknowledges the pioneering support of

George & Pamela Rohr

Since its inception, the Rohr JLI has been a beneficiary of the vision, generosity, care, and concern of the Rohr family.

In the merit of the hundreds of thousands of hours of Torah study by JLI students worldwide, may they be blessed with health, *Yiddishe nachas* from all their loved ones, and extraordinary success in all their endeavors.

THE 5785 ROSH CHODESH SOCIETY COURSE,
A WORK OF HEART, IS DEDICATED
IN LOVING MEMORY OF

Miriam Mintz, OBM

לעילוי נשמת **מרים** ע"ה
בת יבלחט"א **גרשון פנחס**
ד' מנחם אב, תשפ"ד

An exceptional human being and a teacher of special education par excellence, she taught, inspired, and uplifted thousands of students.

Appointed as a *shluchah*, her love and understanding of Torah and Chasidic insight permeated her entire being—always evident in her genuine care for every Jew and visible in her actions every day of her life.

Miriam treasured the gift of connecting with her Creator, cherishing every opportunity for prayer with heartfelt embrace.

The ever-present joyful smile on her beautiful face captivated, encouraged, and strengthened everyone she encountered.

Miriam yearned to build a family and to fulfill the mission of "ושננתם לבניך—You shall teach them diligently to your children." – *Deuteronomy 6:7*

The *Sifrei* writes: "Disciples are called offspring."

The collective Torah study around the world is achieving Miriam's wish. May her global family of students merit to multiply in ever-increasing measure.

May her steadfast spirit and determination continue to inspire and teach us how to surmount every obstacle and achieve every goal.

May her memory stand as a source of blessing and inspiration, and may her light continue to shine.

—

May her dear husband, parents, parents-in-law, and all their loved ones merit the immediate fulfillment of "והקיצו ורננו שוכני עפר—Arise and awake . . . and sing. . . ." – *Isaiah 26:19*

May they go from strength to strength and enjoy health, happiness, *nachas*, and success in all their endeavors, לאורך ימים ושנים טובות.

Dedicated by the family of *shluchim* and *shluchos* worldwide, whose *shlichus* has benefited so greatly through our partnership with JLI

Table of Contents

From The Director's Desk

Dear Rosh Chodesh Society Fellow,

It gives me great pleasure to welcome you to the Rosh Chodesh Society's newest course, *A Work of Heart: Between Me and G-d—How Jewish Prayer Unites Heaven and Earth.* I am honored, privileged, and delighted that you have chosen to join us in this wonderful course of Torah study. With three hundred RCS chapters across the world participating in this curriculum, you are now united with thousands of Jewish women who share a common bond of heritage and sisterhood. Most notably, you are a vital link in the unbreakable chain of our family, maintained by our collective Torah learning, each of us driven to attain a greater state of spiritual sensitivity, personal enlightenment, and the performance of good deeds.

I am excited to spend the year together, learning about how prayer is far more than an instinctive appeal or a regulated duty. *A Work of Heart* will fling the cover off the prayer book, the prayer services, and the synagogue to expose the beating heart of prayer that breathes beneath it all.

Together with your phenomenal instructor, you will delve into the fascinating wisdoms, mystical truths, clarity of purpose, and wondrous structure underlying Jewish prayer and its soulful journey.

It is my sincerest hope and prayer that your life will be enriched by these teachings based on the Torah's injunction to "serve G-d with all your heart," (Deuteronomy 11:13) and that you will be gifted with meaning and serenity to fully inhabit the sacred space where Heaven and earth unite.

Jewish prayer is an art and an opportunity, an enriching exercise, and a journey of self-discovery: a transformative tool and a productive part of life, a perspective changer, and a moment of self-empowerment. And, like every specialized art, prayer must be learned. I am so grateful that we can learn it together. I encourage you to consider inviting others to join us as we soar on the wings of prayer.

There is nothing more powerful than the force of Jewish women united in Torah study and heartfelt prayer. Thank you for keeping our nation strong, proud, and protected.

With respect, blessing, and heartfelt prayers for the Jewish people and our Holy Land,

Shaindy Jacobson
Director, Rosh Chodesh Society
18 Elul, 5784

LESSON ONE

A WORK OF SOUL

A NEW PARADIGM FOR PRAYER

Prayer often gets a bad rap: Dialogue with the Unseen seems unrealistic, prayer gobbles vital time, petitioning is for the needy, prayer services are confusing, etc. This lesson reveals that the core of prayer in Judaism is the soul's craving for a deep and meaningful personal connection with G-d, and demonstrates how to meet this goal through prayer.

I. Setting the Course

Exercise 1.1

1. Why do you pray?

for thanking & asking

2. What do you find difficult about prayer?

hope it reaches Hashem

3. What are you looking for in this course?

Understanding prayer
what to pray for?

II. Personal Connection with G-d

Text 1

I SAMUEL 1:1-2, 10-11, 13

וַיְהִי אִישׁ אֶחָד מִן הָרָמָתַיִם צוֹפִים מֵהַר אֶפְרָיִם, וּשְׁמוֹ אֶלְקָנָה . . .
וְלוֹ שְׁתֵּי נָשִׁים, שֵׁם אַחַת חַנָּה וְשֵׁם הַשֵּׁנִית פְּנִנָּה, וַיְהִי לִפְנִנָּה יְלָדִים
וּלְחַנָּה אֵין יְלָדִים . . .

וְהִיא מָרַת נָפֶשׁ, וַתִּתְפַּלֵּל עַל ה' וּבָכֹה תִבְכֶּה. וַתִּדֹּר נֶדֶר וַתֹּאמַר:
"ה' צְבָאוֹת! אִם רָאֹה תִרְאֶה בָּעֳנִי אֲמָתֶךָ, וּזְכַרְתַּנִי, וְלֹא תִשְׁכַּח אֶת
אֲמָתֶךָ, וְנָתַתָּה לַאֲמָתְךָ זֶרַע אֲנָשִׁים, וּנְתַתִּיו לַה' כָּל יְמֵי חַיָּיו" . . .

וְחַנָּה הִיא מְדַבֶּרֶת עַל לִבָּהּ, רַק שְׂפָתֶיהָ נָּעוֹת, וְקוֹלָהּ לֹא יִשָּׁמֵעַ.

There was a man from Ramataim-Tzofim, in the hill country of Ephraim. His name was Elkanah. . . . He had two wives: one named Chanah and the other Peninah. Peninah had children, but Chanah was childless. . . .

Chanah was embittered. She prayed to G-d and wept profusely. She vowed, "G-d of the many Heavenly and worldly beings! Look upon Your servant's misery and remember me. Do not forget Your servant, and give me a son. If You do this I will dedicate him to G-d all the days of his life. . . ."

Chanah was praying in her heart. Her lips were moving, but her voice was silent.

SAMUEL

Biblical book. The Book of Samuel relates the history of the Jewish people during the lifetime of the prophet Samuel and the reigns of the first Jewish kings, Saul and David, in the 9th and 10th centuries BCE. Samuel wrote the descriptions of the events of his lifetime, and the book was completed by the prophets Gad and Nathan. The book has been artificially divided into I Samuel and II Samuel, but it is essentially one book.

Text 2

PSALMS, CH. 23

מִזְמוֹר לְדָוִד, ה' רֹעִי לֹא אֶחְסָר. בִּנְאוֹת דֶּשֶׁא יַרְבִּיצֵנִי, עַל מֵי מְנֻחוֹת יְנַהֲלֵנִי. נַפְשִׁי יְשׁוֹבֵב, יַנְחֵנִי בְמַעְגְּלֵי צֶדֶק לְמַעַן שְׁמוֹ. גַּם כִּי אֵלֵךְ בְּגֵיא צַלְמָוֶת לֹא אִירָא רָע כִּי אַתָּה עִמָּדִי, שִׁבְטְךָ וּמִשְׁעַנְתֶּךָ הֵמָּה יְנַחֲמֻנִי. תַּעֲרֹךְ לְפָנַי שֻׁלְחָן נֶגֶד צֹרְרָי, דִּשַּׁנְתָּ בַשֶּׁמֶן רֹאשִׁי, כּוֹסִי רְוָיָה. אַךְ טוֹב וָחֶסֶד יִרְדְּפוּנִי כָּל יְמֵי חַיָּי, וְשַׁבְתִּי בְּבֵית ה' לְאֹרֶךְ יָמִים.

A psalm by David:

G-d is my shepherd; I lack nothing.

He lies me down in green meadows; He leads me beside still waters.

He calms my soul; He leads me upon upright paths to show His care.

Even when I walk in the valley of the shadow of death, I fear no harm, for You are with me. Your rod and Your staff, they comfort me.

[I am confident that] you will yet set a laden table before me, in full view of my enemies. You have anointed my head with oil; my cup overflows.

May only goodness and kindness pursue me all the days of my life. May I sit in the house of G-d for the length of my days.

PSALMS

Biblical book. The Book of Psalms contains 150 psalms expressing praise for G-d, faith in G-d, and laments over tragedies. The primary author of the psalms was King David, who lived in the 9th century BCE. Psalms also contains material from earlier figures. The feelings and circumstances expressed in the psalms resonate throughout the generations, and they have become an important part of communal and personal prayer.

Text 3

RABBI YISRAEL BAAL SHEM TOV, *KETER SHEM TOV*, P. 57

מָשָׁל שֶׁהִכְרִיז הַמֶּלֶךְ בְּיוֹם שִׂמְחָתוֹ: כָּל מִי שֶׁיְּבַקֵּשׁ דָּבָר מִן הַמֶּלֶךְ יְמַלְאוּ לוֹ בַּקָּשָׁתוֹ.

וְיֵשׁ מִי שֶׁבִּיקֵּשׁ שְׂרָרָה וְכָבוֹד, וְיֵשׁ שֶׁבִּיקֵּשׁ עוֹשֶׁר, וְנָתְנוּ לְכָל אֶחָד מְבוּקָּשׁוֹ.

וְהָיָה שָׁם חָכָם אֶחָד שֶׁאָמַר שֶׁשְּׁאֵלָתוֹ וּמְבוּקָּשׁוֹ שֶׁיְּדַבֵּר הַמֶּלֶךְ בְּעַצְמוֹ עִמּוֹ ג׳ פְּעָמִים בְּיוֹם, וְהוּטַב מְאֹד בְּעֵינֵי הַמֶּלֶךְ, מֵאַחַר שֶׁדִּיבּוּרוֹ חָבִיב עָלָיו מִן עוֹשֶׁר וְכָבוֹד, לָכֵן יְמוּלָּא בַּקָּשָׁתוֹ שֶׁיִּתְּנוּ לוֹ רְשׁוּת לִיכָּנֵס בְּהֵיכָלוֹ לְדַבֵּר עִמּוֹ, וְשָׁם יִפְתְּחוּ לוֹ הָאוֹצָרוֹת שֶׁיִּקַּח מִן עוֹשֶׁר וְכָבוֹד גַּם כֵּן.

A king once decreed that on his day of celebration, anyone who would request something from him would have their request granted.

One person asked for power and glory; another asked for wealth. Each person's request was granted.

There was one wise man who requested that he be given the opportunity to speak with the king three times a day. The king was very impressed that this man valued speaking with him more than riches and glory. The king therefore fulfilled this man's request and allowed him to enter his chamber thrice daily to speak with him. The king also gave the man access to his treasuries, bestowing him with riches and glory as well.

RABBI YISRAEL BAAL SHEM TOV (BESHT)
1698–1760

Founder of the Chasidic movement. Born in Slutsk, Belarus, the Baal Shem Tov was orphaned as a child. He served as a teacher's assistant and clay digger before founding the Chasidic movement and revolutionizing the Jewish world with his emphasis on prayer, joy, and love for every Jew, regardless of their level of Torah knowledge.

Text 4

THE REBBE, RABBI MENACHEM MENDEL SCHNEERSON, *LIKUTEI SICHOT* 2, P. 410

דִי גֶענוֹיֶע אִיבֶּערְזֶעצוּנְג פוּן "פְּרֵייֶער" - אוֹיף לָשׁוֹן הַקוֹדֶשׁ אִיז - בַּקָשָׁה, אָבֶּער בַּיי אִידְן הֵייסְט עֶס נִיט מִיטְן נָאמֶען בַּקָשָׁה נָאר מִיטְן נָאמֶען תְּפִלָּה.

דֶער אוּנְטֶערְשֵׁייד פוּן בַּקָשָׁה בִּיז תְּפִלָּה אִיז אוֹיךְ אַ הָפְכִית'דִיקֶער:

בַּקָשָׁה מֵיינְט בֶּעטְן, אוּן תְּפִלָּה מֵיינְט בַּאהֶעפְטְן זִיךְ.

בַּקָשָׁה אוּנְטֶערְשְׁטְרַייכְט – בֶּעטְן, מֶען בֶּעט בַּיי דֶעם אוֹיבֶּערְשְׁטְן עֶר זָאל גֶעבְּן - מִלְמַעֲלָה לְמַטָּה - דָאס וָואס עֶס פֶּעלְט. בִּשְׁעַת עֶס פֶּעלְט נִיט אָדֶער עֶס אִיז נִיטָא קֵיין רָצוֹן אוֹיף אַ זַאךְ, אִיז נִיט שַׁיָיךְ קֵיין בַּקָשָׁה.

תְּפִלָּה אוּנְטֶערְשְׁטְרַייכְט – בַּאהֶעפְטְן זִיךְ מִיטְן אוֹיבֶּערְשְׁטְן מִלְמַטָּה לְמַעֲלָה. דָאס אִיז שַׁיָיךְ בַּיי אַלֶעמֶען אוּן אַלֶעמָאל . . .

דֶערְפַאר אִיז אוֹיךְ בַּיי דִי וֶועלְכֶע עֶס פֶּעלְט זֵיי גָארְנִישְׁט, פַּארַאן – אוּן מִיט דֶער גַאנְצֶער שְׁטַארְקַייט - דִי זַאךְ פוּן תְּפִלָּה, וַוייל תְּפִלָּה אִיז נִיט נָאר גֶעבֶּעט אוּן בַּקָשָׁה, נָאר דֶער עִיקָר – דֶער אָפְּפְּרִישׁ פוּן דֶעם פַארְבּוּנְד אוּן דְבֵיקוּת פוּן אִים מִיטְן אוֹיבֶּערְשְׁטְן.

The precise Hebrew equivalent for the English word *prayer* is *bakashah*. Yet, in Jewish tradition, the word *tefilah* is preferred.

These two words—*bakashah* and *tefilah*—imply two very different (even opposite) conceptions of prayer:

While *bakashah* means *to request*, *tefilah* means *to connect*.

Bakashah implies a request of G-d to grant us (in a top-down manner) something that we lack. If, however, we neither lack nor desire anything, there is no need for *bakashah*, an entreaty.

RABBI MENACHEM MENDEL SCHNEERSON 1902–1994

The towering Jewish leader of the 20th century, known as "the Lubavitcher Rebbe," or simply as "the Rebbe." Born in southern Ukraine, the Rebbe escaped Nazi-occupied Europe, arriving in the U.S. in June 1941. The Rebbe inspired and guided the revival of traditional Judaism after the European devastation, impacting virtually every Jewish community the world over. The Rebbe often emphasized that the performance of just one additional good deed could usher in the era of Mashiach. The Rebbe's scholarly talks and writings have been printed in more than 200 volumes.

By contrast, *tefilah* involves connecting with G-d (in a bottom-up manner). Such an activity remains relevant for all people, at all times....

A person might lack nothing in life and nevertheless prayer—in its fullest sense—remains relevant to them. For prayer is not merely a method of conveying requests. Primarily, prayer is the renewal of the bond between an individual and G-d.

Text 5

THE REBBE, RABBI MENACHEM MENDEL SCHNEERSON, IBID.

יֶעדֶער אִיד הָאט אַ נְשָׁמָה וָואס זִי אִיז פַּארְבּוּנְדְן מִיטְן אוֹיבֶּערְשְׁטְן. אָבֶּער מִצַּד דֶעם וָואס דִי נְשָׁמָה אִיז אַרָאפּ אִין גוּף אוּן פַּארְבּוּנְדְן מִיט אִים, מוּז דִי נְשָׁמָה פַּארְבִּינְדְן זִיךְ מִיט גוּפְנִיוּת'דִיקֶע עִנְיָנִים אֲזוֹי וִוי עֶסְן, טְרִינְקֶען אוּן דָאס גְלַייכְן, וָואס אִין דֶער צַייט וֶוערְט אָפְּגֶעשְׁוַואכְט אִיר פַּארְבּוּנְד מִיטְן אוֹיבֶּערְשְׁטְן.

אוּן אוֹיף דֶעם זַיינֶען פַּארַאן גֶעוִויסֶע צַייטְן אִין טָאג אוֹיף תְּפִלָּה, בִּכְדֵי צוּ בַּאנַייעֶן דֶעם פַּארְבּוּנְד מִיטְן אוֹיבֶּערְשְׁטְן, אוּן פַּארְשְׁטַארְקְן אִים.

Every Jew possesses a G-dly soul that is connected to G-d. But, due to the soul's descent and investment into the body, the soul becomes bogged down by the body's needs like eating, drinking, etc. Over time, this weakens the G-dly soul's connection with G-d.

The daily times of prayer, meaning *connection*, serve to renew and strengthen the G-dly soul's connection with G-d.

III. Prayer Meditation

Text 6

PSALMS 69:14 (RECITED IN THE MORNING PRAYERS)

וַאֲנִי תְפִלָּתִי לְךָ ה' עֵת רָצוֹן, אֱלֹקִים בְּרָב חַסְדֶּךָ עֲנֵנִי בֶּאֱמֶת יִשְׁעֶךָ

May my prayer to You, L-rd, be at a propitious time; G-d, in Your abounding kindness, answer me with true deliverance.

Takeaway Exercise

Connecting. Set aside sixty seconds for a brief prayer, with your focus exclusively on seeking to connect with G-d through this exercise. It can be done at home, in a synagogue, or at any location or setting that you consider conducive and appropriate.

We'll discuss how it went during the next lesson.

Key Points

1. Prayer is deeply personal and profoundly individualistic. It is the way a person expresses their deepest thoughts and feelings, in conversation, to G-d. The rituals associated with prayer aren't intended to diminish this.

2. The word *tefilah* implies that there is more to prayer than just making requests of G-d. Prayer is also a time to connect. Even if a person feels that there's nothing they need to tell G-d, prayer, in the sense of connection, is still relevant to them. This—developing one's connection with G-d—is one of the goals of daily prayer.

3. The G-dly soul is a stranger in this world. It yearns for spiritual experience and closeness to G-d. Prayer is its chance. Prayer nourishes the G-dly soul and fills it with spiritual stamina.

4. The prayer book is intended to facilitate—not replace—personal prayer. It is meant to guide our thoughts and articulate our feelings. When we use it properly, its words become our own.

Appendices

Text 7

MAIMONIDES, *MISHNEH TORAH*, LAWS OF PRAYER 1:4-6

כֵּיוָן שֶׁגָּלוּ יִשְׂרָאֵל בִּימֵי נְבוּכַדְנֶצַּר הָרָשָׁע, נִתְעָרְבוּ בְּפָרַס וְיָוָן וּשְׁאָר הָאֻמּוֹת, וְנוֹלְדוּ לָהֶם בָּנִים בְּאַרְצוֹת הַגּוֹיִם. וְאוֹתָן הַבָּנִים נִתְבַּלְבְּלָה שְׂפָתָם, וְהָיְתָה שְׂפַת כָּל אֶחָד וְאֶחָד מְעֹרֶבֶת מִלְּשׁוֹנוֹת הַרְבֵּה. וְכֵיוָן שֶׁהָיָה מְדַבֵּר, אֵינוֹ יָכוֹל לְדַבֵּר כָּל צְרָכוֹ בְּלָשׁוֹן אַחַת אֶלָּא בְּשִׁבּוּשׁ, שֶׁנֶּאֱמַר: "וּבְנֵיהֶם חֲצִי מְדַבֵּר אַשְׁדּוֹדִית, וְאֵינָם מַכִּירִים לְדַבֵּר יְהוּדִית, וְכִלְשׁוֹן עַם וָעָם" (נְחֶמְיָה יג, כד).

וּמִפְּנֵי זֶה, כְּשֶׁהָיָה אֶחָד מֵהֶם מִתְפַּלֵּל, תִּקְצַר לְשׁוֹנוֹ לִשְׁאֹל חֲפָצָיו, אוֹ לְהַגִּיד שֶׁבַח הַקָּדוֹשׁ בָּרוּךְ הוּא בִּלְשׁוֹן הַקֹּדֶשׁ, עַד שֶׁיְּעָרְבוּ עִמָּהּ לְשׁוֹנוֹת אֲחֵרוֹת.

וְכֵיוָן שֶׁרָאָה עֶזְרָא וּבֵית דִּינוֹ כָּךְ, עָמְדוּ וְתִקְּנוּ לָהֶם שְׁמוֹנֶה עֶשְׂרֵה בְּרָכוֹת עַל הַסֵּדֶר: שָׁלוֹשׁ רִאשׁוֹנוֹת שֶׁבַח לַה', וְשָׁלוֹשׁ אַחֲרוֹנוֹת הוֹדָיָה, וְאֶמְצָעִיּוֹת יֵשׁ בָּהֶן שְׁאֵלַת כָּל הַדְּבָרִים — שֶׁהֵן כְּמוֹ אָבוֹת לְכָל חֶפְצֵי אִישׁ וָאִישׁ, וּלְצָרְכֵי הַצִּבּוּר כֻּלָּן, כְּדֵי שֶׁיִּהְיוּ עֲרוּכוֹת בְּפִי הַכֹּל, וְיִלְמְדוּ אוֹתָן, וְתִהְיֶה תְּפִלַּת אֵלּוּ הָעִלְּגִים תְּפִלָּה שְׁלֵמָה כִּתְפִלַּת בַּעֲלֵי הַלָּשׁוֹן הַצָּחָה.

When the Jewish people were exiled in the times of the wicked Nebuchadnezzar, they became interspersed in Persia and Greece and other countries. The children they raised in these foreign countries weren't proficient in any single language; their language was a concoction of many. In the words of the verse, "And their children spoke in both Ashdodite and in other languages. They did not know how to speak the Jewish language" (NEHEMIAH 13:24).

RABBI MOSHE BEN MAIMON (MAIMONIDES, RAMBAM)
1135-1204

Halachist, philosopher, author, and physician. Maimonides was born in Córdoba, Spain. After the conquest of Córdoba by the Almohads, he fled Spain and eventually settled in Cairo, Egypt. There, he became the leader of the Jewish community and served as court physician to the vizier of Egypt. He is most noted for authoring the *Mishneh Torah*, an encyclopedic arrangement of Jewish law; and for his philosophical work, *Guide for the Perplexed*. His rulings on Jewish law are integral to the formation of Halachic consensus.

Consequently, when it came to prayer, these people were unable to adequately request their needs or praise G-d in Hebrew unless they would complement their prayers with other languages.

When Ezra and his court saw this, they established the Amidah prayer, which consists of eighteen blessings. The first three blessings are praises of G-d, and the last three are thanksgiving. The intermediate twelve blessings are requests for all types of matters. They serve as general categories for all the specific requests of both the individual and the community.

The people could thus easily learn these prayers and recite them fluently, enabling them to pray with the same degree of eloquence as those people who did have command over the language.

Text 8

RABBI BACHYA IBN PAKUDAH, *CHOVOT HALEVAVOT* 8:3

וְדַע, כִּי הַמִּלּוֹת תִּהְיֶינָה בַּלָּשׁוֹן וְהָעִיּוּן בַּלֵּב, וְהַמִּלּוֹת כְּגוּף לַתְּפִלָּה וְהָעִיּוּן כְּרוּחַ. וּכְשֶׁיִּתְפַּלֵּל הַמִּתְפַּלֵּל בִּלְשׁוֹנוֹ, וְלִבּוֹ טָרוּד בִּזּוּלַת עִנְיַן הַתְּפִלָּה, תִּהְיֶה תְּפִלָּתוֹ גּוּף בְּלֹא רוּחַ וּקְלִיפָּה בְּלֹא לֵב, מִפְּנֵי שֶׁגּוּפוֹ נִמְצָא וְלִבּוֹ בַּל עִמּוֹ עֵת תְּפִלָּתוֹ . . .

וּלְפִי שֶׁהָיְתָה מַחְשֶׁבֶת הַלֵּב מִתְהַפֶּכֶת הַרְבֵּה, וְאֵין לָהּ קִימָה לַמְּהִירוּת עֲבוּר הַהִרְהוּרִים עַל הַנֶּפֶשׁ, הָיָה קָשֶׁה עָלֶיהָ לְסַדֵּר עִנְיָנֵי הַתְּפִלָּה מֵעַצְמָהּ, תִּקְּנוּ אוֹתָם רַבּוֹתֵינוּ זִכְרוֹנָם לִבְרָכָה בְּמִלִּים מְתוּקָּנוֹת, יְסַדְּרֵם הָאָדָם בִּלְשׁוֹנוֹ, מִפְּנֵי שֶׁמַּחְשֶׁבֶת הַנֶּפֶשׁ הוֹלֶכֶת אַחַר הַמַּאֲמָר וְנִמְשֶׁכֶת אֶל הַדִּבּוּר.

וְהָיְתָה הַתְּפִלָּה מִלּוֹת וְעִנְיָנִים, וְהַמִּלּוֹת צְרִיכוֹת אֶל הָעִנְיָן וְהָעִנְיָן אֵינוֹ צָרִיךְ אֶל הַדִּבּוּר.

Know that the words of prayer should be on the tongue and its correlating meditation in the heart. For, while words are the body of prayer, meditation is its spirit. But when one prays with just their tongue, and their heart is distracted, the prayer is like a body without a spirit; a shell without a kernel. For, during this person's prayer, the body is present, but the heart is not. . . .

Maintaining focus during prayer is difficult, and it is for this reason that the rabbis established the liturgy of the prayer book. The words of the prayer book engage a person's thoughts and thus help the individual to maintain focus.

Prayer is a composite of words and the content they express. The words need the content, but the content does not need the words.

RABBI BACHYA IBN PAKUDAH
11TH CENTURY

Moral philosopher and author. Ibn Pakudah lived in Muslim Spain, but little else is known about his life. *Chovot Halevavot* (*Duties of the Heart*), his major work, was intended to be a guide for attaining spiritual perfection. Originally written in Judeo-Arabic and published in 1080, it was later translated into Hebrew and published in 1161 by Judah ibn Tibbon, a scion of the famous family of translators. Ibn Pakudah had a strong influence on Jewish pietistic literature.

Text 9

RABBI YOSEF YITZCHAK SCHNEERSOHN,
KUNTRES TORAT HACHASIDUT, PP. 6–7

עוּבְדָא הֲוָה בִּימֵי מוֹרֵנוּ הַבַּעַל שֵׁם טוֹב נִשְׁמָתוֹ עֵדֶן, אֲשֶׁר הָיָה קִטְרוּג שֶׁל כְּלָיָה, רַחֲמָנָא לִצְלָן, עַל אַחַת הַקְּהִלּוֹת, וּכְשֶׁרָאָה מוֹרֵנוּ הַבַּעַל שֵׁם טוֹב אֶת כּוֹבֶד הַמַּצָּב הִרְבָּה בִּתְפִלָּה וּבְתַחֲנוּנִים בְּרֹאשׁ הַשָּׁנָה וּבְיוֹם הַכִּפּוּרִים.

וַיְהִי בְּעֵת תְּפִלַּת נְעִילָה הִכִּירוּ הַתַּלְמִידִים הַקְּדוֹשִׁים בִּתְפִלַּת מוֹרֵנוּ הַבַּעַל שֵׁם טוֹב אֲשֶׁר מַצָּבוֹ שֶׁל הַקִּטְרוּג, רַחֲמָנָא לִצְלָן, הוּא רְצִינִי בִּמְאוֹד, וְיִתְאַמְּצוּ גַּם הֵם בִּתְפִלּוֹת תַּחֲנוּנִים בִּבְכִיּוֹת עֲצוּמוֹת מֵעוּמְקָא דְלִבָּא.

כִּרְאוֹת מִתְפַּלְּלֵי בֵּית הַכְּנֶסֶת בְּעֶזְרַת יִשְׂרָאֵל וּבְעֶזְרַת נָשִׁים אֲשֶׁר מוֹרֵנוּ הַבַּעַל שֵׁם טוֹב וְתַלְמִידָיו הַקְּדוֹשִׁים עוֹדָם עוֹמְדִים עַל עָמְדָם מִתְחַזְּקִים וּמִתְאַמְּצִים בִּתְפִלָּתָם, הֵבִינוּ כּוּלָּם כִּי הַמַּצָּב נוֹרָא הוּא, וַיִּבְכּוּ הָאֲנָשִׁים וְהַנָּשִׁים מֵעוֹמֶק נְקוּדַּת לְבָבָם בִּבְכִיּוֹת עֲצוּמוֹת, וַיְהִי רַעַשׁ גָּדוֹל.

זֶה אֵיזֶה שָׁנִים, אֲשֶׁר בָּחוּר עִבְרִי בֶּן כְּפַר רוֹעֶה צֹאן וּבָקָר, בָּא לוֹ לְיָמִים הַנּוֹרָאִים לְבֵית הַכְּנֶסֶת שֶׁל מוֹרֵנוּ הַבַּעַל שֵׁם טוֹב, וּבִהְיוֹתוֹ בּוּר גָּמוּר הָיָה עוֹמֵד מַקְשִׁיב וּמִסְתַּכֵּל בִּפְנֵי הַחַזָּן בְּאֵין אוֹמֵר וּדְבָרִים.

כְּכַפְרִי הָיָה רָגִיל בְּקוֹל בְּהֵמוֹת, הָעִזִּים, הַכְּבָשִׂים, הַצִּפּוֹרִים, וְהָעוֹפוֹת, וְהֶחָשׁוּב בֵּינֵיהֶם הָיָה אֶצְלוֹ קוֹל הַתַּרְנְגוֹל בִּקְרִיאָתוֹ. וּבִרְאוֹתוֹ הַהִתְרַגְּשׁוּת הַגְּדוֹלָה אֲשֶׁר בְּבֵית הַכְּנֶסֶת, וּבְשָׁמְעוֹ הַבְּכִיּוֹת בְּעֶזְרַת יִשְׂרָאֵל וּבְעֶזְרַת נָשִׁים הַצְּעָקוֹת הַנּוֹרָאוֹת, הִנֵּה גַּם לְבָבוֹ נִשְׁבַּר בְּקִרְבּוֹ, וַיִּקְרָא בְּקוֹל גָּדוֹל: "קוּקִי-רֶעקָא-הָאן, גָ-ט הָאבְּ רַחֲמָנוּת!"

בְּהִשָּׁמַע בְּבֵית הַכְּנֶסֶת קוֹל הַקּוֹרֵא כְּתַרְנְגוֹל, נִבְהֲלוּ הָעוֹמְדִים בְּעֶזְרַת יִשְׂרָאֵל וְנִפְחֲדוּ הַשּׁוֹמְעוֹת בְּעֶזְרַת נָשִׁים, וְלֹא יָדְעוּ מִי הוּא

RABBI YOSEF YITZCHAK SCHNEERSOHN (RAYATZ, FRIERDIKER REBBE, PREVIOUS REBBE) 1880–1950

Chasidic rebbe, prolific writer, and Jewish activist. Rabbi Yosef Yitzchak, the 6th leader of the Chabad movement, actively promoted Jewish religious practice in Soviet Russia and was arrested for these activities. After his release from prison and exile, he settled in Warsaw, Poland, from where he fled Nazi occupation and arrived in New York in 1940. Settling in Brooklyn, Rabbi Schneersohn worked to revitalize American Jewish life. His son-in-law Rabbi Menachem Mendel Schneerson succeeded him as the leader of the Chabad movement.

הַקּוֹרֵא, וּכְשָׁמְעָם הַצְּעָקָה "גָ-ט הָאבּ רַחֲמָנוּת", רָאוּ כִּי הַבָּחוּר הַכַּפְרִי הִשְׁמִיעַ קוֹלוֹ.

אֲחָדִים מֵהַמִּתְפַּלְּלִים אֲשֶׁר עָמְדוּ אֵצֶל הַכַּפְרִי גָּעֲרוּ בוֹ לְהַשְׁתִּיקוֹ וְחָפְצוּ לְגָרְשׁוֹ. וַיֹּאמֶר אֲלֵיהֶם: "גַּם אָנֹכִי יְהוּדִי, וֵאלֹקֵיכֶם הוּא גַם אֱלוֹקַהּ שֶׁלִּי". הַשַּׁמָּשׁ הַזָּקֵן רַבִּי יוֹסֵף יוֹזְפָּא הִרְגִּיעַ אֶת רוּחָם שֶׁל הַמִּתְפַּלְּלִים, וַיֹּאמֶר לְהַכַּפְרִי כִּי יִשָּׁאֵר עַל מְקוֹמוֹ כְּבַתְּחִלָּה.

כַּעֲבוּר רְגָעִים אֲחָדִים אַחַר הַמְאוֹרָע עִם בֶּן הַכַּפְרִי, נִשְׁמַע קוֹלוֹ שֶׁל מוֹרֵנוּ הַבַּעַל שֵׁם טוֹב, וְאַחֲרָיו הַתַּלְמִידִים הַקְּדוֹשִׁים הַמְמַהֲרִים לְסַיֵּים תְּפִלַּת הַשְּׁמוֹנֶה עֶשְׂרֵה בִּנְעִילָה, וּפְנֵי קֹדֶשׁ הַבַּעַל שֵׁם טוֹב נָהֲרוּ מְגִיל. בִּנְעִימָה מְיוּחֶדֶת הִתְחִיל מוֹרֵנוּ הַבַּעַל שֵׁם טוֹב חֲזָרַת הַשָּׁלִיחַ צִבּוּר בִּתְפִלַּת נְעִילָה, וּבְהִתְעוֹרְרוּת מְיוּחֶדֶת אָמַר פְּסוּקֵי הַיִּחוּד שְׁמַע יִשְׂרָאֵל, בָּרוּךְ שֵׁם, ה' הוּא הָאֱלֹקִים. וַיָּשִׁיר מוֹרֵנוּ הַבַּעַל שֵׁם טוֹב שִׁירֵי שִׂמְחָה.

כְּשֶׁבֶת מוֹרֵנוּ הַבַּעַל שֵׁם טוֹב עִם תַּלְמִידָיו הַקְּדוֹשִׁים בִּסְעוּדַת מוֹצָאֵי יוֹם כִּפּוּרִים הוֹאִיל לְסַפֵּר כָּל פְּרָטֵי עִנְיְנֵי הַקִּטְרוּג, רַחֲמָנָא לִצְלָן, שֶׁהָיָה — לֹא עָלֵינוּ — עַל עֵדָה בְּיִשְׂרָאֵל, וְכַאֲשֶׁר הִתְאַמֵּץ בִּתְפִלָּתוֹ לְעוֹרֵר רַחֲמֵי שָׁמַיִם עַל הָעֵדָה, הִנֵּה פָּגַשׁ, רַחֲמָנָא לִצְלָן, קִטְרוּג גָּדוֹל עָלָיו, עַל אֲשֶׁר מִשְׁתַּדֵּל לְהוֹשִׁיב בְּנֵי יִשְׂרָאֵל בִּכְפָרִים וּבְפָרָשַׁת דְּרָכִים, אֲשֶׁר יְכוֹלִים הֵם לִלְמוֹד חַס וְשָׁלוֹם מִשְּׁכֵנֵיהֶם.

כְּשֶׁהִתְחִילוּ לִבְדּוֹק בְּמַעֲשֵׂיהֶם וּמַצָּבָם שֶׁל אַנְשֵׁי הַכְּפָר, רָאִיתִי אֲשֶׁר הַמַּצָּב הוּא קָשֶׁה בִּמְאֹד וְהָיִיתִי בְּכָל רָע, אַךְ לְפֶתַע פִּתְאוֹם נִשְׁמַע בַּמָּרוֹם קוֹל קְרִיאָתוֹ שֶׁל בֶּן הַכְּפָר הַתָּם, "קוּקוּ-רֶעקָא-הָאן, גָ-ט הָאבּ רַחֲמָנוּת!" אֲשֶׁר קְרִיאָה תְּמִימָה זוֹ גָּרְמָה קוֹרַת רוּחַ לְמַעְלָה עַד רוּם הַמַּעֲלוֹת. וּבָטְלוּ הַקִּטְרוּגִים מֵעַל הָעֵדָה וּמֵעָלַי.

Once, in the times of the Baal Shem Tov, a Heavenly decree of destruction was issued against a certain community. The Baal Shem Tov sensed the gravity of the decree and prayed fervently that year on Rosh Hashanah and Yom Kippur.

During the Ne'ilah prayers [the concluding prayers of Yom Kippur], the Baal Shem Tov continued to pray intensely. His students sensed the desperateness of the situation, and they, too, prayed intensely, weeping from the depths of their hearts.

The rest of the congregants in the synagogue, both men and women, upon seeing the intensity of the prayers of the Baal Shem Tov and his students, understood that the situation was dire. They, too, burst into tears and cried out their hearts in prayer.

For the past few years, a certain Jewish farm boy from the countryside had been coming to the Baal Shem Tov's synagogue for the Days of Awe. This boy was completely illiterate (and unable to pray from the prayer book), so he would stand silently and listen, and he would watch the face of the cantor.

Being a farm boy, he was familiar with all kinds of animal sounds and had a particular liking for the rooster's cry. The great storm of emotion in the synagogue and the weeping of the men and women broke his heart. He called out aloud, "*Cuckoo-ree-koo-hon!* G-d have mercy!"

The men and women in the synagogue were taken aback. Who had called that out? But when they heard, "G-d have mercy!" they realized that it was the country boy.

Some of the congregants standing near the boy admonished him and tried silencing him. They wanted to remove him from the synagogue. The boy pleaded, "I, too, am a Jew, and we both have the same G-d." The old synagogue secretary, Rabbi Yosef Yozpa, calmed the congregants and allowed the boy to remain in his place.

A few moments after this incident, the Baal Shem Tov and his students proceeded to conclude the silent Amidah of the Ne'ilah prayer. The Baal Shem Tov's face shone with joy. He began the repetition of the Amidah with a special melody. He recited the verses of "Hear O Israel," "Blessed is the name," and "The L-rd is G-d" with great excitement. He followed these verses by singing joyous songs.

At the meal to break the fast after Yom Kippur, the Baal Shem Tov explained the entire story to his students:

"There was a terrible decree against a certain community. When I tried to intercede, I discovered that I, too, was the subject of a negative Heavenly decree, due to my initiative of creating Jewish communities in remote farm areas, where the members of these communities could be negatively influenced by their neighbors.

"When the Heavenly court began to examine the conduct of the Jewish farm people, I realized that I was in trouble. But suddenly, the call of '*Cuckoo-ree-koo-hon!* G-d have mercy!' of this farm boy was heard on High. This wholehearted cry brought G-d tremendous pleasure, causing Him to nullify the decrees that hung over that community and over me."

TECHINOT

Historically, Jewish women have always had a special relationship with prayer. Beyond the standard texts of formal prayer, Jewish women in Europe developed an entire literature of personal prayers known as *techinot* (traditionally pronounced *tchines*), supplications.

Usually written by women and printed for a female audience, these prayers in the vernacular Yiddish supplement the formal daily and festival prayers and address specific occasions and lifecycle events. Many of the *techinot* deal with issues specific to women, and they all provide a personal and intimate window into female Jewish spirituality and piety.

The first collections of *techinot* were published in the seventeenth century, and the genre remains popular until today in the original Yiddish as well as in Hebrew and English translations.

Every lesson in *A Work of Heart* has an appendix containing one or two of these traditional women's prayers, with a translation into English. A brief biographical note is provided for those authors whose identity is known.

A *TECHINA* FOR **THE FAMILY**

A Naye Shas Techinah **(Vilna), pp. 14–15**

Rabbi Yaakov Gordon, trans., *Techinos*
(Jerusalem: Feldheim Publishers, 2011), pp. 8–12

Titled "A Naye Yerushalayim Techinah—A New *Techinah* from Jerusalem," this *techinah* is a prayer for health and blessings for one's family. The *techinah* is preceded by a note: "This precious *techinah* was written by an exceedingly righteous woman from Jerusalem and is intended for daily recitation either before or after the regular prayers."

A New Techinah from Jerusalem

To the Eternal, the G-d of Yisrael, Who rests His Presence upon the Keruvim, my G-d and the G-d of my fathers, I beseech You from the depth of my heart to have mercy on me as a father has mercy on his children. Listen to my petition and save me from all evil; guide me on a straight path and accept the supplications which I present before You each day from the depth of my heart. Do not turn away my prayers unanswered. Enable me and my husband and children to always serve Your holy service.

Merciful King, have mercy on me and on all the people in my household. Do not act toward us with the attribute of strict judgment, but rather, with the attribute of mercy. Remove Your wrath from us and listen to our supplications when we call out to You. Help us with all our needs and make us happy by fulfilling all our wants. Grant the requests that we ask of Your holy Name and help us as You helped our forefathers when they cried out to You while enslaved in Egypt.

Give us children who are good and righteous, who will be pious and learned, and may my husband and I be privileged to raise them for Your holy service. May they find favor in Your eyes and in the eyes of all who behold them. Give us many years with much happiness so that we can witness their joy and great honor.

I ask of You, mighty and awesome G-d, the Eternal, Who is all powerful, merciful, and kind, the King Who is King of kings and the Master of all

א נייע ירושלים תחינה

בשם ה' אלקי ישראל יושב הכרובים, דו גאט פון מיינע עלטערן, איך טו דיך בעטן מיטן גאנצן הארצן, דו זאלסט זיך איבער מיר דערבארעמען כרחם אב על בנים, אזוי ווי א פאטער דערבארעמט זיך איבער זיינע קינדער, און הער מיין געבעט, און היט מיך פון אלע בייזן, און פיר מיך אין דעם רעכטן וועג, און פארנעם מיין געבעט, וואס איך טו אלע טאג בעטן מיט מיין גאנצן הארצן, און לאז מיך נישט אומקערןליידיק מיט מיין תפילה. און לאז מיך מיט מיין מאן און קינדער לעבן צו דיין הייליקן דינסט.

מלך רחמים, דו דערבארעמדיקער קעניג דערבארעם דיך איבער מיר און איבער אלע די מייניקע, און באנעם זיך נישט מיט אונז חלילה מיט מידת הדין, נאר מיט מידת הרחמים, און טו אפ דיין צארן פון אונז, און דערהער אונזער געבעט אלע מאל ווען מיר טוען דיר רופן.

העלף אונז אין אלע אונזערע נויטן, דערפריי אונז מיט וואס מיר ווילן, און זיי ממלא אונזערע בקשות וואס מיר פארלאנגען פון דיין הייליקן נאמען, און זאלסט אונז העלפן אזוי ווי דו האסט געהאלפן אונזערע עלטערן אין זייער גרויסן און שווערן פיין אין מצרים, און גיב מיר גוטע און פרומע קינדער, וואס זאלן זיין צדיקים און חסידים און תלמידי חכמים, און איך זאל זוכה זיין צו דערציען זיי צו דיין הייליקן דינסט, און זיי זאלן האבן חן און חסד אין דיינע אויגן און אין די לייט'ס אויגן, און מיר זאלן אויסלעבן אונזערע

יארן אין גרויס פרייד, און מיר זאלן זוכה זיין אויסצוגעבן אונזערע קינדער בכבוד גדול.

איך בעט דיך, דו אלמאכטיקער גאט, בארמהארציקער פאטער, הער, איבער אלע הערן, אז דו זאלסט הערן אלע מיינע תפילות, און דו זאלסט היטן מיך און מיין מאן און מיינע קינדער פון אלע בייזן, דו זאלסט מיך דערפרייען ווי דו האסט אונזער מוטער חנה עליה השלום דערפרייט מיט דאס וואס זי האט באגערט פון דיין הייליקן נאמען.

מלך רחמים דו דערבארימדיקער פאטער, קעניג פון דער וועלט, איך טו דיר רופן טאג און נאכט. אלע טעג פון לעבן פארלאז אונז נישט, און גיב אונז פרנסה און אלע אונזער באדערפעניש פון דיין הייליקע געטרייע מילדע האנט, און נישט חלילה דורך לייט הילף, און גיב אונז אלע באדערפיניש בנחת און נישט מיט צער, און לאז מיר זוכה זיין צו לעבן ביז הונדערט יאר מיט מיין מאן און קינדער צו זיצן ביי מיין טיש, און מיר זאלן האבן גוטע מליצים לעולם הבא.

מלך מלכי המלכים הקדוש ברוך הוא, איך טו דיר אנרופן אין אלע צייטן, דען דו ביסט נאר איין גאט, און דא ביסט מיין שפייזער, און דו גיבסט מיר אלע מיינע באדערפינשן, און דא האסט מיך דערנערט און געשפייזט און דערצויגן פון מיין יוגנט אן ביז היינטיקן טאג. היט מיך און מיין מאן און קינדער פון א מיתה משונה, און זאלסט אונז געדענקען און אלע צייטן, און אונז אנשרייבן צו א גוט יאר, צו לאנג לעבן אויף דער וועלט. זאלסטו אונז געדענקען שטענדיק צו גוטן און צו א בענטשונג, און זאלסט אונזערע תפילות אלע צייטן דערהערן, אזוי ווי דו האסט געהערט די תפילה פון מנשה מלך יהודה. און זאלסט אונז תפילה נישט פארשעמען און נישט לאזן אומקערן זיך ליידיק פון דיר, דען דו ביסט דער גאט וואס הערט אלע געבעטן פון די וואס רופן מיטן גאנצן הארצן, אמן, וכן יהי רצון.

masters, to listen to all of our prayers and supplications. Protect me, my husband, and my children from all evil, and accept my prayer just as You accepted the prayer of Chanah, and You fulfilled the request that she asked of Your holy Name.

King of mercy, King of the world, I call to You, do not abandon us! Provide for our livelihood and all our needs from Your broad and full hands, and not from the hands of men, G-d forbid. Give us all that we need easily, and without hardship. May my husband and I merit long life and may we see our children "like olive saplings" around our table, and may they be good advocates for us in the next world.

King, the King of kings, the Holy One, Blessed is He, I call out before You, for You alone are our G-d and there is no one but You. You are the One Who feeds us and provides for all our needs, and from the time I was created and until now, You have fed me and raised me. Protect me and my husband and children from early and abnormal death, and remember us for good and for blessing each day. Listen to our prayers always and do not turn away from them. May they not return unanswered from before You, for You hearken to the prayers of those who plead before You with all their heart. Amen, and may it be Your will.

ADDITIONAL READING

Prayers, Synagogue, Worshippers

By Herman Wouk

HERMAN WOUK, PHD, 1915–2019

American novelist and playwright. Wouk was born in New York City to a Jewish-Russian immigrant family. When the U.S. entered World War II, he joined the Navy, serving in the Pacific Theater for four years. Wouk's wartime experiences gave him the material and background for his bestseller and Pulitzer-Prize-winner, *The Caine Mutiny*. *This Is My G-d* was his best-selling affirmation of faith in traditional Judaism, penned after much self-examination and exposure to many secular influences. His later works included the novel *Inside, Outside*, which discusses Judaism in private life and in politics, and *The Will to Live On: This Is Our Heritage*.

A VISIT TO THE SYNAGOGUE

Even the most convinced unbeliever is likely to have an occasional religious mood or fancy, no matter how much he may disapprove of it; as the most devoted husband feels an unwanted stir of pleasure now and then when a pretty girl passes by. Nature will win out. The human impulse—if the secularist prefers, the human weakness—that has created and perpetuated religion is not absent from any breast. In such a passing religious moment, the Jewish skeptic may go so far as to wander into a synagogue to see what the faith of his fathers has to offer him.

He is handed a prayer book that strikes him as a jumble, with English translations that for long stretches make little sense. He is apt to observe preoccupied and inattentive worshippers reeling off Hebrew with few external symptoms of devotion, or whispering together while a reader chants a long singsong. Now and then everybody stands, he cannot say why, and there is a mass chant, he cannot say what; or if he dimly recalls it from childhood, he cannot find it in the prayer book. The time comes when the Holy Scroll is taken from the Ark for a parade to the reading desk, the bells tinkling on its silver crown. The reading in a strange Oriental mode seems endless, and he observes that it seems endless to some other worshippers too, who slump in an unfocussed torpor, or chat, or even sleep. If there is a sermon, especially from a young rabbi, the chances are that it is a digest of articles from the past week's liberal newspapers and magazines, with a few references to the Bible. The skeptic leaves—early, if he can—well satisfied that his views are sound, that his religious fancy was a temporary touch of melancholia, and that if the Jewish G-d exists, there is no reaching him through the synagogue.

The experience will be somewhat different, probably, if he happens into a synagogue so old-fashioned that its rabbi is a bearded ancient who speaks Yiddish. In that case the worshippers may seem more fervid in their devotions, though no less apt to chat now and then. The sermon—if the visitor remembers his Yiddish—is likely to strike at least a momentary response from him with vivid racy imagery, with insights into life that are curiously phrased but dig deep. He may leave with a wisp of regret for days and ways that are done; for of course there is no reviving Yiddish as a community tongue or teaching it to his children, who probably attend a progressive private school.

All this presumes a visit to a traditional synagogue. Conservative and Reform temples, with some differences in manner and custom, offer parts of the same substance. When the whole has no good effect on him, we can assume that parts probably will not either.

A NIGHT AT THE OPERA

The reader will perhaps remember, in this connection, his first visit to the opera. The chances are that he went sometime in his late teens or early twenties, urged on by an enthusiastic companion, perhaps female. The chances are, too, that he was skeptical about grand opera and suspected it might all be an elaborate boring fraud, a dead transplanted art form which American snobs and phonies pretended to enjoy because going to the opera was a high-class European habit. For all I know, this is the present opinion of opera that many of my readers hold.

But those who have changed their minds will recall that they did not do so on their first visit. Then, on the contrary, they probably saw confirming evidence of their suspicions. Fat old men slumped asleep in the boxes, their stiff shirts buckling; their wives more interested in the clothes and faces in the other boxes than in the stage performance; soulful creatures needing haircuts standing in the back of the orchestra, or squatting on the floor, in self-conscious poses of rapture; on the stage a fat screechy woman pretending to be a demure little country bride, a little man with a potbelly and short jerking arms impersonating Don Juan, a chorus of aging painted ladies, and men with ridiculous matchstick legs in tight hose, making tired clumsy gestures at acting now and then; while the orchestra tootled and tinkled without cease one monotonous kind of sugary noise; that, in all likelihood, was his first impression of one of the miracles of human inspiration, Mozart's *Don Giovanni*.

Sir Thomas Beecham once said that *Don Giovanni* has never had an adequate performance—that is, a troupe of singers capable of singing it, and an audience equipped to hear it. The run of singing artists does not produce in one generation enough voices to match Mozart's demands. The people who fill an opera house on any night are—people; some wonderful, some ordinary, some stupid, some insufferable, some dragged there by wives, some coming there to prove they are intelligent, some coming out of habit, some to tell the folks back home that they saw a New York opera, and some who love Mozart as they love the sunlight, and who are willing to endure all the coarseness and failure of another performance for the sake of the shafts of lovely light that despite all will break through now and then.

As performers and audience cannot usually rise to Mozart, the rabbi and his congregation cannot usually rise to Moses. That does not mean that the law of Moses is less sublime than world opinion acknowledges it to be, or that the forms of popular worship it has inspired are not capable of carrying its message down the years. The fact is that the synagogue, for all its human weaknesses, has done so. Every synagogue at every service has worshippers to whom the words and the ceremonies are transfusions of strength and intelligence; perhaps a few, perhaps many. The visitor's quick look cannot go inside their heads and hearts; in the good phrase of the jazz addicts, he does not dig what he is seeing.

WHAT THE SYNAGOGUE IS

The synagogue began as a kind of popular law school well over two thousand years ago. In classic synagogue architecture there are always study tables placed where the light is best. The tables have become vestigial or have disappeared in many American structures, as the synagogue, with the rest of Judaism, has undergone the dislocation of a shift of hemispheres. It is a pretty good guess that where an old rabbi sermonizes in Yiddish the tables will still be found; and the old rabbi will be found at one or another table with his followers, expounding the law.

It is a social axiom of Judaism—like our American doctrine that all men are created equal, which we know to be romantic, but which nevertheless stands as our working ideal—that all Jews are law students, commencing their studies at five. From this course in Torah law nobody graduates. Advanced students become rabbis; that is, literally, teachers. But in the Jewish diction rabbis do not teach; they learn with their students. One says quite literally of a master of the Talmud, "He knows how to learn." The theoretical norm of Jewish conduct includes enough labor in the marketplace to support one's family, the rest of one's time going to the law. Since this norm operates for perhaps one percent of Jewry, it is a somewhat abnormal norm; admirably intellectual, perhaps, but not geared to the distribution curve of human traits. Nevertheless, as a working ideal it deeply stamps our institutions and our manners.

It determines, for instance, the liturgy and the atmosphere of the synagogue; what we do there, and the way we do it. The very heart of synagogue practice is the reading of the Torah, week by week, in fifty-two sections, so that once a year in perpetuity we review and discuss our whole statutory law.

When the First Temple fell and the great daily service in Jerusalem stopped, the vacuum at the core of the religion might have brought on a total collapse. But Jewry, with the regenerative power that is its magic, created a new institution. In the houses of law study that existed everywhere in Judea and Babylon, the Jews took to offering devotions like those that had gone with the priestly ceremonies, adding prayers for an end to the exile and a restoration of the Temple. The house of study evolved into a house of worship. It kept its character as the law school of the masses, but services became fixed in its pattern.

The Second Temple revived Jewish life in the Holy Land, but much of Jewry remained in Babylon. The synagogue held its place as a center of worship as well as of study. When the Romans levelled the Second Temple, the synagogue became the fortress of the faith, the place where Jews gathered, learned the law, and prayed; the intellectual fortress, and in times of attack often the physical fortress.

In this form, the institution successfully traversed twenty centuries.

Naturally, such an immense stretch of time left its marks. The liturgy kept gathering layers of new devotions. A simple structure became overlaid with additions from Bible and Talmud, and with fresh compositions by rabbis of different centuries. Copyists and printers tended to cut nothing that had once been added, for that approached sacrilege. The prayer books became steadily longer, the Hebrew more difficult—pure, clear Hebrew is usually ancient—and the forms more complicated. By the nineteenth century, a morning festival service contained enough material to take up, if spoken with due attention, six or seven hours. The habit of racing through prayers arose. When I was a boy, I marveled at the ability of the adults in the synagogue to proceed at such breakneck speed through difficult medieval poetry. I looked forward to the day when I too would have such mastery of Hebrew and such powers of concentration. Now I know that nobody has such powers.

A change in such a state of affairs had to come. The Reform movement tore the liturgy to bits, retained a few fragments translated into German—later into English—and that was that. The Conservatives kept more of the liturgy and more Hebrew, but drastically modified or cut out prayers and ceremonies going back to Temple times. In the traditional synagogue there has been a slow process of bringing the prayer book back to its classic form. More and more we tend to skip the cabalistic acrostics of the Middle Ages, which not one worshipper in a thousand can understand—though those who do maintain that they are deep and lovely—and to give more time and attention to the pure and transparent Hebrew of the prayers that come down from the oldest times, that are the core of the service, and that anyone who knows even a little Hebrew can easily say.

This process is not a smooth one. Old pietists naturally dig in against omission of any prayers they have come to know. Youngsters can hardly be trained to handle the essential liturgy in the time given to Hebrew study. The mere machinery of an American religious center—membership drive, building drive, committee meetings, men's club, sisterhood, youth league, and so forth—tends to overwhelm all. The young rabbi comes out of his ordination with a head full of Talmudic lore and plunges into a vortex where everybody is an authority: the synagogue's president, the chairlady of the sisterhood, or even a novelist who pokes into the Talmud now and then. He is told to comment on the news; not to comment on the news; that he speaks above the people's heads; that he is debasing himself to the popular level; that a modern rabbi must be a social leader, a fundraiser, an inspirational orator, a jolly good fellow, a passable card player, and a pious figure no less awe-inspiring than his bearded forebears in the old country; and in this whirl of contradictions and impasses he must spend his days and gain his bearings. The wonder is that we still have young rabbis, that the number of synagogues is increasing, and that the outlines of a stable modern service are appearing. The vitality of Judaism is the reason. While controversy waxes over the coming shape of the tree, the old tree slowly and steadily puts out its new branches. And as the French say, the more it changes the more it becomes what it was.

THE CREED AND THE SERVICE

At the heart of all our liturgies—the forty minutes of an ordinary Tuesday morning, as well as the twelve solid hours of the Day of Atonement—lie two devotions. I will call them the Creed and the Service, to indicate their nature. In the synagogue their names are the *Sh'ma* and the *Shmone Esrai*—that is, literally, Hear, and The Eighteen.

Around these two key prayers cluster excerpts from the classics of Jewish literature and law: the Torah, the Prophets, the Psalms, the Talmud: for the synagogue remains, as it always was, a study hall. The worshipper, repeating the day's prayers, traverses the main fields of Judaic learning, fulfilling his formal duty of perpetual study.

The two basic prayers are short. The Creed itself you can say in a few seconds, the Service in a few minutes. A worshipper pressed for time, reciting these two devotions, performs the ritual of Hebrew worship; for the Sh'ma is the essence of our law, and The Eighteen is the link between the synagogue and the ancient Temple. The full texts of both are in a note to this chapter, so the reader who is wholly strange to the prayer book can know what they are.

The Sh'ma contains the one verse of Scripture that probably every Jew in the world knows by heart, or has at least heard often, Deuteronomy 6:4:

> ***Hear, O Israel, the L-rd our G-d, the L-rd is One.***

The observant Jew says it in the morning and at nightfall every day of his life, with three related passages from the Torah. It is the first Hebrew sentence a child learns, and it is the utterance with which every Jew is supposed to breathe his last.

On this point I will obtrude a short personal anecdote. I used to wonder whether, in the last extremity, a man could really call to mind and recite the Creed. Then once during a typhoon in the Pacific I was almost blown off the deck of a ship, and I remember quite clearly thinking, as I went sliding toward my fate, "Well, if I drown, let me say the Sh'ma as I go." Luckily for me the lifeline I grabbed happened to hold; and so I postponed the utterance, and the world has a few plays and novels it could well have wagged along without, and the patient reader is enduring the present harangue. I believe there are one or two literary critics who may wish I had gotten to say that watery Sh'ma, but I cannot help that, a man hangs on if he can.

The Service is an extremely old litany of eighteen blessings. A nineteenth was added in Talmudic times; and on Sabbaths and festivals there are only seven; but The Eighteen is still what everybody calls the devotion. There are three Eighteens, morning and afternoon and evening, to parallel the Temple rites.

MUST PRAYER BE IN HEBREW?

The first tractate of the Talmud, Benedictions, fixes the times and customs of saying the Sh'ma, does the same for The Eighteen, and then develops the blessings for all occasions of life. The antiquity of the Creed and the Service is evident in the matter-of-fact way the Talmud discusses them.

Benedictions lays down the rule that one should bless the Creator for every good in this world; and it even contains a remarkable blessing on evil news. Perhaps the most startling passage in it, for a modern reader, is an open authorization to pray in English, that is, in any language one understands. The popular notion is that English prayer is a shattering heresy. Our common law allowed it two thousand years ago.

Despite that, the Jews have always clung to a Hebrew liturgy. In previous times it might have caused less trouble and disaffection if the prayers had been in Greek, Aramaic, Latin, Egyptian, Arabic, Spanish, French, Turkish, German, Polish, or Russian. But the community, by a continuing mass instinct, has held to the Scripture tongue. That instinct is asserting itself today in the United States, in the Reform and Conservative movements, which year by year bring back more Hebrew into their devotions.

Today we have printed translations. In olden times, when knowledge of Hebrew was sometimes scantier than it is today, there was an important synagogue officer, the *meturgeman*, or translator, who called out line by line the vernacular meaning of Torah readings. In certain Sefard prayer books you will still find interlinear Spanish. Our people have put themselves to all this awkwardness and difficulty and persisted in praying in Hebrew. My guess is that they will always do so.

A language has a genius. Some works translate well, others are untranslatable. Moliere is effective only in French. Without knowing Arabic nobody has ever understood the Koran. Pushkin remains a possession of the Russian people, though the world has acquired Tolstoy. In general, the higher the charge of peculiarly national identity and emotion, the less translatable a work is.

The Hebrew Bible speaks with power in all the tongues of earth, but it sounds to nobody else as it does to the Jews. The Second Table of the Ten Commandments reads in Hebrew something like this: "Don't kill; don't be vile; don't steal; don't tell lies about others; don't envy any man his wife or house or animals, or anything he has." This sounds shockingly wrong in English. For the English genius, religion is solemn and stately; Canterbury Cathedral, not a shul. The grand slow march of "Thou Shalt Nots" is exactly right. Religion for the Jews is intimate and colloquial, or it is nothing.

Our liturgy, at least the classic part, is as colloquial and easy-flowing as the Torah. No adequate or even approximate translation of the prayer book exists (this situation is improving. – HW [1985]). The King James Bible serves as a mine for splendid translations of Psalms and other Scripture stretches. Even so, the change from Hebrew to English drastically alters the feeling. Translators of other sections use the King James diction–*wouldst* and *thou* and *vouchsafe* and *loving-kindness* and all the rest–and the tone and texture of our prayers nearly evaporate. People complain sometimes that praying in English makes them feel as though they were in a church. It is a just reaction. They experience the English genius, not the Hebrew.

All the same, half a loaf is assuredly better than none. If prayer in the current language resulted in a stronger and better-informed Jewry, whatever the watering down of meaning, every man of sense would be for it. But on that head we have twenty centuries of experimental evidence. Translated prayer has been, in the communities that have adopted it, a first step toward general loss of Hebrew. Loss of Hebrew has always been a long step toward loss of law, custom, and knowledge, and toward oblivion by absorption.

The fact is that Judaism always has worked by raising the small cadre of Jews to an extraordinary cultural level. The Jews to stay alive have had to know two or three languages. All of them have always had to read and write. It is everlastingly uphill work. Nothing else seems to answer.

During the war I led many services in English, and I have prayed in English. The Talmud surely is right to advise a man to pray in any language that he understands rather than to give up prayer because he does not know Hebrew. For all that, I do not imagine that I can spare my children the old Jewish task of mastering the holy tongue. This was true before the birth of Israel made it an important modern language. Goethe in his day, Edmund Wilson in ours, learned Hebrew to find out what the Bible was driving at. So in all times have many Christian scholars. We learn it to find out what our Torah is telling us and what we truly mean by our prayers. It is work. But any intelligent adult in a year can command the simple Hebrew of our liturgy if he wishes.

One worshipper becomes the prayer leader, or "messenger of the assembly." His special status lasts for one service, then he returns to his place. Anybody who can read Hebrew aloud correctly can take a turn at the reading stand. Most congregations use a prayer leader with a good singing voice—a cantor—on Sabbaths and festivals. The purpose is to add charm to the service and draw crowds. Of course, the piety of the cantor, who week after week leads the service, becomes a matter of concern. The mistaken impression thereby arises that a cantor holds some kind of religious office. He is, however, simply a Jew who knows Hebrew and can sing.

Every Jew has the same prayers to say. There is no intercession, no praying by proxy, and the most pious and world-revered rabbi has no different duties or offices to perform in worship than any thirteen-year-old boy.

The prayer leader keeps order by chanting the first and last lines of prayers. He repeats aloud the Eighteen Benedictions, with the congregation responding, "Amen." The task is an easy one. Many a neophyte who knows Hebrew goes confidently to the reading stand and leads the prayers, and nobody has anything but praise for him. After some attendance in the synagogue he realizes he is missing all the refinements of *nigun* (melody) and he becomes shaky and self-conscious. But in a lifetime of worship he will always encounter Jews who know nigun better than he does, so there is nothing for it but to plunge in and do his best. Any man who speaks the Hebrew loud and clear performs the office.

A truly necessary office is the *shamas*, or sexton. An expert in nigun, he is the factotum of the synagogue. He cares for the library, prayer books, and shawls, serves as prayer leader when no qualified worshipper appears, ensures a quorum of ten at all times, and reads the Holy Scrolls. A synagogue can get along without a rabbi and a cantor. But there must be a shamas, or some worshipper must do a shamas's work.

SOME MAJOR VARIATIONS

After the Roman dispersion, the Jews pulled together in two general communities: the Ashkenaz of North and East Europe, and the Sefard of the Mediterranean lands. They came to pronounce Hebrew differently. Their customs and their liturgies branched into distinct forms. This split exists today. Israeli Hebrew, for instance, is Sefard. It takes some relearning for a Jew who has the Ashkenaz education usual in America.

In New York there is an important Sefard congregation more than three hundred years old, founded by the first Spanish-Jewish settlers in the New World. In this charming Spanish-Portuguese

Synagogue, at Seventieth Street and Central Park West, the Sefard liturgy lives on, different in rite and melody from the Ashkenaz worship that wholly surrounds it, and to some tastes more evocative and picturesque.

A number of the congregants bear old names of the original Spanish founders, whose families are a roll of honor in American history.

The interesting thing about Jewish worship, considering the long dispersion, the total absence of a governing religious body, and the difficulty of communications until recently, is not the variation in customs and text but the underlying sameness. One finds in the Talmud, written before the nations of Europe even existed, minute discussions of how to say prayers that Jews still recite today in Tokyo, Johannesburg, London, and Los Angeles. An American or British Jew wandering into a Sefard synagogue in Israel full of dark-skinned Yemenites will feel temporarily at sea; but once he is handed a book he can follow the service and say his prayers.

Utter silence during prayer is the rule, and words spoken during the Sh'ma and The Eighteen are especially serious violations. In the old-time East European synagogue this rule suffered partial eclipse.

The poverty of the ghetto forced synagogues to support themselves by auctioning off Sabbath and holy day honors. Calls to the Torah, opening of the Ark, and so forth, all went for a price. The auctions were colorful and exciting enough, but the mood of prayer naturally vanished while they went on. They were often quite long. During the reading of the Torah, moreover, it became the practice for each man, as he was called to his aliya, or reading turn, to announce his contributions to the synagogue's many charities. For each announcement he or his family received a public blessing by the shamas. Again, this was a process of high economic value, but not attuned to thoughts of the higher world.

These customs came to America with the great waves of Jewish immigrants at the turn of the century. They enabled many tiny congregations to survive and grow into majestic synagogues and fashionable temples. With the prospering of the Jewish community, these devices of desperation have gradually given way to conventional fund-raising. The auction atmosphere of the Torah-reading time, and the exodus of sidewalk gossipers during this part of the service, are only memories now. There has been a fairly effective restoration of the rule of silence.

I would not give up for anything, all the same, my remembrance of the mournful auction chant of the shamas: "*Finif Tollar um shlishi!* Five dollars for the third reading!" Nor do I want to forget the historic auction one Yom Kippur afternoon nearly forty years ago, in a synagogue in a Bronx cellar, when my father outbid men with far more money (though they were all poor struggling immigrants) for the reading of the Book of Jonah. One by one the competitors dropped out as the bidding went up past a hundred, a hundred twenty-five, to the incredibly magnificent sum of two hundred dollars, bid in one devastating leap by my father. I can still hear the crash of the sexton's palm on the table, and his shaken happy shout, "*Zwei hunderd tollar um maftir Yena!*"

My father made this tremendous and costly beau geste because his own father, a shamas in Minsk, had had the prerogative of reading the Book of Jonah, and he was determined to keep the custom in the family. He did, too. In that synagogue nobody ever seriously bid against him for the honor again. To this day my brother and I read the Book of Jonah at Yom Kippur services wherever we can. We have done so in places as far apart as Chicago, Hawaii, and Okinawa.

The auctions are a thing of the past and it is better so, but they served a purpose. Children in such synagogues learned unmistakably what a precious thing a call to the Torah was.

SOME DIFFICULTIES

The newcomer in a synagogue will of course feel strange and ill at ease; he will be put off by the matter-of-fact manner of many of the worshippers; he will find the process hard to follow, and he will be an exceptional person not to feel discouragement at first. But persevering attendance, especially linked with any kind of elementary Hebrew training, will in a short time give him back the key to the storehouse of Jewish prayer. Then when he wants to, he will pray in the measured and fine words of the tradition; at the synagogue if he can go there, at home if he cannot.

The difficulties of a newcomer are matched, possibly overshadowed, by the problems that face the pious. If the newcomer is not at home, the novelty at least excites his attention. The synagogue-goer is too much at home. The prayers are too familiar. Years of repetition have grooved the words into his memory. If he is not at pains to concentrate, they slide by like water.

The fact is, prayer is never easy. True prayer is as demanding—at least as demanding—as the carrying on of a business conversation or the writing of a letter. It purports to be a communication with a Listener. The child and the newcomer struggle with their unfamiliarity. Devout worshippers struggle with their overfamiliarity. All men of any training or any faith are put to the greatest mental effort, I imagine, to get at any real sense of talking to G-d.

That being the case—since so much praying is, by the limits of human nature, doomed to fall short of what it sets out to be—the question arises, Is not prayer three times a day, in forms long fixed, mere empty machinery? It might be so, perhaps, except that the synagogue always remains what it was in origin: a study hall. One learns worship by worshipping or by trying to—there is absolutely no other way. The natural outpouring of the heart in moments of crisis is not, as the romantic would imagine, prayer at its best. Those who have been through such experiences know that they find themselves reduced to incoherent, shamefaced stammering. Improvised prayer is honored in Judaism, and some inspired improvisations have entered the liturgy. The fixed prayers are the base for a man to stand on, in everyday devotion and in extremity.

Daily prayer, at the very least, is a review of one necessary instrument of the good life as Judaism knows it. It is a duty done, a link in the chain going back to Abraham's acknowledgment of One G-d, a link we add as G-d adds a new day to time. And there is no such thing as wholly absent, wholly mechanical prayer. A glint of the light in the words and the thoughts of the Jewish liturgy falls at some instant, at several instants, into the mind of the most preoccupied worshipper. At least he is there, praying to G-d, so that the glints can come.

Perhaps for saints and for truly holy men fully conscious prayer is really an everyday thing. They live, in that case, in clarity that plain people do not know. For the ordinary worshipper, the rewards of a lifetime of faithful praying come at unpredictable times, scattered through the years, when all at once the liturgy glows as with fire. Such an hour may come after a death, or after a birth; it may strike after a miraculous deliverance, or on the brink of evident doom; it may flood the soul at no marked time, for no marked reason. It comes, and he knows why he has prayed all his life.

This Is My G-d: The Jewish Way of Life (Garden City, N.Y.: Doubleday & Co., Inc., 1959), pp. 92–108

LESSON TWO

A WORK OF PLEAS

UNDERSTANDING THE MECHANICS OF PETITION

Praying includes petitions, but is it impudent or heretical to seek alterations to what G-d has given us? Why would G-d want mortal appeals? This lesson dabbles in mysticism to identify the mechanics that make prayer effective. It defines the most favorable approach, and then we come to discover the benefits to our personal relationship with G-d from prayers of petition.

I. Introduction

Exercise 2.1

List two recent occasions during which you prayed that something would change.

1

2

How comfortable are you with praying to G-d for something you need?

1. Very Comfortable
2. Comfortable
3. Ambivalent
4. Uncomfortable

Questions for Discussion

1. Hasn't G-d already determined my fate? Can my prayer modify G-d's decision?
2. If G-d is all-knowing, is He not aware of my needs without my informing Him?
3. Countless individuals benefit from many blessings in life without having prayed for them. Doesn't that indicate that praying for our needs is superfluous?
4. Many prayers appear to go unanswered. What, then, is the function of prayer?

Text 1a

REFA'ENU, EIGHTH BLESSING OF WEEKDAY AMIDAH

רְפָאֵנוּ ה' וְנֵרָפֵא, הוֹשִׁיעֵנוּ וְנִוָּשֵׁעָה כִּי תְהִלָּתֵנוּ אָתָּה. וְהַעֲלֵה אֲרוּכָה וּרְפוּאָה שְׁלֵימָה לְכָל מַכּוֹתֵינוּ . . .

Heal us, O L-rd, and we will be healed.

Help us, and we will be saved.

For You are our praise.

Grant complete cure and healing to all our wounds. . . .

Text 1b

BARECH ALEINU, NINTH BLESSING OF WEEKDAY AMIDAH

בָּרֵךְ עָלֵינוּ ה' אֱלֹקֵינוּ אֶת הַשָּׁנָה הַזֹּאת וְאֶת כָּל מִינֵי תְבוּאָתָהּ לְטוֹבָה, וְתֵן טַל וּמָטָר לִבְרָכָה עַל פְּנֵי הָאֲדָמָה . . .

Bless for us, L-rd our G-d, this year,

and all the varieties of its produce, for good.

And bestow dew and rain for blessing upon the face of the earth. . . .

II. The Mechanics of Prayer

Text 2

RABBI DAVID SHLOMO EIBESHITZ,
ARVEI NACHAL, *PARSHAT* BALAK 1

הַמֶּחְקָרִים הִקְשׁוּ בְּמַה שֶּׁאָנוּ רוֹאִין בְּכָל עֵת שֶׁיֵּשׁ אֵיזֶה צַעַר בָּעוֹלָם וּגְזֵירָה אֲזַי מְבַטְּלִין עַל יְדֵי תְּפִלָּה . . . וְאֵיךְ יְצוּיַּיר אֶצְלוֹ שִׁינּוּי רָצוֹן עַל יְדֵי הַתְּפִלָּה?

אָכֵן בְּשַׁ"ס יֵשׁ תֵּירוּץ עַל זֶה. וְהוּא אֲמָרָם זִכְרוֹנָם לִבְרָכָה: (חוּלִּין ס, ב) "מְלַמֵּד שֶׁיָּצְאוּ דְשָׁאִים וְעָמְדוּ עַל פֶּתַח קַרְקַע, וְלֹא יָצְאוּ עַד שֶׁבָּא אָדָם הָרִאשׁוֹן וּבִיקֵּשׁ עֲלֵיהֶם רַחֲמִים, וְיָרְדוּ גְשָׁמִים וְצָמְחוּ, מְלַמֵּד שֶׁהַקָּדוֹשׁ בָּרוּךְ הוּא מִתְאַוֶּה לִתְפִלָּתָן שֶׁל צַדִּיקִים".

אֲשֶׁר לְפִי זֶה אֵין כָּאן שִׁינּוּי רָצוֹן, כִּי כָּךְ הָיָה הָרָצוֹן מִתְּחִלָּה לְהַעֲצִיר הַגְּשָׁמִים כְּדֵי שֶׁיִּתְפַּלְלוּ וְאַחַר כָּךְ יֵרְדוּ גְשָׁמִים.

The philosophers ask about the fact that whenever we are in distress, we attempt to change things through prayer. . . . Is it conceivable that prayer could change G-d's will?

The Talmud (CHULIN 60B) provides an answer to this question. It states, "[On the third day of Creation], vegetation emerged from the earth, but only slightly. It did not grow until Adam came into existence and prayed on its behalf, whereupon rain descended and the vegetation grew. This teaches us that G-d thirsts for the prayers of the righteous."

Accordingly, G-d does not change His plans through prayer. G-d's intention from the outset was to withhold rain so that man would pray and that only then rain would fall.

RABBI DAVID SHLOMO EIBESHITZ
1755–1814

Rabbi and Chasidic thinker. After serving in numerous rabbinical posts in Ukraine, Rabbi Eibeshitz moved to Safed, Israel. His most noted works are *Arvei Nachal*, a Chasidic and kabbalistic commentary on the Torah; and *Levushei Serad*, a commentary to the Code of Jewish Law.

III. A New Will, a New Way

Text 3a

II KINGS 20:1

בַּיָּמִים הָהֵם, חָלָה חִזְקִיָּהוּ לָמוּת. וַיָּבֹא אֵלָיו יְשַׁעְיָהוּ בֶן אָמוֹץ
הַנָּבִיא, וַיֹּאמֶר אֵלָיו: כֹּה אָמַר ה', צַו לְבֵיתֶךָ, כִּי מֵת אַתָּה וְלֹא תִחְיֶה

In those days, Hezekiah fell terminally ill. Isaiah the prophet, son of Amotz, came to him and said, "This is what G-d says, 'Set your house in order, for you are going to die; you will not live.'"

KINGS

Biblical book. The Book of Kings, part of the Prophets section of the Hebrew Bible, relates the history of the Israelites and their kings and prophets, from the final days of King David in 837 BCE until the destruction of the first Temple in 423 BCE. Written by the prophet Jeremiah, Kings is a single work that was later split into 2 parts.

Text 3b

TALMUD, BERACHOT 10A

אָמַר לֵיהּ: כְּבַר נִגְזְרָה עָלֶיךָ גְּזֵירָה.

אָמַר לֵיהּ: בֶּן אָמוֹץ, כַּלֵּה נְבוּאָתְךָ וְצֵא! כָּךְ מְקוּבְּלַנִי מִבֵּית אֲבִי
אַבָּא: אֲפִילוּ חֶרֶב חַדָּה מוּנַּחַת עַל צַוָּארוֹ שֶׁל אָדָם, אַל יִמְנַע עַצְמוֹ
מִן הָרַחֲמִים.

Isaiah responded, "The decree against you has already been issued."

Said Hezekiah, "Son of Amotz, cease prophesying and leave! I have received the following tradition from my ancestors: 'Even if a sharp sword is held against a person's neck, do not refrain from praying for mercy!'"

Yhi Ratzone May it be the will of G-d

BABYLONIAN TALMUD

A literary work of monumental proportions that draws upon the legal, spiritual, intellectual, ethical, and historical traditions of Judaism. The 37 tractates of the Babylonian Talmud contain the teachings of the Jewish sages from the period after the destruction of the 2nd Temple through the 5th century CE. It has served as the primary vehicle for the transmission of the Oral Law and the education of Jews over the centuries; it is the entry point for all subsequent legal, ethical, and theological Jewish scholarship.

Text 3c

II KINGS 20:2-6

וַיַּסֵּב אֶת פָּנָיו אֶל הַקִּיר וַיִּתְפַּלֵּל אֶל ה' לֵאמֹר:

אָנָּה ה'! זְכָר נָא אֵת אֲשֶׁר הִתְהַלַּכְתִּי לְפָנֶיךָ בֶּאֱמֶת וּבְלֵבָב שָׁלֵם,
וְהַטּוֹב בְּעֵינֶיךָ עָשִׂיתִי. וַיֵּבְךְּ חִזְקִיָּהוּ בְּכִי גָדוֹל.

וַיְהִי יְשַׁעְיָהוּ לֹא יָצָא חָצֵר הַתִּיכֹנָה, וּדְבַר ה' הָיָה אֵלָיו לֵאמֹר: שׁוּב
וְאָמַרְתָּ אֶל חִזְקִיָּהוּ נְגִיד עַמִּי: כֹּה אָמַר ה' אֱלֹקֵי דָּוִד אָבִיךָ, שָׁמַעְתִּי
אֶת תְּפִלָּתֶךָ, רָאִיתִי אֶת דִּמְעָתֶךָ, הִנְנִי רֹפֵא לָךְ.

Hezekiah turned to face the wall, and he prayed to G-d.

"Please, O G-d! Remember now how I have walked before you truthfully and sincerely, and I did that which is good in your eyes." And Hezekiah wept profusely.

Even before Isaiah was able to leave the middle courtyard [of Hezekiah's palace], G-d told him to go back and tell Hezekiah, "So says G-d, the G-d of your ancestor David, 'I have heard your prayers, and I have seen your tears; I will heal you.'"

Text 4

THE REBBE, RABBI MENACHEM MENDEL SCHNEERSON,
SEFER HAMAAMARIM MELUKAT, VOL. 2, PP. 271–272

וְעִנְיַן הַתְּפִלָּה הוּא בַּקָּשָׁה מֵהַקָּדוֹשׁ בָּרוּךְ הוּא שֶׁגַּם בְּאִם לֹא יֶשְׁנָהּ חַס וְשָׁלוֹם הַהַשְׁפָּעָה גַּם בְּהַמָּקוֹר, וְלֹא עוֹד אֶלָּא שֶׁנִּגְזַר עָלָיו שֶׁיִּהְיֶה חוֹלֶה חַס וְשָׁלוֹם וְכַיּוֹצֵא בָּזֶה, מִכָּל מָקוֹם, תּוּמְשַׁךְ לוֹ הַשְׁפָּעָה חֲדָשָׁה מֵאוֹר אֵין סוֹף שֶׁלְּמַעְלָה מֵהִשְׁתַּלְשְׁלוּת.

דְּזֶהוּ שֶׁאוֹמְרִים בְּכַמָּה תְּפִלּוֹת יְהִי רָצוֹן, דְּפֵירוּשׁ יְהִי רָצוֹן הוּא שֶׁיִּהְיֶה רָצוֹן חָדָשׁ.

Even if no blessing has been allotted to us in the spiritual source of blessing—or worse yet, even if it has been determined in Heaven that something negative will occur, such as an illness, G-d forbid—our prayers serve as appeals to G-d to change our reality through generating an entirely new bestowal of Divine energy from His Infinite Self that transcends the entire spiritual system.

This explains the terminology included in many of our prayers, "May it be Your will." The implication of "may it *be*" is that we are asking for a completely new will to be issued.

RABBI MENACHEM MENDEL SCHNEERSON 1902–1994

The towering Jewish leader of the 20th century, known as "the Lubavitcher Rebbe," or simply as "the Rebbe." Born in southern Ukraine, the Rebbe escaped Nazi-occupied Europe, arriving in the U.S. in June 1941. The Rebbe inspired and guided the revival of traditional Judaism after the European devastation, impacting virtually every Jewish community the world over. The Rebbe often emphasized that the performance of just one additional good deed could usher in the era of Mashiach. The Rebbe's scholarly talks and writings have been printed in more than 200 volumes.

Text 5

RABBI SHNEUR ZALMAN OF LIADI, *TORAH OR*, MIKETZ 42B

הַתְּפִלָּה הִיא בַּקָּשַׁת יְהִי רָצוֹן - שֶׁיִּתְהַוֶּה בְּחִינַת רָצוֹן, שֶׁכְּמוֹ שֶׁכְּבָר נִמְשַׁךְ רָצוֹן הָעֶלְיוֹן בְּחָכְמָה, הִנֵּה הַחָכְמָה מְחַיֶּיבֶת עַל פִּי הַתּוֹרָה . . . שֶׁהֶעָוֹן גּוֹרֵם יִסּוּרִים, חַס וְשָׁלוֹם. אֲבָל עַל יְדֵי הַתְּפִלָּה יְהִי רָצוֹן, נִמְשַׁךְ רָצוֹן הָעֶלְיוֹן שֶׁלְּמַעְלָה מִבְּחִינַת חָכְמָה, וְשָׁם הוּא רַחֲמִים פְּשׁוּטִים, וְרַבּוּ פְּשָׁעֶיךָ כו'.

Prayer is a request that a new Divine will come into being, as we say, "May it be Your will." This is necessary because the current will that has already descended into the spiritual system of bestowal . . . corresponds to our merits and can therefore produce an outcome that we would wish to avoid. Our prayers, however, elicit a fresh Divine will that transcends this spiritual system; they tap into a sublime source in which undiscriminating mercy prevails and where blessing is not contingent upon our actions.

RABBI SHNEUR ZALMAN OF LIADI (ALTER REBBE)
1745–1812

Chasidic rebbe, Halachic authority, and founder of the Chabad movement. The Alter Rebbe was born in Liozna, Belarus, and was among the principal students of the Magid of Mezeritch. His numerous works include the *Tanya*, an early classic containing the fundamentals of Chabad Chasidism; and *Shulchan Aruch HaRav*, an expanded and reworked code of Jewish law.

Text 6

THE REBBE, RABBI MENACHEM MENDEL SCHNEERSON,
LIKUTEI SICHOT 29, P. 187

בַּיי תְּפִלָּה, אַף עַל פִּי אַז תַּכְלִיתָה אִיז עֶס זָאל אוֹיפְגֶעטָאן װֶערְן אַ שִׁינּוּי בְּגַשְׁמִיּוּת, "שֶׁיִּתְרַפֵּא הַחוֹלֶה וְיֵרֵד הַגֶּשֶׁם מִשָּׁמַיִם לָאָרֶץ וְיוֹלִידָה וְיַצְמִיחָה", אִיז דָאס אָבֶּער אַ תּוֹצָאָה דֶערְפוּן וָואס מֶען פּוֹעֶל'ט אַ רָצוֹן חָדָשׁ כִּבְיָכוֹל בַּיי הַקָּדוֹשׁ בָּרוּךְ הוּא, אוּן דָאס קוּמְט בְּעִיקָּר דוּרְךְ כַּוָּונַת הַלֵּב פוּן מִתְפַּלֵּל, "שֶׁיְּפַנֶּה אֶת לִבּוֹ מִכָּל הַמַּחֲשָׁבוֹת וְיִרְאֶה עַצְמוֹ כְּאִילּוּ הוּא עוֹמֵד לִפְנֵי הַשְּׁכִינָה" (מִשְׁנֶה תּוֹרָה, הִלְכוֹת תְּפִלָּה ד, טז).

בְּשַׁעַת אַ אִיד אִיז מְפַנֶּה לִבּוֹ פוּן אַלֶע זַיינֶע מַחֲשָׁבוֹת וּרְצוֹנוֹת אוּן אִיז זִיךְ מְבַטֵּל כְּעַבְדָּא קַמֵּיהּ מָרֵיהּ צוּם אוֹיבֶּערְשְׁטֶען אִיז דָאס פּוֹעֵל, אוֹיךְ לְמַעֲלָה כִּבְיָכוֹל (כַּמַּיִם הַפָּנִים לְפָנִים) אַז עֶס זָאל זַיין אַ רָצוֹן חָדָשׁ, וָועלְכֶער אִיז נִיט לוֹיט דִי הַגְבָּלוֹת פוּן סֵדֶר הָעוֹלָם, בִּיז אֲפִילוּ נִיט לוֹיט דֶעם סֵדֶר וְהַגְבָּלָה פוּן תּוֹרָה, עֲשִׂיַּית רָצוֹן חָדָשׁ.

The point of petitioning G-d in prayer is to effect a change in the physical world—that the sick be healed, that rain fall and cause the crops to grow, and so forth. Such changes are the result of our eliciting a new Divine will. We precipitate this fresh Divine will primarily through our state of mind during prayer by "freeing the mind from all other concerns and seeing ourselves as though we are standing before G-d" (MAIMONIDES, *MISHNEH TORAH*, LAWS OF PRAYER 4:16).

When we free ourselves from all of our personal thoughts and interests and completely surrender ourselves to G-d, this moves G-d to respond in kind with a freshly minted will that disregards the limitations of nature as well as the limitations set out by the Torah.

Text 7

TALMUD, BERACHOT 34B

מַעֲשֶׂה בְּרַבִּי חֲנִינָא בֶּן דוֹסָא, שֶׁהָלַךְ לִלְמוֹד תּוֹרָה אֵצֶל רַבִּי יוֹחָנָן בֶּן זַכַּאי, וְחָלָה בְּנוֹ שֶׁל רַבִּי יוֹחָנָן בֶּן זַכַּאי.

אָמַר לוֹ: חֲנִינָא בְּנִי, בַּקֵּשׁ עָלָיו רַחֲמִים וְיִחְיֶה!

הִנִּיחַ רֹאשׁוֹ בֵּין בִּרְכָּיו, וּבִקֵּשׁ עָלָיו רַחֲמִים, וְחָיָה.

אָמַר רַבִּי יוֹחָנָן בֶּן זַכַּאי: אִלְמָלֵי הִטִּיחַ בֶּן זַכַּאי אֶת רֹאשׁוֹ בֵּין בִּרְכָּיו כָּל הַיּוֹם כּוּלוֹ, לֹא הָיוּ מַשְׁגִּיחִים עָלָיו . . . הוּא דוֹמֶה כְּעֶבֶד לִפְנֵי הַמֶּלֶךְ, וַאֲנִי דוֹמֶה כְּשַׂר לִפְנֵי הַמֶּלֶךְ.

Rabbi Chanina ben Dosa went to study Torah under the tutelage of Rabbi Yochanan ben Zakai.

Rabbi Yochanan's child fell ill. Rabbi Yochanan turned to his student and said, "Chanina! Pray for my son that he should survive!"

Chanina buried his head in his lap and prayed for G-d's mercy. The child recovered.

Said Rabbi Yochanan, "Had I placed my head in my lap and prayed all day long, I would not have been answered. . . . For I am like a minister before the king, whereas Chanina is like a servant before the king."

Takeaway Exercise

Tangible Relationship. Make a brief prayer in which you request something from G-d. Be mindful that your goal is not simply to have a particular wish granted, but that you strongly desire to witness G-d's hand in your life for the sake of forging a deeper, more personal relationship with G-d. Hopefully, your prayer will indeed be granted, and when that occurs, take a moment to reflect not only on the blessing you received but on the ultimate gift of the Creator's overt presence in your life.

We'll discuss how it went during the next lesson.

Key Points

1. While there are some blessings that G-d grants without our making a request, there are others that G-d wills to only grant us upon our prayer and request. G-d engineered this in order to facilitate our communication with Him, thereby expressing and developing our relationship with Him.

2. There are various forms of prayer, but there is something special about our prayers of petition. These are fundamental to building a relationship with G-d, similar to the special closeness that emerges after a friend aids us in a crisis. Moreover, the act of reaching out to a friend for assistance is itself a powerful demonstration of an important bond. And when we turn to G-d for help, as opposed to any other purported power, we make a strong statement about our belief and connection with Him.

3. Prayer can also trigger a new Divine will by bypassing the spiritual system to reach G-d Himself, Who transcends the spiritual order. Whereas Heaven's default decisions are largely merit-based, undiscriminating mercy prevails in G-d Himself as He transcends His spiritual system.

4. Overriding the spiritual merit-based system is possible because G-d mimics our actions. Brushing aside our natural instincts and desires to focus profoundly on relating to G-d—surrendering ourselves to His will and internalizing our dependence on Him—causes G-d to respond in-kind: He brushes aside His default merit-based system of granting blessings and focuses on relating directly with us from His Transcendent Self.

TECHINOT FOR

SHABBAT CANDLE LIGHTING

The following two *techinot* are written for recital after lighting Shabbat candles.

Sarah bat Tovim, *Techinah Sheloshah She'arim* (Vilna, 1850), p. 4*

רִבּוֹנוֹ שֶׁל עוֹלָם מיין מִצְוָה פוּן דיא ליכט אָן צינדין זאָל אזוֹא אָן גינוּמען זיין וויא דיא מִצְוָה פוּן דעם כֹּהֵן גָדוֹל ווען ער האָט די ליכט אין ליבִין ב"ה אָן גיצוּנדין איז זיין מִצְוָה אָן גינוּמען גיוואָרין אזוֹ זאָל מיין מִצְוָה אויך אָן גינוּמען ווערין

Master of the universe, may the *mitzvah* of my lighting the candles be accepted like the *mitzvah* of the High Priest when he lit the candles in the beloved Holy Temple. Just as his *mitzvah* was accepted, so may mine be accepted.

נֵר לְרַגְלִי דְבָרֶךָ וְאוֹר לִנְתִיבָתִי דאָשׂ איז טייטש דיינע רייד איז איין ליכט צוּא מייני פיס אוּנ מיינע קינדער זאָלין גיין אין גאָטש וועג אוּנ דיא מִצְוָה פוּן מיינע ליכט צינדין זאָל אָן גינוּמען ווערין אז מיינע קינדרשׁ אויגין זאָלן לייכטן

"Your words are a lamp for my foot, and light for my path" (Psalms 119:105). This means that Your words are a lamp for my feet so that all my children should walk in G-d's path, and

*The Yiddish text for these *techinot* use old Yiddish terms and spelling conventions.

SARAH BAT TOVIM
17TH–18TH CENTURY

Sarah was born in Sataniv, Ukraine, where her grandfather served as the rabbi. Known as Sarah bat Tovim (Sarah from a good family), she writes that she lived a sad life as a wanderer. Sarah authored the extremely popular *Sheloshah She'arim –Three Gates*, a handbook containing instructions and prayers for the three *mitzvot* traditionally cherished by Jewish women: Shabbat candles, chalah, and family purity.

אין דער ליבער הייליגער תּוֹרָה אויך טוא איך בעטין ביי די ליכט דעם ליבין גאָט ב"ה אז מיין מִצְוָה פון די ליכט זאָל אָן גינומען ווערין וויא דאָשׂ ליכט האָט גיברענט פון דעם בוים אייל אין בה"מ אונ איז ניט פאר לאָשין גיוואָרין.

בִּזְכוּת דאָשׂ ליכט פון דעם ליבין שַׁבָּת זאָל מַגִין זיין וויא דר ליבער שַׁבָּת האָט מַגִין גיוועזן אויף אָדָם הָרִאשׁוֹן ווי ער איז בַּהיט גיוואָרין פר איין גיכין טויט אזוֹ זאָל אונזר זְכוּת פון די ליכט מַגִין זיין אז אונזרי קינדרשׂ ליכט זאָל לייכטין אין דר תּוֹרָה זייערי מַזָלוֹת זאָל לייכטן אין הימיל זיי זאָלין קענען פַּרְנָסָה געבין צו ווייב אונ קינדר בְּעַיִן יָפֶה

בִּזְכוּת דאָשׂ ליכט פון דעם ליבין שַׁבָּת זאָל מַגִין זיין וויא דר ליבער שַׁבָּת האָט מַגִין גיוועזן אויף אָדָם הָרִאשׁוֹן ווי ער איז בַּהיט גיוואָרין פר איין גיכין טויט אזוֹ זאָל אונזר זְכוּת פון די ליכט מַגִין זיין אז אונזרי קינדרשׂ ליכט זאָל לייכטין אין דר תּוֹרָה זייערי מַזָלוֹת זאָל לייכטן אין הימיל זיי זאָלין קענען פַּרְנָסָה געבין צו ווייב אונ קינדר בְּעַיִן יָפֶה

אונ אונזערי מִצְוֹ ת זאָלין אָן גינומן ווערן ווי די מִצְוֹ ת פון אונזרי אָבוֹת וְאִמָהוֹת אונ די שְׁבָטִים הַקְדוֹשִׁים מיר זאָלן זיין אזוֹא ריין וויא איין קינד ווערט גיבּאָרין פון זיין מוטער אָמֵן:

may the *mitzvah* of my candle lighting be accepted so that my children's eyes should be illumined by the beloved holy Torah.

Dear G-d, I also ask as I stand by the candles that my *mitzvah* of lighting candles be accepted like the candle of the *menorah* that was lit from olive oil in the Holy Temple and was never extinguished.

May the merit of the beloved Shabbat candles protect me, just as the beloved Shabbat protected Adam, the original human, from swift death. So may our merit of lighting the candles protect our children, that their candles should shine with the study of Torah, and their stars of luck shine in the heavens so that they may be able to earn a decent living to comfortably provide for their wives and children.

May our *mitzvot* be accepted like the *mitzvot* of our patriarchs and matriarchs and those of the holy tribes, so that we may be as pure as a child newly born of its mother. Amen.

Techinot Rachel Imenu (Jerusalem, 1954), pp. 44–45

גָאט פוּן דַיין פָאלְק יִשְׂרָאֵל דוּא בִּיסְט הֵיילִיג אוּנ דוּא הָאסְט גִיהֵילִיגְט דַיין פָאלְק יִשְׂרָאֵל אוּנ דוּ הָאסְט גִיהֵיילִיגְט דֶעם שַׁבָּת אוּנ דוּ בִּיסְט אֵיינֶר אוּנ דִי יִשְׂרָאֵל הָאסְטוּ אוֹס דֶר וֵוֶילְט פוּן אַלֶע פֶעלְקֶער צוּא דַיין דִינְסְט אוּנ דֶעם שַׁבָּת צוּ עֶהְרִין אוּנ צוּ לַייכְטִין מִיט לֵיכְט אוּנ צוּא הָאבִּין פְרֵייד אוּנ לוּסְט אִין דַיינֶעם דִינְסְט אִין דַיינֶעם הֵיילִיגְן שַׁבָּת

דָס מִיר זֶענִין שׁוּלְדִיג עֶרְלִיךְ צוּ הַאלְטֶן מִיט אַלֶע זַאכֶן אַזוֹ וִוי אַמֶלֶךְ דֶר הַאלְט עֶרְלִיךְ זַיין מַלְכָּה אָדֶער וְויא אַחָתָן הַאלְט עֲרְלִיךְ זַיין כַּלָה. אוּנ נָאךְ רֵיידֶן פִיל חֲכָמִים דָאס זֵייא הָאבְּן גְרוּפִין דֶעם שַׁבָּת בַּת מַלְכָּה אוּנ כַּלָה.

אִיךְ דַיין טָאכְטֶער הָאבּ שׁוֹן לִיכְט גְצוּנְדִין צֵוויי לִיכְט וִיא דַיינֶע חֲכָמִים הָאבְּן גְהֵייסְן דִי וָוס וֵוייסֶען דַיין הֵיילִיגֶע תּוֹרָה צוּ עֶהְרֶן אוּנ צוּ הֵיילִיגֶן דַיין נָאמֶן אוּנ דִי תּוֹרָה אוּנ דֶעם שַׁבָּת.

אַלְמֶעכְטִיגֶר גָאט גִיבּ מִיר אוּנ מַיין מַאן אוּנ מֵיינֶע קִינְדֶר אוּנ מַיין גַאנְץ הוֹז גְזִינְד דֶעם הֵיילִיגִין שַׁבָּת צוּ רוּעֶן אוּנ צוּ הֵיילִיגֶן מִיט נַחַת . . .

שִׁיק אוּנְז דִי בְּרָכָה מִיט דֶעם גוּטִין מַלְאָךְ דֶר דָא גֵייט אוֹיף דִי רֶעכְטֶע הַאנְט פוּן דֶעם מֶענְטְשִׁין אוּנ דֶער בֵּייזֶער מַלְאָךְ זָאל דרוֹף זָאגֶן אָמֵן אוּנ לָאז אוּנז זוֹכֶה זַיין דָס מִיר זָאלֶן אַרְבֶּען דֶעם טָאג דֶר דָא אִיז אֵייטֶל שַׁבָּת דֶר דָא רוּהְט דֶר דָא לֶעבְּט אֵייבִּיג עֶס זָאל בַּאוּוִילִיגְט זַיין פַאר דִיר גָאט מַיין בַּאשֶׁעפֶער אוּנ מַיין דֶער לֵייזֶער אָמֵן.

G-d of Your people Israel, You are holy, and You have made Your people Israel and the Shabbat holy. You are One, and from among all the peoples You have chosen Israel alone to serve You. You have chosen the Shabbat alone for glory, for lighting candles, and for rejoicing and delighting in Your service.

Today is Your holy Shabbat, which we are obligated to observe with great care, as a king cares for his queen, and as a groom cares for his bride. Many of our sages spoke about this, comparing Shabbat to a queen and a bride.

I, Your daughter, have already lit the candles as instructed by Your sages, those who know Your holy Torah and who know how to study it and glorify and sanctify Your Name, the Torah, and Shabbat.

Almighty G-d, give me and my husband and my children and my entire household this holy Shabbat for rest, for holiness, and *nachas*. . . .

Send us a blessing with the good angel who walks at a person's right hand, and may the evil angel respond "Amen." May we merit that You cause us to inherit the day that is entirely Shabbat and rest [the messianic era], when we will live forever. May this be Your will, G-d my Creator. Amen.

ADDITIONAL READINGS

Why Pray?

By Chani Weinroth

A good friend of mine, whose lifestyle differs from my own, once asked me whether she could pose a frank question.

"Tell me, Chani, why do you still pray? You've been ill for eight years now, which means that you have been praying for eight years straight. Don't you see that it doesn't help? Besides, you've told me many times that no one has recovered from such an advanced stage of the disease. What's the point of praying when you don't believe it can help you?"

It must admit that she posed an excellent question.

Let me rewind to the earliest dawn of my prayer for recovery. It was born after that fateful meeting with a doctor who informed me I had no more than six months to live.

"This figure is based on statistics," he intoned, "but statistics are occasionally at odds with reality. In other words, I cannot guarantee that you will last even six months."

Those were his final words on the matter. With that, our meeting ended, but not my life. I began praying, and I am still here. So who can claim that it does not help?

Of course, what I prayed for has not exactly emerged. I prayed for health and I remain ill.

However, prayer is not a shopping list, where you compare your list with your purchases and mark off what you did or did not find in the store that day. Prayer provides something different altogether that is not necessarily measured by answers to our requests.

THE PURPOSE OF PRAYER

What prompts us to pray in the first place? In the majority of cases, it is some kind of lack. He needs money? He prays. She needs a husband? She prays. They have no children? They pray. Health, shelter, and even pressure over a critical exam—these are the kind of matters that compel us to open our hearts in prayer. We pray that our wishes be granted.

If matters such as the above are indeed our motivation for praying, then what happens if our prayers are apparently not accepted—at least in relation to the contents of our prayers? We have set ourselves up for disappointment or even despair. It then becomes all too easy to view our prayer as a disintegrated illusion or like childish naiveté that has passed and been disproven. But this approach to prayer is a grave error.

I will not deny that to request something repeatedly for eight long years, only to have the request

---

CHANI WEINROTH, 1983–2017

Mother, author, and lecturer. Throughout her 8 year battle with cancer, she wrote inspirational letters to her children in which she shared her life, wisdom, and faith. She published these letters under the title *B'Eretz Hachayim* and went on to publish 2 more books.

flatly rejected, is unquestionably disappointing. However, I would like to describe what prayer has indeed given me over these past eight years:

For me, prayer is not a means to achieving an end. True, I desire good health, and I certainly introduce this deepest desire into my prayers, but I view prayer as a goal in itself. I pray for the sake of praying. Requests for good health and so many other things for which we plead in prayer serve to invigorate our prayer experience, but they are not there for the sake of testing the reliability of prayer in terms of fulfilling someone's shopping list.

We do not always pay attention to the fact that our prayers are not formulated to read like a shopping list or the like. Take for example the prayer for healing. It begins, *refa'enu... ve-nerafe,* "Heal us, G-d, and we will be cured; rescue us and we will be saved. . . ." The blessing, however, is not yet complete. It continues, *ki... melech rofe ne'eman ve-rachaman atah*, "For You, Almighty King, are a faithful and merciful healer." I stand before G-d in prayer, but not merely for the sake of lodging a request. Rather, a prayer for something I lack is an opportunity to remind myself of G-d's sheer awesomeness.

If you have ever experienced the mitzvah of *hafrashat challah*, which involves separating a piece of raw dough before baking bread, you can relate to the kind of experience I am describing. But this experience is not restricted to the performance of a mitzvah. Anyone who has burst into tears due to pain or grief can testify to experiencing some sort of relief once the tears subside. Why is that? Has the issue been resolved? Did the problem disappear at the first sight of tears? Certainly not. But internally, something has been unloaded. There is a sense that someone higher is listening, and that the tears were not in vain. That feeling is more or less what I am delighted to experience after a good prayer.

DON'T END!

I remind myself of two things before launching into prayer. First, G-d is not some kind of Santa Claus who we might ask for a present and he'll tuck it under a tree for us. In addition, G-d does not need our prayers. The prayers were designed to serve as gifts for us, not gifts for G-d. He wants us to pray, but He does not need our prayers. We are the ones who need our prayers.

If you have ever experienced a truly powerful prayer that caused you to feel exceptionally close to G-d, you know that in that blissful moment a tremendous fear creeps in, when you wonder, "What will happen when this prayer is over? I'm soaring and desperately wish to avoid landing. I want to stay close to Him for just a little longer."

HEALTHY SOUL

Our prayer for healing lumps two concepts together: *refu'at ha-nefesh u'refu'at ha-guf*, "healing of the body and healing of the soul." I often wonder if it is indeed possible to differentiate between the two.

I used to volunteer at a service that provides healing for the soul. I remember the day I arrived at the center shortly after giving birth to my daughter Shirah. I was not feeling well, and it was difficult for me to rise from my seat. I noticed a sturdy, muscular young man who was being treated at the center. If asked to guess his profession, I would suggest boxing. I turned to him with a small request for assistance.

"Please do a favor and pass me that cup."

He stared at me with dull eyes, and without the faintest hint of cynicism, he replied, "I don't have the strength."

Believe me, I believed him. Despite my low hemoglobin following the birth I am convinced that I had greater strengths than the bulging muscles threatening to rip through this strapping young man's shirt.

If we encounter a person whose legs have been amputated, we do not tell him, "What are you waiting for? Try to walk! Don't panic, you can do it. . . ." By contrast, when we meet someone suffering from such severe depression that they cannot remove their noses from their blankets, we approach them illogically with a rational sounding demand, "Get up! Let's go! What is this nonsense? With a little bit of will, you can be up on your feet."

As for me, I focus ever stronger on my prayers for health of body and health of soul.

To my friend who asked, "Chani, why on earth do you still pray?" I respond:

I need to feel close to G-d. And this need is fully met through prayer. As for your inquiry, "Don't you see that it doesn't help?" I place my hand on my heart and declare in full sincerity that there are moments of prayer in which I feel so very close to G-d that I feel fully well and healthy. That is the honest truth. It is difficult for me to put it precisely into words, just as it is difficult to describe the precise taste of coffee to someone who has never tasted coffee in their lives. But one who tasted, knows.

Translated from *Olam Hafuch Ra'iti* (Weinroth Books 2016), pp. 46–49

Divine Providence

By Rabbi Jacob Immanuel Schochet

It is quite apparent that the acts of man will not necessarily prove successful. Man may do all that is necessary, and do so in a proper way, and still fail to realize his goals. It is likewise with prayer: one may pray properly, at the right time and with the right devotion, yet his request is not fulfilled.

Now the reason may be that G-d refuses to assent as a form of punishment or trial, or because the petitioner is not yet fully prepared and ready. Then, again, there may be some other, external impediment.

Another, and possibly most frequent reason, is that "No" may also be an answer, and in fact the best possible answer. The request may not have been assented to by Divine Providence for a good reason: Omniscient G-d knows that the favour requested is ultimately not in the best interest of the petitioner. For many of man's prayers are inappropriate and unreasonable. They are mere personal desires which we, thinking in terms of 'here and now,' imagine to be needs or essential for our welfare and happiness. Of this it has been said, "'The needs of Your people are many and their wit is scant': because their wit is scant, that is why their needs are many."

In this context we must consider two things. On the one hand, a man must always retain faith and trust in G-d, and hope that his requests (insofar that they are proper, reasonable, and suitable) will be fulfilled. This trust in G-d must be strong and sincere, to the extent that "even when a sharp sword is already on your neck, do not refrain from asking for G-d's mercy."

On the other hand, one must be careful not to fall prey to the sin of presumptuous calculation on prayer (*iyun tefilah*), that is, to expect that G-d will definitely accept and grant the request as compensation due for praying. To be sure, one ought to hope, wait patiently, "Hope in G-d, be strong . . . and hope in G-d" (Psalms 27:14). Nonetheless, one must also keep in mind and consider that (as stated) there are various reasons why requests may be refused. Thus there is no reason to despair. On the contrary: contemplation on this principle should lead man to "examine his deeds, as it is written, (Lamentations 3:40), 'Let us search our ways and investigate'" (Berachot 5a).

The proper attitude to prayer, and its most suitable content, therefore, would be some form of the prayer of R. Eliezer: "L-rd of the Universe! Do Your will in heaven above, and give repose of spirit to those that fear you below; and do what is good in your eyes. Blessed are You, G-d, who hears prayer." This means: "Do not attend to my words or to my requests to do what *my heart* desires or what *I* ask; for oftentimes I pray for something which is bad for me, because I imagine and think that it is good. You, however, know better than I whether it is good for me or bad. Therefore: *You* decide, and not I; do what *You* know is good—'do what is good in Your eyes.'"

"Salvation belongs to G-d" (Psalms 3:9). G-d alone, and not man, knows the way of salvation. Thus

---

RABBI JACOB IMMANUEL SCHOCHET, PHD, 1935–2013

Torah scholar and philosopher. Rabbi Schochet was born in Switzerland. Rabbi Schochet was a renowned authority on kabbalah and Jewish law and authored more than 30 books on Jewish philosophy and mysticism. He also served as professor of philosophy at Humber College in Toronto, Canada. Rabbi Schochet was a member of the executive committee of the Rabbinical Alliance of America and of the Central Committee of Chabad-Lubavitch Rabbis, and served as the Halachic guide for the Rohr Jewish Learning Institute.

"Cast your burden upon G-d and He will sustain you" (Psalms 55:23). "Commit your way unto G-d and trust in Him, and He will act" (Psalms 37:5) to provide what is good and beneficial for you.

ALL PRAYERS ANSWERED

It would seem that some prayers are not answered. This does not mean, however, that they were in vain or not effective.

First of all, the principal objective of prayer is not that it be answered according to wish. Thus we are taught that he who sets his mind in prayer on the anticipation of seeing it fulfilled (*iyun tefilah)*, will suffer heartache, as it is written, "Hope deferred makes the heart ache" (Proverbs 13:12). The ultimate goal, therefore, is not the actual fulfillment of the request submitted, but the awareness "that in the whole universe there is none to whom it is fitting to pray other than G-d," and the recognition that man is altogether deficient "and only G-d can provide whatever he lacks."

The mental, emotional and spiritual results of prayer, as defined above, are more than sufficient to render *tefilah* worthwhile and effective.

To be sure, this does not mean that one should ignore the literal or common meaning of prayer, to petition G-d for all and any needs. On the contrary: when one sees that he prayed and was not answered, he should pray again and again, as it is said, "Hope in G-d, be strong and let your heart be valiant, and hope in G-d." Nonetheless, one must not lose sight of the essence and underlying premises of the principle of *tefilah*.

Secondly: Some objectives, as, for example, the Messianic redemption, require multiple prayers—both in terms of the prayers articulated as well as in terms of petitioners. Though the literal results of these prayers are not perceived at the time, each of them is and remains significant: each of these prayers is effective, albeit partially, insofar that each contributes to the necessary sum-total, the ultimate whole.

Moreover, these individual prayers are not only part of a whole, which takes time to complete, but they effect partial or 'miniature' responses of the very genus of the request submitted to G-d. For throughout the period of the *galut* there are many forms of 'miniature' salvations and redemptions.

Thirdly, and most importantly: Every single prayer is effective and answered, though not necessarily on the level of the petitioner. In the words of the Baal Shem Tov:

> *One must believe that as soon as the prayer has been uttered, one is answered for what has been requested. It may be asked, that at times the fulfillment of the request is not perceived. In fact, however, (the prayer has been answered, except that) it is in a manner hidden from the petitioner. For example, one may have prayed specifically for the removal of his distress, and this request was granted in terms of the world in general. (The petitioner's personal anguish may remain, but) that itself is actually for his own good, or to expiate some sin, and the like. When man's mind is set on awaiting the actual fulfillment on the specific, personal level, he brings materialism into the prayer, which in fact should be completely spiritual, for the sake of the* Shechinah *and not for the sake of the mundane. (The ulterior motive, therefore,) becomes a separating barrier.*

In another version, recorded by the Baal Shem Tov's grandson and disciple R. Mosheh Chaim Ephrayim of Sudylkov:

My master and grandfather said that all prayers are effective in the upper worlds, and sometimes in other parts of the earth. (Sometimes one may ask for one thing, and he is given something else; and sometimes the prayer's effects are limited to the upper worlds.) He based this on the verse, "When the exalted things are debased among the children of man" (Psalms 12:9)—i.e., "the things that stand in the pinnacle of the universe, yet people debase them." This refers to prayer which effects awesome things in the highest places of the worlds, yet people think that their prayers are not accepted and therefore treat them lightly.

For sometimes the effect of prayer is in the upper realms of the universe, and not below, and people, therefore, think that their prayer was, Heaven forbid, in vain. In truth, however, this is not the case. All prayers are accepted, but their effect is according to what omniscient G-d determines to be for the best interests of man and the world.

> *Excessive self-deprecation on the part of man, thinking his prayers to be of no avail, is in effect false humility, and may lead him astray. False humility causes man to think that his service of G-d, his prayers and Torah, is of no consequence. In truth, however, he must realize that he is a 'ladder set on the earth, and its top reaches into heaven': all his motions, his speech, his conduct and involvements, leave impressions in the uppermost realms. By thinking to himself, 'Who am I that I could blemish or correct anything above or below, that my doings will leave a mark,' he will be led to follow the inclinations of his heart, imagining that he has nothing to worry about.*

Thus we are taught, '*Da mah lema'alah mimach*'—know, that whatever is Above—it is all *from and through you yourself*! All of man's actions are of cosmic significance. All of man's actions elicit commensurate reactions.

Deep Calling Unto Deep (Brooklyn: Kehot Publication Society, 1990), pp. 89–96

LESSON THREE

A WORK OF ASCENT

MAKING SENSE OF LITURGY, ONE STEP AT A TIME

Many attempt to pray, but struggle to generate a genuine experience. Others struggle with deciphering the structure and texts of the Jewish prayer book. This lesson exposes the brilliance, beauty, and objectives behind the prayer book's ladder-like structure; and identifies the ways in which its texts coax and guide a genuine prayer experience.

I. Prayer Ladder

Exercise 3.1

Caption each of the following five illustrations:

Text 1

THE REBBE, RABBI MENACHEM MENDEL SCHNEERSON,
SEFER HAMAAMARIM MELUKAT, VOL. 2, PP. 266–267

הַהֶפְרֵשׁ בֵּין עוֹלָמוֹת הָעֶלְיוֹנִים לְעוֹלָם הַזֶה: דִּבָעוֹלָם הַזֶה נִרְגָשׁ שֶׁמְּצִיאוּתוֹ מֵעַצְמוּתוֹ.

וּכַּמְבוֹאָר . . . הַהֶפְרֵשׁ בֵּין נִבְרָא וְאוֹר.

דְּאוֹר הוּא רְאָיָה עַל הַמָּאוֹר, דִּכְשֶׁאָנוּ רוֹאִים אוֹר, הָאוֹר עַצְמוֹ מַרְאֶה וּמְגַלֶּה שֶׁיֵּשׁ מָאוֹר.

מַה שֶּׁאֵין כֵּן יֵשׁ הַנִּבְרָא הִנֵּה לֹא זוּ בִּלְבַד שֶׁאֵינוֹ מְגַלֶּה בּוֹרֵא, אֶלָּא עוֹד זֹאת שֶׁהוּא מַעֲלִים וּמַסְתִּיר עַל זֶה, וְאַדְּרַבָּה נִרְגָשׁ שֶׁמְּצִיאוּתוֹ מֵעַצְמוּתוֹ (אֶלָּא שֶׁמִּצַד הַשֵּׂכֶל מוּכְרָח שֶׁאֵינוֹ כֵּן).

The unique quality of our physical world, which distinguishes it from all spiritual worlds, is that the beings of this world feel as though they exist independently.

This can be explained . . . by analyzing the difference between G-d's "light" and G-d's "creations."

Light is a reflection of a luminary. The very existence of light demonstrates to the onlooker that there is a luminary.

Creations, however, are different. Not only do they not reflect their Creator; they conceal Him. Creations feel as though they exist independently. Only through logic can they realize this is not so.

RABBI MENACHEM MENDEL SCHNEERSON 1902–1994

The towering Jewish leader of the 20th century, known as "the Lubavitcher Rebbe," or simply as "the Rebbe." Born in southern Ukraine, the Rebbe escaped Nazi-occupied Europe, arriving in the U.S. in June 1941. The Rebbe inspired and guided the revival of traditional Judaism after the European devastation, impacting virtually every Jewish community the world over. The Rebbe often emphasized that the performance of just one additional good deed could usher in the era of Mashiach. The Rebbe's scholarly talks and writings have been printed in more than 200 volumes.

Text 2

THE REBBE, RABBI MENACHEM MENDEL SCHNEERSON,
TORAT MENACHEM 5715:2, PP. 268-269

דְהִנֵּה תְּפִלָּה הִיא בַּעֲלִיָּה מִלְמַטָּה לְמַעְלָה, דְהַסֵּדֶר בַּעֲבוֹדַת הַתְּפִלָּה הוּא שֶׁהַהַתְחָלָה הוּא מִמַּדְרֵיגוֹת נְמוּכוֹת בְּיוֹתֵר, וְאַחַר כָּךְ עוֹלֶה בְּעִילוּי אַחַר עִילוּי, עַד שֶׁבָּא לְמַדְרֵיגוֹת הַנַּעֲלוֹת בְּיוֹתֵר. וּכְמוֹ שֶׁכָּתוּב (בְּרֵאשִׁית כח, יב), "סוּלָּם מוּצָּב אַרְצָה וְרֹאשׁוֹ מַגִּיעַ הַשָּׁמָיְמָה", שֶׁהַתְחָלַת הַתְּפִלָּה הוּא מֵעִנְיָנִים נְמוּכִים שֶׁמּוּצָּבִים אַרְצָה, וְכָךְ הוּא עוֹלֶה בְּעִילוּי אַחַר עִילוּי בְּסֵדֶר וְהַדְרָגָה, עַד שֶׁבָּא לְעִנְיָנִים הַנַּעֲלִים בְּיוֹתֵר, וְעַד שֶׁמַּגִּיעַ הַשָּׁמָיְמָה.

Prayer is a process of ascent. It starts from the lowest spiritual point and ascends, step-by-step, to the pinnacle of spirituality. It is like the ladder in Jacob's dream, "A ladder planted in the earth that reaches up to Heaven" (GENESIS 28:12). Similarly, prayer begins in a lowly "earthlike" state and ascends gradually until it reaches the spiritual pinnacle, reaching "up to Heaven."

Figure 3.1

The Ladder of Prayer

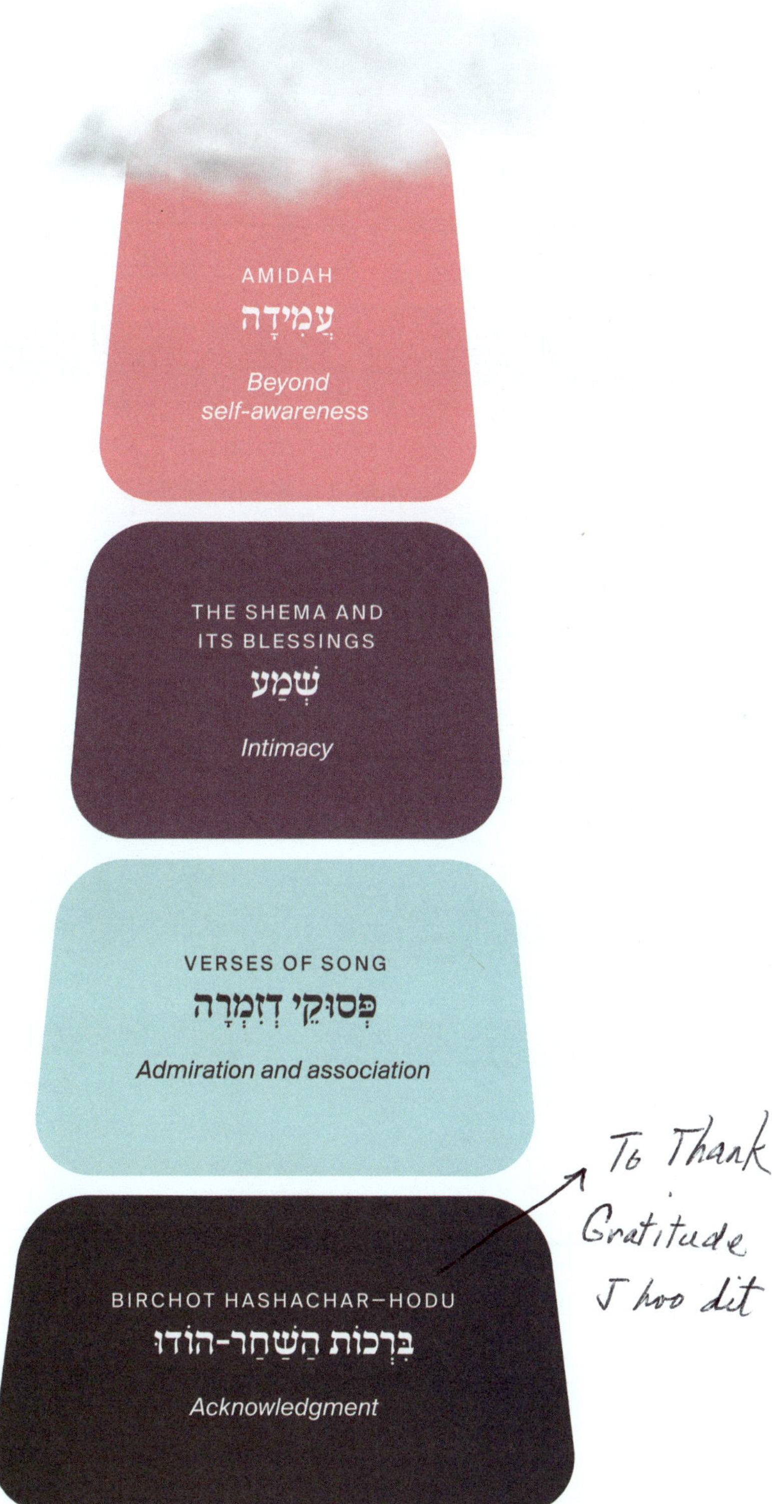

Text 3

RABBI CHAIM ELIEZER BICHOVSKY,
GINZEI NISTAROT, OR NE'ERAV, P. 21

הָרַב הַמַּגִּיד הָיָה שׁוֹהֶה בִּתְפִלָּתוֹ כַּמָּה שָׁעוֹת, וְהָיָה בִּסְבִיבָה שֶׁלּוֹ אִישׁ אֶחָד לַמְדָן וִירֵא שָׁמַיִם וּמִתְפַּלֵּל עַל פִּי כַּוָּנַת אֲרִי זַ"ל, וְלֹא הָיָה מַאֲרִיךְ כָּל כַּךְ, וְהָיָה לוֹ לְפֶלֶא.

הָאִישׁ הַנִּזְכָּר לְעֵיל הָיָה עָשִׁיר, וְהָיָה נוֹסֵעַ פַּעַם בְּשָׁנָה לְלַייפְּצִיג, וְשׁוֹהֶה כְּדֵי מִסְחָרוֹ וְחוֹזֵר לְבֵיתוֹ, וְיוֹשֵׁב כָּל הַשָּׁנָה עַל הַתּוֹרָה וַעֲבוֹדָה.

פַּעַם אַחַת, עָבַר לְרֶגֶל מִסְחָרוֹ דֶּרֶךְ מֶעזְרִיטְשׁ וְנִשְׁאַר שָׁם לִרְאוֹת הַתְּפִלָּה שֶׁל הַמַּגִּיד. וְנִכְנַס אֵלָיו וְשָׁאַל מִמֶּנּוּ שֶׁהוּא מִתְפַּלֵּל גַּם כֵּן עַל פִּי כַּוָּנַת הָאֲרִי זַ"ל, וְאֵינוֹ מוּכְרָח לְהַאֲרִיךְ כָּל כַּךְ?

שָׁאַל לוֹ הַמַּגִּיד, מִמַּה הוּא מִתְפַּרְנֵס?

וְאָמַר לוֹ, שֶׁיֵּשׁ לוֹ מְעַט סְלָעִים, וְנוֹסֵעַ פַּעַם בְּשָׁנָה עַל יָרִיד וּמֵבִיא סְחוֹרוֹת הַיְדוּעִים לוֹ, וּמוֹכֵר אוֹתָם בְּעִירוֹ תֵּיכֶף, וּמֵהָרֶיוַח מִתְפַּרְנֵס

שָׁאַל לוֹ [הָרַב הַמַּגִּיד]: "וּמֵהֵיכָן תֵּדַע שֶׁהִרְוַחְתָּ?"

אָמַר לוֹ: "אֲנִי כּוֹתֵב הַסַּךְ שֶׁהוֹצֵאתִי עַל הַסְּחוֹרָה וְהַהוֹצָאוֹת, וְכַאֲשֶׁר אֲנִי מוֹכֵר אֲנִי כּוֹתֵב כַּמָּה פָּדִיתִי, וַאֲנִי מְנַכֶּה הַקֶּרֶן וְהַהוֹצָאוֹת מִסַּךְ הַנִּפְדֶּה, וּמַה שֶּׁנִּשְׁאַר הוּא הָרֶיוַח".

אָמַר לוֹ הָרַב הַמַּגִּיד: "וְלָמָּה לְךָ לְבַלּוֹת זְמַן לִנְסוֹעַ עַל הַיָּרִיד וְלָבוֹא? תִּכְתּוֹב עַל הַנְּיָיר הַקֶּרֶן וְהַהוֹצָאוֹת, וְתִכְתּוֹב הַפִּדְיוֹן, וּתְנַכֶּה הַקֶּרֶן וְהַהוֹצָאוֹת מִן הַפִּדְיוֹן!"

וְהִתְחִיל הַסּוֹחֵר לִצְחֹק, "וְכִי מִן הַכְּתִיבָה יָבוֹא הָרֶיוַח בְּלֹא נְסִיעָה וּקְנִיָּה? וּבְהֶכְרֵחַ צָרִיךְ לִנְסוֹעַ וְלִקְנוֹת וּלְבַלּוֹת זְמַן וְלִמְכּוֹר, וְאָז יוּכַל לִהְיוֹת רֶיוַח".

אָמַר לוֹ הַמַּגִּיד: "הַכַּוָּנוֹת הֵם גַּם כֵּן כְּמוֹ הַסְּחוֹרָה: אִם לֹא תִּהְיָה קָשׁוּר בְּדַעְתְּךָ כְּאִלּוּ אַתָּה שָׁם, הוּא כְּאִלּוּ כּוֹתֵב הַקֶּרֶן וְהָרֶיוַח,

RABBI CHAIM ELIEZER BICHOVSKY
D. 1924

Chasidic philosopher and publisher. Rabbi Bichovsky lived in the Ukraine and moved to Israel toward the end of his life. He was a student of Rabbi Shemariah Noach of Babruysk and is noted for publishing many manuscripts of Chabad Chasidic philosophy. He served as bookkeeper and chairman of Colel Chabad, a charity in Israel established by Rabbi Shneur Zalman of Liadi in 1788.

אֲשֶׁר מִזֶּה לֹא יֵשׁ שׁוּם תּוֹעֶלֶת. אֲבָל אִם תִּקְשׁוֹר נַפְשְׁךָ שָׁמָּה, וִיהְיֶה שְׁהוּת לִקְנוֹת דָּבָר חֵפֶץ, אָז תַּרְוִיחַ בְּהַכַּוָּונוֹת. וְעַל כֵּן צָרִיךְ עַל זֶה שְׁהוּת זְמַן בְּעֵת הַתְּפִלָּה".

The Magid of Mezeritch would pray for hours at a time, meditating on the kabbalistic themes explained by the Arizal. In a nearby town, there lived another learned and G-d-fearing man who similarly prayed with the Arizal's kabbalistic meditations. However, this man completed his prayers in a far shorter time than the Magid, leaving him puzzled at the Magid's slow pace.

Now, this fellow happened to be a wealthy businessman. Once a year, he traveled to the grand fair at Leipzig to pursue his business affairs. He remained there for a while, but once he had finished, he returned home and spent the rest of the year engrossed solely in Torah study and Divine service.

On one of his trips to Leipzig, this merchant first stopped in Mezeritch to again observe the Magid in prayer. Once the Magid had completed his prayers, the fellow entered the Magid's room and asked, "Why does it take you so long to pray? I also pray with the Arizal's meditations, but it doesn't take me nearly as long!"

The Magid replied with a question, "What is your source of income?"

"Once a year, I travel to the business fair in Leipzig to buy merchandise," he explained with surprise. "When I get back home, I sell it immediately and make a profit from the sales."

"How do you know that you've made a profit?" challenged the Magid.

"Why, I document the prices that I buy and sell the merchandise for!" the merchant responded. "I then subtract the buying price and my other business expenses from the sales price. The remaining sum is my profit."

"But why do you waste so much time traveling to and from Leipzig?" the Magid pressed further. "Why don't you just document the buying and selling prices and subtract the former from the latter?"

The businessman chuckled at the absurdity and retorted, "Will documentation on its own really make any money? I need actual merchandise for that! I need to travel to Leipzig and take the time to actually buy and sell the merchandise. Only then can I make a profit."

The Magid responded, "The meditations of prayer are just like merchandise. If you do not actually experience the meditation, it is like simply documenting buying and selling prices. This is ineffective. You need to apply yourself to the meditation and take the time to actually 'buy something.' Only then will the meditations be effective. This is why it takes me so long to pray."

II. Acknowledgment

Text 4

MODEH ANI, PRAYER UPON AWAKENING

מוֹדֶה אֲנִי לְפָנֶיךָ מֶלֶךְ חַי וְקַיָּם, שֶׁהֶחֱזַרְתָּ בִּי נִשְׁמָתִי בְּחֶמְלָה. רַבָּה אֱמוּנָתֶךָ.

I offer thanks to You, living and enduring King, for You have mercifully restored my soul within me; Your faithfulness is great.

Text 5

MORNING BLESSINGS

בָּרוּךְ אַתָּה ה' אֱלֹהֵינוּ מֶלֶךְ הָעוֹלָם, הַנּוֹתֵן לַשֶּׂכְוִי בִינָה לְהַבְחִין בֵּין יוֹם וּבֵין לָיְלָה.

בָּרוּךְ אַתָּה ה' אֱלֹהֵינוּ מֶלֶךְ הָעוֹלָם, פּוֹקֵחַ עִוְרִים.

בָּרוּךְ אַתָּה ה' אֱלֹהֵינוּ מֶלֶךְ הָעוֹלָם, מַתִּיר אֲסוּרִים.

בָּרוּךְ אַתָּה ה' אֱלֹהֵינוּ מֶלֶךְ הָעוֹלָם, זוֹקֵף כְּפוּפִים.

Blessed are You, L-rd our G-d, King of the universe, Who gives the rooster understanding to distinguish between day and night.

Blessed are You, L-rd our G-d, King of the universe, Who opens the eyes of the blind.

Blessed are You, L-rd our G-d, King of the universe, Who releases the bound.

Blessed are You, L-rd our G-d, King of the universe, Who straightens the bowed.

Text 6

THE REBBE, RABBI MENACHEM MENDEL SCHNEERSON,
TORAT MENACHEM 5715:2, PP. 232-233

וּלְהָבִין מַהוּ עִנְיַן הַהוֹדָאָה שֶׁמּוֹדִים לוֹ יִתְבָּרֵךְ, וַהֲרֵי אֵינוֹ שַׁיָּךְ מַחֲלוֹקֶת נֶגְדוֹ יִתְבָּרֵךְ, עַד שֶׁיִּצְטָרְכוּ לְהוֹדוֹת לוֹ?

אַךְ הָעִנְיָן בָּזֶה הוּא, שֶׁאֵין זוֹ מַחֲלוֹקֶת בְּגוּף הָעִנְיָן, כִּי אִם, שֶׁהֶרְגֵּשׁ הַנִּבְרָאִים הוּא שֶׁלְּמַטָּה יֵשׁ וּלְמַעְלָה אַיִן, וְלָכֵן אִי אֶפְשָׁר לִהְיוֹת בְּהַשָּׂגָתָם הַדֵּיעָה הָעֶלְיוֹנָה שֶׁלְּמַעְלָה יֵשׁ וּלְמַטָּה אַיִן . . .

אָמְנָם אַף שֶׁעִנְיָן זֶה אֵינוֹ בְּהַשָּׂגַת הַתַּחְתּוֹן, מִכָּל מָקוֹם מוֹדִים אֲנַחְנוּ לָךְ, שֶׁאָנוּ מוֹדִים שֶׁהָאֱמֶת הוּא כְּמוֹ שֶׁהוּא בְּהַדֵּיעָה הָעֶלְיוֹנָה, שֶׁלְּמַעְלָה יֵשׁ וּלְמַטָּה אַיִן.

The theme of conceding to G-d requires explanation: How is it possible to argue with G-d, making it necessary to concede to Him?

The "argument" we are discussing is not over objective reality. It is a difference in feeling. We and G-d differ in how we feel about the world: while G-d experiences Himself as a genuine entity and the world as a created entity, we experience the world as a genuine entity and G-d's existence as theoretical. We are simply not capable of experiencing the world the same way G-d does....

Nevertheless, despite our innate feeling, we concede to G-d's experience of reality. We concede that His existence is genuine and ours is only created.

Figure 3.2

Morning Blessings

Based on Rabbi Menachem Mendel of Lubavitch, *Or HaTorah, Maamarei Razal–Inyanim;* and Rabbi Shalom Dovber Schneersohn, *Sefer Hamaamarim* 5672, vol. 2, p. 738

BLESSED ARE YOU . . . WHO:	DEEPER THEME
Gives the rooster understanding to distinguish between day and night.	Distinguishing between good and bad
Opens the eyes of the blind.	Seeing the full context
Releases the bound.	Freeing our Divine soul from its bodily "captivity"
Straightens the bowed.	Placing our mind above our emotions

Takeaway Exercise

Acknowledging. Identify a specific area in your life in which you feel it is important for you to work harder on advancing beyond superficial function and tapping into that experience's G-dly and core purpose. Meditate on this each morning while reciting the Morning Blessings.

We will discuss how it went during our next lesson.

Key Points

1. The morning prayers are structured like a ladder. We begin prayer at the bottom, feeling naturally distant from G-d, and we slowly climb closer to Him. Each day, we begin this climb anew.

2. The first stage of prayer is *acknowledgment*. The simple function of this stage of prayer is to acknowledge G-d as the Source of all the blessings in our lives and to express our gratitude to Him for them.

3. Our animalistic soul views itself and the world as independent of G-d; it is focused on pursuing its base desires. Our Divine soul views ourselves and the world as perpetually connected to G-d and as instruments of His will.

4. The deeper meaning of the *acknowledgment* stage is "concession": the animalistic perspective is more instinctive, and so the *acknowledgment* stage of prayer guides us in the process of conceding to the Divine perspective and identifying with it.

TECHINOT FOR
THE SEPARATION OF CHALAH

The following *techinot* are written for recital before the separation of chalah, a small chunk of dough symbolically discarded before baking bread. Chalah has been a *mitzvah* traditionally practiced and cherished by women in particular.

***Seder Techinot*, Amsterdam 1791**

Devra Kay, trans., *Seyder Tkhines*
(Philadelphia, PA: Jewish Publication Society, 2004)

דיא תחנה זאגט מן אז מן חלה נעמט מיט גרושר כוונה :

גלויבט ביסט דוא גאט אונזר הער · גאט אונזר עלטרן דוא האסט געהייליגט
דיין פֿאלק ישראל איבר אז אלי דיא פֿעלקר אויף ערדן אונ׳ האסט אונז
געבאטן דיין געבאט · אונ׳ האסט אונז געבאטן ווען איר קנעטן איין טייג אונזרט ברוט
צו אב טיילן דר פֿון איין טייל צו דיר גאט אלמעכטיגר אונ׳ האסט אונז בפֿולן צו
געבן דעם כהן דער דא איז ריין פֿון אלי אום רייניגקייט · דען דוא האסט אב
גשייטן איין טייל פֿון דר ערדן אונ׳ האסט בשאפֿן דער פֿון דען מענטשן אונ׳
האסט אים געבן איין זיל איין רייני פֿון שטאט דאש רייני וואו דר כהן גדול דר
רייניגר שטיט דא איז קיין אונרייניגקייט : נון זייא איר געטראפֿט אום ווילן אונזרי
זינד אונ׳ אונזר עלטרן דאש עס איז פֿר שטערט געווארן ירושלים שטאט דיא
הייליגי · אונ׳ דאש הייליג הויז דאז זיין נאמן איז געהייליגט דאריק דורך דיא כהנים
דיא דא האבן געברענגט אופפֿר אויף דען אופפֿר שטאל מיט גרושר רייניגקייט :
דא דורך זייא זיא ווערדיג געווזן צו עסין דאש הייליג ברוט צו פֿר דיר גאט איין גאט ·
אונ׳ איצונד האבן איר קיין כהן דער זיך קאן ריין האלטן נאך געבאט דיין הייליגה
תורה גלייך וואל וויל איך האלטן דיין געבאט אונ׳ וויל אב טיילן איין טייל פֿון טייג
צו לובן אונ׳ צו עהרן דיין הייליגן נאמן אונ׳ וויל עש פֿר ברענן דז קיינר פֿון ישראל
זאל דראן שטרויכלן · אונ׳ בית דיך גאט איין הער דאז דוא איך אונ׳ איין מאן אונ׳
איין קינדר זאלטש לאזן זוכה זיין צו דער נעבן דאש דאש הייליג הויז זאל ווידר
גיבויאט ווערן אונ׳ ירושלים זאל ווידר זיין אז פֿאר אלטש אונ׳ דיין פֿאלק ישראל
זאל ווידר וואונן אין דען הייליגן לאנד דאז דוא האסט געהייליגט דיין הייליגן נאמן
לויטן אין אונ׳ צו געבן דיא אב טיילונג דעם כהן דער דא איז ריין פֿון אלר
אונרייניגהייט אין גרויסן פֿרייד מיט פֿאר זאמלונג ישראל דש זייא וואר אין גאטש
נאמן אמן : אונ׳ אויך דיא ברכה :

Image courtesy of the National Library of Israel.

You are beloved, G-d our G-d,
And G-d of our forefathers.
You have sanctified Your people Israel
Above all people,
And have commanded
That when we bake our Sabbath bread,
We should separate one part of the dough
For You, G-d Almighty,
As it was done for the Priest,
Who was free of all impurity,
Just as You separated a part of the earth
From which You created humankind,
And gave each one a pure soul.
Where the High Priest stood
There was no corruption.
Now we are punished for our sins
And the sins of our forefathers.
And His city, Jerusalem, is destroyed,
As is the Holy House
In which Your Name was made holy
Through the Priests
Who brought offerings
To the offering stool,
According to the law.
Through the worthiness of the Priest,
The holy bread was eaten
For You, G-d, my G-d.
But now we have no Priest
To keep the Commandment
Of Your holy Torah.
I wish to keep Your Commandment,
And wish to divide off
Part of the dough
To praise and honor
Your Holy Name.
And I wish to burn it,
So none of Israel
Shall be tempted to eat it.
And I beg You,
G-d, my G-d,
To allow me and my children
To live to see Your Holy House
Built again in Jerusalem as before,
And all Your people living again
In the Holy Land
That You made holy with Your Name,
So that we may again
Give the separated portion of dough
To the Priest,
Who is free from all impurities,
In great happiness
With Israel gathered together
In G-d's name
Amen.

Sarah bat Tovim, *Techinah Sheloshah She'arim* (Vilna, 1850), pp. 3–4*

מיין חַלָה זאָל אזוֹ אָן גינוּמען זיין אז איין קָרְבָּן אויף דעם מִזְבֵּחַ איז אָן גינוּמען גיוואָרין מיין מִצְוָה זאָל אָן גינוּמן זיין גלייך ווי איך האָבּ זי רעכט מְקַיֵים גווען.

פר צייטן איז דאָס אָן גקוּמן דעם כֹּהֵן אוּנ ער האָט פר דעם פר געבִּין די זינד אזוֹ זאָל מיר אויך פאר געבִּין ווערין מיינע זינד איך זאָל זיין גלייך ווי איין נאיי גיבּאָרין קינד איך זאָל קענען מיינע ליבּע שַׁבָּתִים אוּנ יָמִים טוֹבִים עהרין ער זאָל מיך בּשׂערין איך זאָל מיך קענען מיט מיין מאן אוּנ מיט מיינע קינדר דר נערין עשׂ זאָל אָן גנוּמען ווערן מיין מִצְוָה פוּן חַלָה נעמען אז מיינע קינדרלעך זאָלין גשׂפּייזט ווערן פוּן דעם ליבּן גאָט בּ"ה מיט גרוישׂ רַחֲמָנוּת אוּנ מיט גרויס דער בּארימקייט עשׂ זאָל גגליכין זיין מיין מִצְו ת חַלָה גלייך וויא איך האָבּ מַעְשֵׂר גיגעבִּין. וויא איך טוּא מיין מִצְוָה פוּן חַלָה מיטין גאנצין הארצין. אזוֹא זאָל גאָט בּ"ה מיך היטין פאר פּיין אוּנ שמארצין:

May my chalah be accepted as a sacrifice on the holy altar and may my *mitzvah* be accepted as if it had been properly executed there.

In olden times, this chalah dough was set aside for the priest, and our sins were forgiven in return. May my sins be forgiven now so that I may become like a newborn child. May I be able to honor my beloved Shabbat and festivals. May G-d destine for me that I, my husband, and my children be well nourished, and may my *mitzvah* of separating chalah be accepted so that my little children should be sustained by our dear G-d with great compassion and with great mercy. May my observance of the *mitzvah* of chalah be considered equal to having given the tithe. Just as I observe the *mitzvah* of chalah with my whole heart, so may G-d protect me from anguish and pain.

*The Yiddish text for this *techinah* uses old Yiddish terms and spelling conventions.

SARAH BAT TOVIM
17TH–18TH CENTURY

Sarah was born in Sataniv, Ukraine, where her grandfather served as the rabbi. Known as Sarah bat Tovim (Sarah from a good family), she writes that she lived a sad life as a wanderer. Sarah authored the extremely popular *Sheloshah She'arim –Three Gates*, a handbook containing instructions and prayers for the three *mitzvot* traditionally cherished by Jewish women: Shabbat candles, chalah, and family purity.

Count Your Blessings

A series of blessings customarily recited each morning is collectively known as *Birchat Hashachar*—the Morning Blessings. Each of these calls attention to another element of the daily human experience that is otherwise taken for granted. These daily blessings provide an opportunity to pause and reflect on our good fortune for the basic underpinnings and purpose of life, and they encourage us to express gratitude to G-d for gifting us with the functions and roles described in the blessings.

Taking the time to enter a gratitude mindset each morning is a surefire method of channeling goodness and positivity into your day. All it takes is a little mindfulness and a couple of minutes.

Brief explanations have been added to the following excerpt from the first part of the Morning Blessings:

1 The Rooster

בָּרוּךְ אַתָּה ה׳, אֱלֹקֵינוּ מֶלֶךְ הָעוֹלָם,
הַנּוֹתֵן לַשֶּׂכְוִי בִינָה לְהַבְחִין בֵּין יוֹם וּבֵין לָיְלָה.

Blessed are You, G-d, King of the universe,
Who grants the rooster the understanding
to distinguish between day and night.

Before electrical alarm clocks, people relied on nature's alarm clock—the rooster—to awaken at dawn. This blessing was a way to thank G-d for providing a reliable method of timely arousal from sleep. As we recite the blessing today, we bear in mind (a) whichever of G-d's marvels we use to wake up each morning, and (b) the diverse wonders of nature found in the animal kingdom.

Each prayer offers multiple layers of significance. A deeper insight notes[1] that the text employs a rare Hebrew term for rooster, *sechvi*, which carries an alternate translation, "heart." We thank G-d for granting us the mental and emotional capacity to distinguish between moral day and night—between that which is good, sacred, and worthy, and the opposite. This is a morning blessing, to remind us that throughout our day we will face choices that require a moral compass and an inner strength to embrace the good and distance ourselves from its opposite.

1. Rosh, Berachot 9:23.

② Vision

בָּרוּךְ אַתָּה ה', אֱלֹקֵינוּ מֶלֶךְ הָעוֹלָם,
פּוֹקֵחַ עִוְרִים.

Blessed are You, G-d, King of the universe, Who opens the eyes of the blind.

The human eye is an astonishing, complex organ. To avoid taking this major miracle for granted, we thank G-d each day for the blessing of sight.

Helen Keller (who was blind) famously said, "Recently I was visited by a very good friend who had just returned from a long walk in the woods, and I asked her what she had observed. 'Nothing in particular,' she replied. I might have been incredulous had I not been accustomed to such responses, for long ago I became convinced that the seeing see little."

A Chasidic deeper insight[2] views this blessing as addressing the gift of being able to see the bigger picture. Poor decisions are often due to shortsightedness or a failure to see beneath the surface. Conversely, positive and Divine choices arrive upon exercising our mental ability to view the larger truth: a truly valuable gift.

—

2. Rabbi Menachem Mendel of Lubavitch, *Or HaTorah Maamarei Chazal*, p. 306.

③ Stretching the Limbs

בָּרוּךְ אַתָּה ה', אֱלֹקֵינוּ מֶלֶךְ הָעוֹלָם,
מַתִּיר אֲסוּרִים.

Blessed are You, G-d, King of the universe, Who releases the bound.

Our limbs barely move or stretch as we sleep; we largely appear as if we were bound. Upon awakening we begin to move and stretch, and we thank G-d for the gift of movement.

A deeper insight[3] sees this as a reference to the battle between the two souls within us. Our natural, impulsive soul holds a greater grip on our conscious character and daily choices. By contrast, our pristine, Divine soul is largely a prisoner of the former. The Divine soul longs to find joy in sacred endeavors but is shackled by our animalistic impulses and goals. There are moments, however, when our Divine soul succeeds in breaking free from captivity and it shines through our noble deeds. Our ability to tip the scales in favor of our Divine soul is a gift from G-d. Each morning, we thank G-d for the power to overcome our baser instincts and to act in accordance with our Divine core.

—

3. Rabbi Dovber of Lubavitch, *Torat Chayim*, Shemot 1, p. 74c.

4 Sitting Up

בָּרוּךְ אַתָּה ה', אֱלֹקֵינוּ מֶלֶךְ הָעוֹלָם,
זוֹקֵף כְּפוּפִים.

Blessed are You, G-d, King of the universe, Who straightens those who are stooped.

After lying prone in a horizontal position for hours, we thank G-d for the ability to prop our bodies up.

Looking deeper,[4] our head and the rest of our body are of similar altitude while we rest horizontally. We are similar to animals, whose heads are more or less on the same level as their bodies. A feature of human uniqueness is our ability to stand erect, with our head securely above and leading our body. This posture implies that our minds can control our impulses. As we thank G-d for our ability to sit up, we reflect on the Divine gift—the ability to use the mind to regulate emotions, thereby warding off pettiness, anger, and similar destructive emotional forces.

4. See Rabbi Menachem Mendel of Lubavitch, *Or HaTorah*, *Maamarei Chazal*, p. 306.

5 Clothing

בָּרוּךְ אַתָּה ה', אֱלֹקֵינוּ מֶלֶךְ הָעוֹלָם,
מַלְבִּישׁ עֲרֻמִּים.

Blessed are You, G-d, King of the universe, Who clothes the naked.

We thank G-d for the clothing we wear each day. At the dawn of time, G-d personally fashioned clothing for Adam and Eve, who realized their nakedness after committing the first sin. The Torah subsequently commanded us to follow G-d's example, including providing clothing for those in need.

Included in this blessing is a reminder and appreciation for our inherent sense of modesty and decency that, among other things, instinctively compels us to don clothing.

A deeper reflection draws our attention to the clothing of our soul—namely, the *mitzvot*. As clothing and work gear enable us to operate, so do soul-garments allow the soul to function in this world. We thank G-d at the start of each day for the tremendous opportunity to connect with Him through the gift of *mitzvot*.[5]

thought
speech
action
> Clothing of the soul

5. See *Or HaTorah*, Ibid.

6 Strength to the Weary

בָּרוּךְ אַתָּה ה׳, אֱלֹקֵינוּ מֶלֶךְ הָעוֹלָם,
הַנּוֹתֵן לַיָּעֵף כֹּחַ.

Blessed are You, G-d, King of the universe,
Who gives strength to the weary.

After awakening, moving, and getting dressed, we begin to internalize that refreshed morning feeling—and thank G-d for our new dose of energy.

Looking deeper, there are moments in our lifelong spiritual journey when fatigue sets in, inspiration runs dry, and we are left feeling lifeless in terms of zeal or motivation. Then, G-d reaches out and awakens us with a jolt—we are reenergized and eternally grateful.[6]

6. See *Or HaTorah*, Ibid.

7 Habitable Land

בָּרוּךְ אַתָּה ה׳, אֱלֹקֵינוּ מֶלֶךְ הָעוֹלָם,
רוֹקַע הָאָרֶץ עַל הַמָּיִם.

Blessed are You, G-d, King of the universe,
Who spreads out the earth upon the water.

As we move to take our first steps of a fresh day, we thank G-d for terra firma. The Torah relates that at the start of Creation, all the earth was covered by deep water, until on the third day of Creation, G-d divided the surface of the globe between oceans and dry land, although water may be present deeper within. We thank G-d for His kindness in providing us with habitable terrain and the ability to maneuver across it.

Digging deeper, the vast ocean symbolizes unlimited aspirations, big ideas. However, without demarcation to ensure a concrete start and end, it all remains a dream. Every vision requires a line in the sand to contain and channel it, like the earth contains and stems the tide of the endless ocean. We thank G-d for our internal oceans—aspirations and visions—and even more so for the land spread upon it: the ability for practical implementation.[7]

7. Rabbi Avraham Yitzchak Hakohen Kook, *Olat Rei'yah*, Morning Blessings.

Count Your Blessings *continued*

8 The Steps of Humankind

בָּרוּךְ אַתָּה ה', אֱלֹקֵינוּ מֶלֶךְ הָעוֹלָם,
הַמֵּכִין מִצְעֲדֵי גָבֶר.

Blessed are You, G-d, King of the universe,
Who directs the steps of humanity.

As parents cheer excitedly for a baby's first step, this blessing reminds us to reflect and experience wonder and gratitude for *each* step we take, each day of our lives. Repetition dulls our attention to the marvel of walking, but a moment of reflection restores it.

From a deeper perspective, we cannot take a single step in life—in the sense of implementing a decision—without Divine direction. Our logical and emotional motivations for making a move exist only because G-d previously ordained that precise move, to serve a purpose of which we may be entirely unaware. All the unique elements of our life story that shape our character and experience are steps guided by G-d, placing us into settings in which we are uniquely outfitted to accomplish in this world.[8]

8. See Rabbi Menachem Mendel of Lubavitch, *Or HaTorah*, *Maamarei Chazal*, p. 307.

9 Provides All My Needs

בָּרוּךְ אַתָּה ה', אֱלֹקֵינוּ מֶלֶךְ הָעוֹלָם,
שֶׁעָשָׂה לִי כָּל צָרְכִּי.

Blessed are You, G-d, King of the universe,
Who has provided me with all my needs.

Our sages[9] associate this blessing with tying shoes or securing footgear. The "steps of humanity" (previous blessing) are made easier with protected feet. Indeed, on the two dates in the Jewish calendar (Yom Kippur and the Ninth of Av) on which leather footwear is prohibited, we omit this blessing.

In a mystical sense, "all my needs" includes spiritual requirements. We thank G-d for a universe filled with material and also spiritual potential.[10]

The blessing employs the past tense—"*Who has provided*." G-d has already allocated our needs and has orchestrated methods of delivering those blessings. The work we do to earn a profit or paycheck is simply a tool to channel those blessings to us—a concept worth recalling before leaving for work, to exchange pressure and panic for positivity and trust.

9. Talmud, Berachot 60b.

10. Rabbi Avraham Yitzchak Hakohen Kook, *Olat Rei'yah*, Morning Blessings.

10 Belt

בָּרוּךְ אַתָּה ה׳, אֱלֹקֵינוּ מֶלֶךְ הָעוֹלָם,
אוֹזֵר יִשְׂרָאֵל בִּגְבוּרָה.

Blessed are You, G-d, King of the universe,
Who girds Israel with might.

The Talmud[11] associates this blessing with tying a belt around the waist, the common way of securing the loose robes of antiquity before leaving home. It also carried the connotation of strength—a tight belt supports the torso during strenuous activities—and also power and prestige, for the belt held money pouches and weapons. We thank G-d for our strength as well as any honor G-d provides us.

Looking deeper, the belt is a tool that binds two entities, holding them in a mighty embrace. For a Jew, it symbolizes our close attachment to G-d. We thank G-d for His incredible closeness to us, and we acknowledge that our unique Divine intimacy empowers us to overcome the hardships of our history and the challenges of daily life.

On a more personal note, we bless G-d for girding us with the moral strength to overcome our base impulses.[12]

—

11. Talmud, Berachot 60b.

12. Rabbi Menachem Mendel of Lubavitch, *Or HaTorah, Maamarei Chazal*, p. 307.

11 Hat

בָּרוּךְ אַתָּה ה׳, אֱלֹקֵינוּ מֶלֶךְ הָעוֹלָם,
עוֹטֵר יִשְׂרָאֵל בְּתִפְאָרָה.

Blessed are You, G-d, King of the universe,
Who crowns Israel with glory.

Our ancient sages[13] associate this blessing with headgear—no Jew would leave home without it.

For millennia, headgear has been a hallmark feature of a Jewish individual. Males wear a *kipah* or another traditional head covering, and married females wear feminine hair coverings, according to the era and locale. A Jew is forever conscious of the One Above and walks constantly in the presence of the King of the universe. As we don our covering each morning, we thank G-d for the opportunity to maintain such an empowering and transformative consciousness throughout our day.

—

13. Talmud, Berachot 60b.

ADDITIONAL READING

Is G-d a He?

By Tamar Frankiel, PhD

Over the past few decades, a new and distinctive movement has emerged among Jews who are attempting to reclaim some kind of spiritual meaning for their lives. The question has been: If we are recovering our connection to the Divine, can we find that connection in traditional Judaism?

The question has been particularly difficult for many Jewish women because of the picture of G-d we inherited. The G-d we learned about as youngsters, that distant, kingly figure who watched over us seemed, for women discovering their feminine consciousness, too blatantly male. In popular feminism, the G-d of the Hebrew Bible, of Jewish, Christian, and Muslim tradition, has gotten a bad reputation as the patriarchal G-d of Western culture. Some turned to other religions in search of a G-d beyond gender or a philosophy that did not require a belief in G-d at all.

Is it true that G-d in Jewish teachings is patriarchal, that is, thoroughly imbued with male characteristics and values? On first glance, it would seem so. After all, G-d appears to be male. The siddur (prayer book) and the Bible refer to G-d only as He. Traditional Jewish teachings point out that G-d is really beyond all attributes, including those of gender. But, feminist writers have argued, while that is a nice theory, we as human beings need to use symbols and words to express our experience of the Divine. Can we not call G-d She? Further, the words we have inherited for G-d—Father, judge, Creator, L-rd—seem to spring from male experience, not female. Can a woman have an authentic relation to a G-d named only by male titles? Feminists have suggested that the titles reflect deeper levels of experience and perception that are also thoroughly male. The feminine experience of the Divine, whatever that might be, is simply not available in the tradition.

This longing for something authentically feminine is deep and significant. From it has come the desire to create new women's rituals and new feminine interpretations of the Bible. But how can these be also authentically Jewish? As serious Jewish feminists have recognized, we cannot create a new Judaism out of whole cloth. It might be possible in some other religion to create something new and still call it by the name of that religion, but not in Judaism: we are connected, intimately and deeply, to Torah

---

DR. TAMAR FRANKIEL, PHD, 1946–

Dean of Academic Affairs and Professor of Comparative Religion at the Academy for Jewish Religion in Los Angeles, California. Her areas of interest include Jewish women, spirituality, and prayer. She has authored several books on these subjects, including *Loving Prayer*.

itself, the Torah that was given at Sinai and has been passed down faithfully among our people through the ages. New creations lack depth unless they are connected to the tradition we have received, to our history, even if that history seems thoroughly male.

Two responses to this issue have emerged. One is a radical rereading of the Torah from a modernist historical perspective, suggesting that Jewish women in ancient times had religious resources which were not acknowledged by the men who handed down the Torah. Some feminists argue that we can resurrect the goddess-symbols of the ancient Near East. They suggest that the matriarchs themselves may have worshipped goddesses, and that Israelite women are known certainly to have done so. (We know of these practices from the criticisms heaped on goddess-worship by the prophets, but feminists dismiss those criticisms as mere propaganda of the zealous male followers of the patriarchal G-d.) Therefore, they say, we can borrow from goddess worship its rich feminine imagery; we can speak of the Queen of Heaven rather than just the King; we can use images of birth and fertility as well as of creation and conquest.

A second, more moderate view suggests that we do not need to return to goddesses. But, since G-d is neither male nor female, we can use feminine language and symbols to express uniquely feminine aspects of G-d. We can creatively retranslate Hebrew words, giving them a different nuance that is either beyond gender or has a feminine flavor. We can say Ruler of the universe rather than King, for example, to give a more neutral description. We can speak of G-d as our Father and Mother; we can mention the matriarchs as well as the patriarchs in our prayers and stories. Thus, the remembering and retelling of the tradition can come to have a less masculine cast, while remaining true to the words of the tradition as we have received it, and without passing over into idolatry.

Imaginative as these might seem, there are certain problems with such proposals. First, on ancient goddesses: these figures are not as beneficent as they might seem. We might like to fantasize a goddess as an all-beneficent mother in contrast to a harsh, legalistic father figure. But this is not true to what we know of ancient religions. Goddesses were not always sweet and beneficent. Some of the ritual practices connected to the goddesses were violent and, by modern standards, inhumane. In some cases the rituals involved sexual practices unacceptable to Jewish sensibilities.

Moreover, goddesses were not forbidden merely because they were feminine. Male gods were forbidden also, the Baals as well as the Asherahs. The prophets, from Moses onward, were struggling to unify the worship of G-d in order to ensure that the Jewish people remained connected to their unique historical experience of G-d, the G-d who brought them out of Egypt. We cannot forget that, no sooner had the newly freed slaves received the Torah, they began worshipping the golden calf, a favorite image of a Canaanite male god, even though they said, "This is the god that brought us out of Egypt." It would have been easy to extend the confusion, to become involved in the worship practiced by the Canaanite inhabitants of the land of Israel, and ultimately to forget our own history. In fact, that is exactly what we did; that is why the prophets repeatedly had to call the people to stop worshipping idols. They were reminding us that the Jewish perception of the Divine was connected with history, with purpose and direction that transcended any given place. The G-d who brought us out of Egypt had something bigger in mind, something more than sustaining our life, bringing us success and prosperity, or even life after death.

That sense of larger vision, of greater purpose, has sustained the Jewish people through the ages; and that larger vision assures us also that our G-d is ultimately beyond gender. To borrow from other religious experiences just because they are female can, and in our history almost always did, dilute the reality of our unique Jewish experience.

Women are attracted to goddess figures because it is possible to see in them characteristics women can imitate: strength, creativity, compassion. But this has been for centuries a major emphasis of Jewish thought about G-d: Recognizing that we cannot know G-d's essence, we focus on the Divine attributes or characteristics in order to learn the *derech Hashem*, the way of G-d, the things we can imitate and bring into our own lives. When we ask whether G-d is patriarchal or matriarchal, male or female, we are asking about these characteristics. How indeed has G-d revealed Himself/Herself, that aspect of the Divine that we can understand, to our people?

One would think, from feminist criticisms, that the Jewish view of G-d's attributes would list predominantly negative male characteristics: strength, warlikeness, imperialistic control, jealousy. But what in fact are the attributes which our sages have found in G-d? We can take them from the Kabbalah of Isaac Luria: wisdom, knowledge, lovingkindness, strength, harmony, perseverance, beauty, generativity, presence in earthly life. We can take them from the thirteen attributes: merciful, compassionate, slow to anger, abundant in kindness and truth, preserving kindness for thousands of generations, ever-forgiving. Indeed, our tradition finds a multitude of ways—more than we can easily translate into English—to describe the love and compassion of G-d for human beings. In any case, there is clearly no justification for criticizing the Jewish view of G-d as full of undesirable male characteristics.

Yet the gender-specific language remains. If G-d's characteristics really transcend gender, why do we speak of G-d only as He?

Actually, there is nothing wrong with an individual using feminine words for G-d to address her as mother or imagine oneself talking to an intimate female friend. For some individuals, this helps to develop a richer and more intimate relationship to G-d. We can also write and share our own interpretations of G-d's compassion, G-d's judgment, G-d's creative work in the world in feminine terms. This may help us to come to experience the fullness of G-d in our lives.

But this is not a full answer, for there is still the arena of public prayer, where tradition insists that we should adhere to the established text of the siddur. Here many feminists are eager for changes in language and substance. Some Jewish organizations have rushed ahead to revise translations of the prayer book, eliminating gender references, sometimes eliminating portions of the prayers themselves.

We must say, first of all, that this does injustice to the Hebrew language itself, not to mention the centuries of prayer of the Jewish people, who cherished these words as the channels by which we might address G-d. The issue is not merely introducing some feminine language for our personal enrichment, but our relation to the whole of Jewish tradition and the whole Jewish people.

Nor is it only a matter of dutifully respecting the communal tradition. We are easily led astray here because of our cultural disposition to value individual self-expression. We tend to honor the tradition only so long as it feels authentic to us. But what this really means is that we do not well understand communal expression, so we tend to brush it aside.

We must ask: are there not some powerful reasons why our sages have, through the centuries, kept a certain kind of language for our address to G-d, and have been very careful about what comes to be included in our siddur? Indeed there are.

The mystics tell us, following images used by the prophets, that our relation to G-d, as a people, can be conceived in sexual terms. G-d is male, the Jewish people is female. The Shir HaShirim, Song of Songs, which accompanies the celebration of Pesach and which, in some communities, is sung every Friday night, represents G-d and Israel as two lovers. The holidays can be mystically conceived as representing seasons in the relationship between Israel and G-d: Pesach is the first commitment of the two lovers, the engagement, so to speak; Shavuot is G-d's giving us his ketubah or wedding contract; and Sukkot is the consummation of the marriage. In a related set of images, all souls of Israel together is the Shabbat Queen, who is also the Shechinah (feminine aspect of the Divine), who unites with her husband, G-d, on Shabbat.

These images are a way to convey to us that the relation between G-d and human beings is a dynamic model, of which our best understanding is the relation between male and female. If our imagination fails at this point, it is partly a failure of our society, particularly of the widespread weakening of marriage and family in our times. Our grasp of the true meaning of the marriage relationship is dim and vague. We tend either to idealize it as romance (the teenagers Romeo and Juliet), or we criticize it as an instrument of patriarchal oppression, where the husband owns and dominates the wife.

Thus, some feminist writers have severely criticized the Jewish image of the Divine/human marriage. For example, Rosemary Reuther attacks the images found in some of the prophetic writings which accuse Israel of being the harlot while G-d acts like a petty, jealous husband.

This criticism totally fails to understand the depth and richness of the husband/wife experience in Judaism and, in particular, the notion of fidelity as part of marriage. Most of us today can barely grasp this, so we miss how the symbol of G-d as the husband and the Jewish people as the wife is the deepest imaginable relationship. Yet this image, this metaphor for G-d and the Jewish people, holds the secret of the apparently patriarchal language of Bible and siddur, the masculine terms we use for G-d.

In our days of new feminine consciousness, when we are asking what it means to be female or male, this language turns us back to our fundamental relationship to G-d. A woman discovering herself as woman first questions G-d: Why do you appear as male? Or she questions the rabbis: Why did you write about Him as like you and not like us? But we must push the question to a deeper level: what do masculine and feminine, male and female, really mean? How are they unique and how do they come together?

We must certainly reject the interpretation that the male (G-d) has all the power and the female (Israel) is his instrument. That would be thoroughly un-Jewish. We need only recall the famous Talmudic story of Rabbi Eliezer, who was intent on having G-d put his personal seal on a certain halachic decision. The sages, however, decided the matter another way. G-d's response was, "Thus my children have decided." G-d might well have said, in the above anecdote, "Thus my wife has decided." For, in another context, G-d tells Abraham, "In all that Sarah tells you, listen to her voice." The feminine has power, influence, and impact on the world just as does the masculine. They are in continuous interaction, an ongoing dance, in which each elevates and enriches the other.

This metaphor of G-d and Israel as husband and wife helps us understand that when we address G-d as a community, we address Him as male. When we pray in the traditional ways, we are not merely doing our duty by honoring what has been passed down. We are entering into a relationship with G-d by our speech, helping to create a relationship that has its own dynamic, the dynamic of the people, Israel, speaking, in love and intimacy, to her Divine partner. And, as with a marriage, it is only with years of practice that the full richness of this communication becomes a reality for us.

The so-called patriarchal G-d thus turns out to be only one face of G-d. The question once was asked why, in our prayers, we address G-d as G-d of Abraham, G-d of Isaac, and G-d of Jacob rather than more simply as G-d of Abraham, Isaac, and Jacob. The sages answered: Because G-d showed a different face to each one. So also with us. We live in a time when many are speaking of the feminine faces of G-d; this brings to our awareness dimensions of G-d that we might have forgotten. We may also see Him in more traditional terms as Creator, Ruler, Redeemer, Giver of the Torah. We need not reject any of these, male or female, but only use them to deepen our understanding of ourselves as individuals, of our people, and of G-d. Learning to live with and think deeply into our words for G-d is part of our spiritual growth, part of the deepening of consciousness we see in our times.

"G-d and Patriarchy," published in *Feeding Among the Lilies: The Wellsprings Reader,* by Baila Olidort (editor) (Brooklyn, NY: Wellsprings Journal, 1999), pp. 245-253

LESSON FOUR

A WORK OF PRAISE

FINDING G-D IN OUR WORLD

Jewish prayer involves singing G-d's praises for the universe He created, but does G-d need our acclaim? Daily? This lesson reframes our perspective on praising G-d, unveiling the act as a beautiful bridge across the Divine space between Creator and created, and revamping our view of ourselves, our universe, and our purpose in life.

I. Admiration

Text 1

RABBI YOSEF YITZCHAK SCHNEERSOHN,
LIKUTEI DIBURIM 1, P. 75B

אוּן דָאס אִיז דֶער זִין פוּן דֶעם וָוארְט "תְּהִלָּה" דִי לוֹיב אוּן דֶערְצֵיילוּנְג וֶועלְכֶע פַארְבִּינְדְט דֶעם לוֹיבֶּער אוּן דֶערְצֵיילֶער מִיט דֶעם וֶועמֶען עֶר לוֹיבְּט, אַז בְּשַׁעַת עֶר זָאגְט דִי לוֹיב וֶוערְטֶער פִילְט עֶר זִיךְ אִין אַ נָאהֶענְטֶער בַּאצִיהוּנְג מִיט דֶעם וֶועמֶען עֶר לוֹיבְּט.

וִוי מִיר זֶעהֶען בְּמוּחָשׁ, וֶוען אֵיינֶער דֶערְצֵיילְט וִוי אִים אִיז אוֹיסְגֶעקוּמֶען צוּ זֶעהֶען דֶעם גְרוֹיסֶען כָּבוֹד וָואס אַ מְדִינָה הָאט גֶעגֶעבֶּען אִיר מוֹשֵׁל אִין אֵיינֶעם פוּן דִי פַייֶערְטֶעג וֶועלְכֶע וֶוערֶען גֶעפַייֶערְט אִין יֶענֶער מְדִינָה, אוּן עֶר דֶערְצֵיילְט דָאס מִיט אַלֶע פְּרָטִים — דִי רַייכְקַייט אוּן שֵׁיינְקַייט אוּן דִי גְרוֹיסֶע מֶענְשֶׁען וֶועלְכֶע עֶר הָאט אִין יֶענֶעם טָאג גֶעזֶעהֶען — אִיז בְּשַׁעַת עֶר דֶערְצֵיילְט, שְׁטֵייט עֶר אִין אַ גֶעהוֹיבֶּענֶעם שְׁטִימוּנְגְס-גֶעפִיהל וָואס מִיט דֶעם אַלֵיין גֵייט עֶר אַרוֹיס פוּן זַיין וָואכֶעדִיגֶען לֶעבֶּען אוּן שְׁטֵייט הֶעכֶער אוּן אֵיידֶעלֶער.

דֶערְפַאר וֶוערְט תְּפִלָּה אָנְגֶערוּפֶען בְּשֵׁם סוּלָם, וִוי עֶס שְׁטֵייט, "וְהִנֵה סֻלָּם מֻצָּב אַרְצָה וְרֹאשׁוֹ מַגִיעַ הַשָּׁמָיְמָה". תְּפִלָּה אִיז דֶער סוּלָם וֶועלְכֶער פַארְבִּינְדְט דֶעם מִתְפַּלֵל עִם הַקָּדוֹשׁ בָּרוּךְ הוּא, וָואס דוּרְךְ דִי שִׁירוֹת וְתִשְׁבָּחוֹת שֶׁבִּתְפִלָּה וֶוערְט דִי הִתְקַשְׁרוּת הַמִתְפַּלֵל עִם הַקָּדוֹשׁ בָּרוּךְ הוּא.

Praise creates a connection between the individual providing the praise and the person they are praising; while articulating their compliment, an individual experiences a sense of closeness with the subject of their praise.

RABBI YOSEF YITZCHAK SCHNEERSOHN (RAYATZ, FRIERDIKER REBBE, PREVIOUS REBBE) 1880–1950

Chasidic rebbe, prolific writer, and Jewish activist. Rabbi Yosef Yitzchak, the 6th leader of the Chabad movement, actively promoted Jewish religious practice in Soviet Russia and was arrested for these activities. After his release from prison and exile, he settled in Warsaw, Poland, from where he fled Nazi occupation and arrived in New York in 1940. Settling in Brooklyn, Rabbi Schneersohn worked to revitalize American Jewish life. His son-in-law Rabbi Menachem Mendel Schneerson succeeded him as the leader of the Chabad movement.

Say, for example, that someone had the opportunity to witness the tremendous honor that a country showered upon its ruler during a national celebration. When they later describe the scene in all its detail—the opulence, the grandeur, and the presence of preeminent dignitaries—the person becomes inspired by their own recounting. Articulating their admiration serves to transport them from the mundanity of day-to-day life, and they feel uplifted and more refined.

This is why prayer is referred to as a ladder; it connects the individual with G-d, in the spirit of the verse, "A ladder planted in the earth that reaches into the heavens" (GENESIS 28:12). The bond between the individual and G-d is formed through the songs and praises of prayer.

Figure 4.1

Structure of the Verses of Song

PRAYER(S)	FUNCTION/THEME	ORIGIN
Baruch She'amar, p. 30*	Introductory blessing	Men of the Great Assembly
Ashrei-Halelukah, pp. 31-35	G-d's Creation of and involvement with His magnificent world	King David (Psalms 146-150)
Vayevarech-Vecharot, pp. 35-36	Various praises of G-d	King David (I Chronicles 29)
	Early history of the Jewish people	Nehemiah (Nehemiah 9)
Vayosha-Az Yashir, pp. 36-37	Splitting of the Sea	Exodus 14-15
Yishtabach, p. 38	Concluding blessing	Men of the Great Assembly (or King Solomon)

*The page number references are to the Siddur Tehilat Hashem prayer book (New York: Merkos L'Inyonei Chinuch, 2004).

Exercise 4.1

Below are four excerpts from the Morning Prayers' Verses of Song, each expressing a distinct theme. Indicate which quote(s) conveys each of the themes.

QUOTE(S)	THEME
A	G-d's control over the universe
B	G-d's kindness toward His creations
C	The vastness of the universe
C	The multitudes within the universe
D	The ingenious design of the universe

Quote A

Baruch She'amar

Blessed is He Who spoke and the world came into being; blessed is He. Blessed is He Who says and does; blessed is He Who decrees and fulfills.

Quote B

Ashrei

You open Your hand and satisfy the desire of every living thing.

Quote C

Psalms 147

He counts the number of the stars; He gives a name to each of them. Great is our Master and abounding in might; His understanding is beyond reckoning.

Quote D

Vayevarech David

You have made the heavens, the heavens of heavens, and all their hosts; the earth and all thereon; the seas and all therein.

Text 2

MIDRASH TEHILIM 19

"הַשָּׁמַיִם מְסַפְּרִים כְּבוֹד אֵ-ל" (תְּהִילִים יט, ב).

מָשָׁל לְגִבּוֹר שֶׁנִּכְנַס בַּמְּדִינָה וְלֹא הָיוּ יוֹדְעִין מַה כֹּחוֹ. אָמַר לָהֶן פִּקֵּחַ אֶחָד: מֵאַבְנָא דַּהֲוָא מִתְעַשֵּׁשׁ אַתּוּן יוֹדְעִין מַה כֹּחוֹ.

כַּךְ מֵהַשָּׁמַיִם אָנוּ לְמֵידִין כֹּחוֹ שֶׁל הַקָּדוֹשׁ בָּרוּךְ הוּא.

"The skies recount the praise of G-d" (PSALMS 19:2).

This can be understood through the following analogy: A mighty man was a newcomer in town, and the townsmen sought a way to gauge the extent of his strength. A wise person told them, "From the rock that this man raises, you will be able to determine his strength."

Similarly, we can determine the strength of G-d from the skies.

MIDRASH TEHILIM

A rabbinic commentary on the book of Psalms. Midrash is the designation of a particular genre of rabbinic literature usually forming a running commentary on specific books of the Bible. This particular Midrash provides textual exegeses and develops and illustrates the principles of the book of Psalms.

Text 3

MAIMONIDES, *MISHNEH TORAH*,
LAWS OF THE FOUNDATIONS OF THE TORAH 2:2

בְּשָׁעָה שֶׁיִּתְבּוֹנֵן הָאָדָם בְּמַעֲשָׂיו וּבְרוּאָיו הַנִּפְלָאִים הַגְּדוֹלִים, וְיִרְאֶה מֵהֶם חָכְמָתוֹ שֶׁאֵין לָהּ עֵרֶךְ וְלֹא קֵץ, מִיָּד הוּא אוֹהֵב, וּמְשַׁבֵּחַ, וּמְפָאֵר, וּמִתְאַוֶּה תַּאֲוָה גְדוֹלָה לֵידַע הַשֵּׁם הַגָּדוֹל.

When one meditates on G-d's great and wondrous creations and sees how they reflect G-d's infinite genius, one will immediately be aroused to love, praise, and glorify Him and yearn with a tremendous desire to know His great name.

RABBI MOSHE BEN MAIMON (MAIMONIDES, RAMBAM) 1135–1204

Halachist, philosopher, author, and physician. Maimonides was born in Córdoba, Spain. After the conquest of Córdoba by the Almohads, he fled Spain and eventually settled in Cairo, Egypt. There, he became the leader of the Jewish community and served as court physician to the vizier of Egypt. He is most noted for authoring the *Mishneh Torah*, an encyclopedic arrangement of Jewish law; and for his philosophical work, *Guide for the Perplexed*. His rulings on Jewish law are integral to the formation of Halachic consensus.

II. Association

Text 4

BARUCH SHE'AMAR, VERSES OF SONG, MORNING PRAYERS

בָּרוּךְ שֶׁאָמַר וְהָיָה הָעוֹלָם.

Blessed is He Who spoke and the world came into being.

Text 5

RABBI SHNEUR ZALMAN OF LIADI, *TANYA*, *SHAAR HAYICHUD VEHA'EMUNAH*, CHAPTER 11

מִדּוֹתָיו שֶׁל הַקָּדוֹשׁ בָּרוּךְ הוּא, כְּשֶׁבָּאוֹת לִבְחִינַת הִתְגַּלּוּת פְּעוּלָּתָן בַּתַּחְתּוֹנִים, נִקְרָא גִּילּוּי זֶה וְהַמְשָׁכַת פְּעוּלָּה זוֹ בְּשֵׁם "מַאֲמָר" וְ"צֵירוּף אוֹתִיּוֹת"...

כְּמוֹ אוֹתִיּוֹת הַדִּבּוּר בָּאָדָם עַל דֶּרֶךְ מָשָׁל, שֶׁהֵן מְגַלּוֹת לַשּׁוֹמְעִים מַה שֶּׁהָיָה צָפוּן וְסָתוּם בְּלִבּוֹ.

The tools G-d uses to reveal Himself in the act of Creation are referred to as "speech" and "combinations of letters"....

Their function is similar to that of human speech: to reveal to others that which was originally hidden in the heart.

RABBI SHNEUR ZALMAN OF LIADI (ALTER REBBE) 1745–1812

Chasidic rebbe, Halachic authority, and founder of the Chabad movement. The Alter Rebbe was born in Liozna, Belarus, and was among the principal students of the Magid of Mezeritch. His numerous works include the *Tanya*, an early classic containing the fundamentals of Chabad Chasidism; and *Shulchan Aruch HaRav*, an expanded and reworked code of Jewish law.

Text 6

RABBI SHALOM DOVBER SCHNEERSOHN, *SEFER HAMAAMARIM* 5659, P. 35

הַדִּיבּוּר וְהָאוֹתִיּוֹת דְּמַלְכוּת דַּאֲצִילוּת הֵם מַעֲלִימִים וּמַצְפִּינִים עַל הַחָכְמָה בִּינָה דַּעַת וְהַמִּדּוֹת הַמִּתְלַבְּשִׁים בְּדִיבּוּר, שֶׁלֹּא יִתְגַּלֶּה כְּלָל בַּבְּרִיאָה, כִּי אִם אֵיזֶה הֶאָרָה מוּעֶטֶת מְאֹד.

The content contained in the "speech" of G-d—be it intellectual or emotional—is concealed from the entities it creates. The created entities therefore perceive only a minute amount of the content they hold.

RABBI SHALOM DOVBER SCHNEERSOHN (RASHAB) 1860–1920

Chasidic rebbe. Rabbi Shalom Dovber became the 5th leader of the Chabad movement upon the passing of his father, Rabbi Shmuel Schneersohn. He established the Lubavitch network of *yeshivot* called Tomchei Temimim. He authored many volumes of Chasidic discourses and is renowned for his lucid and thorough explanations of kabbalistic concepts.

Exercise 4.2

This chart lists four features of life. Take a moment to consider and record the practical function of each. Then identify a possible spiritual function for each item.

ITEM	PRACTICAL FUNCTION	SPIRITUAL FUNCTION
The body	breath	Prayer
The sun		
Career		
Family		

Text 7

RABBI SIMON JACOBSON, *TOWARD A MEANINGFUL LIFE*
(NEW YORK: WILLIAM MORROW AND CO., 1995), PP. 220-221

By opening our mind to a new possibility—that our human reality is really but a small part of an all-encompassing reality—we are able to move beyond the boundaries of human existence. We begin learning to think like G-d Himself....

Your very perspective of the world begins to change; you begin to glimpse the "light" within the "container." You recognize G-d in everything around you. When you eat, you understand that you are nourishing yourself for constructive and G-dly purposes. You realize that every object has a divine purpose greater than the mere fulfillment of your own needs. Your table is meant for study, your living room for meaningful conversations. Your job is no longer just a means to earn a living, but an opportunity to behave more morally and ethically, and to introduce G-d into our world. A doctor recognizes the divine wonder within the human body and an engineer sees in his work a reflection of divine design and unity.

And finally, you learn to be sensitive to divine providence. You recognize that everything from the fluttering of a leaf in the wind to the movement of the galaxies is driven by G-d's hand. Instead of looking at life from the outside in, you learn to look from the inside out.

RABBI SIMON JACOBSON

Author of the best-selling *Toward a Meaningful Life* (New York: William Morrow, 1995), which has been translated into 12 languages, and founder of the Meaningful Life Center, which seeks to bridge the secular and the spiritual. For over 14 years, Rabbi Jacobson headed a team of scholars responsible for publishing the public talks of Rabbi Menachem M. Schneerson, the Lubavitcher Rebbe. He is also the publisher of *The Algemeiner* (formerly *Der Algemeiner Journal*), a New York-based newspaper covering American and international Jewish and Israel-related news.

Words that hurt
Words that heal } Book
Telushkin

Your Body is not an ornament
It is an instrument

Text 8

YISHTABACH, VERSES OF SONG, MORNING PRAYERS

. . . בּוֹרֵא כָּל הַנְּשָׁמוֹת, רִבּוֹן כָּל הַמַּעֲשִׂים, הַבּוֹחֵר בְּשִׁירֵי זִמְרָה,
מֶלֶךְ יָחִיד חֵי הָעוֹלָמִים.

... Creator of all souls, Ruler of all creatures, Who takes pleasure in songs of praise; You are the only King, the Life of all the worlds.

Text 9

RABBI YOSEF YITZCHAK SCHNEERSOHN,
SEFER HAMAAMARIM 5689, P. 59

וּכְמוֹ עַל דֶּרֶךְ מָשָׁל בְּאִילָן, שֶׁכּוֹרְתִים הָעֲנָפִים הַיְבֵשִׁים וְהַמְקוּלְקָלִים בִּכְדֵי שֶׁהָעֲנָפִים הַחַיִּים יִצְמְחוּ בְּטוֹב יוֹתֵר . . .

כְּמוֹ כֵּן הוּא בְּהָאָדָם שֶׁנִקְרָא עֵץ הַשָּׂדֶה, צְרִיכִים לְהַכְרִית הַחוֹחִים וְהַקּוֹצִים הַמוֹנְעִים וּמְעַכְּבִים, בִּכְדֵי שֶׁיִהְיֶה צְמִיחַת הָאִילָן, שֶׁיַעֲלֶה לְמַעֲלָה . . .

דְלִהְיוֹת שֶׁבְּטִבְעוֹ הוּא חוּמְרִי וְעַל כֵּן מְקוֹמוֹ הוּא בְּחוּמְרִיוּת הָעוֹלָם . . . וּצְרִיכִים לְהוֹצִיאוֹ (אֶת הַנֶּפֶשׁ הַבַּהֲמִית) מִמְקוֹמוֹ וּמֵרְשׁוּתוֹ.

וְהוּא עַל יְדֵי הַהִתְבּוֹנְנוּת דִּפְסוּקֵי דְזִמְרָה.

A gardener cuts away the dried-out and damaged branches of a tree so that its living branches can thrive. . . .

The same is true of the human—whom the Torah refers to as a "tree of the field." It is necessary to cut off the thorns and briars that impede and hinder growth so that the "tree" can grow and rise higher. . . .

Due to the reality that the animal soul is by nature materially oriented, which is why it is planted in the materiality of the world . . . we need to remove the animal soul from its familiar habitat.

This is achieved through the meditation of Pesukei Dezimrah (the Verses of Song).

III. Prayer Meditation

Text 10

PSALMS 148, VERSES OF SONG, MORNING PRAYERS

הַלְלוּיָ-ה,

הַלְלוּ אֶת ה' מִן הַשָּׁמַיִם, הַלְלוּהוּ בַּמְּרוֹמִים.

הַלְלוּהוּ כָל מַלְאָכָיו, הַלְלוּהוּ כָּל צְבָאָיו. הַלְלוּהוּ שֶׁמֶשׁ וְיָרֵחַ, הַלְלוּהוּ כָּל כּוֹכְבֵי אוֹר. הַלְלוּהוּ שְׁמֵי הַשָּׁמָיִם, וְהַמַּיִם אֲשֶׁר מֵעַל הַשָּׁמָיִם.

יְהַלְלוּ אֶת שֵׁם ה', כִּי הוּא צִוָּה וְנִבְרָאוּ. וַיַּעֲמִידֵם לָעַד לְעוֹלָם, חָק נָתַן וְלֹא יַעֲבוֹר.

הַלְלוּ אֶת ה' מִן הָאָרֶץ,

תַּנִּינִים וְכָל תְּהֹמוֹת. אֵשׁ וּבָרָד, שֶׁלֶג וְקִיטוֹר, רוּחַ סְעָרָה עֹשָׂה דְבָרוֹ. הֶהָרִים וְכָל גְּבָעוֹת, עֵץ פְּרִי וְכָל אֲרָזִים. הַחַיָּה וְכָל בְּהֵמָה, רֶמֶשׂ, וְצִפּוֹר כָּנָף. מַלְכֵי אֶרֶץ וְכָל לְאֻמִּים, שָׂרִים וְכָל שֹׁפְטֵי אָרֶץ. בַּחוּרִים וְגַם בְּתוּלֹת, זְקֵנִים עִם נְעָרִים. יְהַלְלוּ אֶת שֵׁם ה' כִּי נִשְׂגָּב שְׁמוֹ לְבַדּוֹ,

הוֹדוֹ עַל אֶרֶץ וְשָׁמָיִם.

Praise the L-rd!

Praise the L-rd from the heavens; praise Him in the celestial heights.

Praise Him, all His angels; praise Him, all His hosts. Praise Him, sun and moon; praise Him, all the shining stars. Praise Him, heavens of heavens and the waters that are above the heavens.

PSALMS

Biblical book. The book of Psalms contains 150 psalms expressing praise for G-d, faith in G-d, and laments over tragedies. The primary author of the psalms was King David, who lived in the 9th century BCE. Psalms also contains material from earlier figures. The feelings and circumstances expressed in the psalms resonate throughout the generations, and they have become an important part of communal and personal prayer.

Let them praise the name of the L-rd, for He commanded and they were created. He has established them forever, for all time; He issued a decree, and it shall not be transgressed.

Praise the L-rd from the earth, sea monsters and all [that dwell in] the depths; fire and hail, snow and vapor, stormy wind carrying out His command; the mountains, all hills, fruit-bearing trees, and all cedars; the beasts and all cattle, creeping things, insects, and winged fowl; kings of the earth and all nations, rulers and all judges of the land; young men as well as maidens, elders together with young lads. Let them praise the name of the L-rd, for His name is sublimely transcendent, it is unto Himself; [only] its radiance is upon the earth and heavens.

Text 11a

RABBI ZALMAN GOPIN, *LILMOD EICH LEHITPALEL*, 3, P. 129

וְנִשְׁאֶלֶת הַשְּׁאֵלָה: כֵּיצַד יְכוֹלִים הַבְּהֵמוֹת וְהַחַיּוֹת אוֹ עֲצֵי הַפְּרִי וְהָאֲרָזִים, לְשַׁבֵּחַ אֶת הַקָּדוֹשׁ בָּרוּךְ הוּא? יֶתֶר עַל כֵּן: כֵּיצַד יְכוֹלִים הַנִּבְרָאִים הַדּוֹמְמִים, כְּמוֹ שֶׁלֶג וְקִיטוֹר אוֹ הָרִים וּבְקָעוֹת, לְשַׁבֵּחַ אֶת הַקָּדוֹשׁ בָּרוּךְ הוּא?

This psalm begs the question: Can beasts and animals, trees and cedars, actually praise G-d? The wonder is even weightier in regard to entirely inanimate phenomena such as snow and vapor, or the mountains and hills. How can they praise G-d?

RABBI ZALMAN GOPIN
1945–

Chasidic mentor, lecturer, and author. Rabbi Gopin serves as lead Chasidic mentor at the Chabad yeshiva of Kfar Chabad, Israel. He also serves as senior educator at Mayanei Yisrael, an adult education institute for Chasidic teachings. He has authored a number of books on Chasidic philosophy and is a frequent lecturer on the subject.

Text 11b

RABBI ZALMAN GOPIN, IBID., 3, PP. 109–110

אֶלָּא הַכַּוָּונָה לַחַיּוּת הָאֱלֹקִית הַמְחַיָּה אֶת הַנִּבְרָאִים וְהִיא הַמְשַׁבַּחַת וּמְהַלֶּלֶת אֶת ה' . . .

וְכֵיוָן שֶׁהַשֶּׁבַח הוּא עִנְיָן פְּנִימִי וְנַפְשִׁי, לָכֵן הַחַיּוּת שֶׁל כָּל נִבְרָא מְשַׁבַּחַת אֶת הַקָּדוֹשׁ בָּרוּךְ הוּא בְּהֶתְאֵם לְדַרְגָּתָהּ: הַשָּׁמַיִם חֲפֵצִים לְהִתְקָרֵב לַה' כְּפִי שֶׁהֵם מַשִּׂיגִים אֶת הַקָּדוֹשׁ בָּרוּךְ הוּא, וְהַחַיּוּת שֶׁל הַגְּבָעוֹת, מִשְׁתּוֹקֶקֶת לַחֲזוֹר לִמְקוֹרָהּ כְּפִי שֶׁהִיא מַרְגִּישָׁה אוֹתוֹ, וְכָךְ גַּם כָּל נִבְרָא וְנִבְרָא.

The psalm refers not to the physical bodies of these entities, but to the G-dly energies that enliven them—those indeed offer praise to G-d. . . .

Praise is personal and soulful. Consequently, the G-dly energy within each entity praises G-d in its own way. The energies within the skies and the hills each desire to become closer to G-d in a different way, according to how they identify with Him. The same is true of the G-dly energy within each creature.

Takeaway Exercise

Creation and Creator. Take two or three minutes to meditate on the magnificence and brilliance of G-d's creation, and the ways in which creation reflects on its Creator. Focus on at least two components in your life and identify their Divine spiritual purpose. Follow this up immediately with an out-loud recital of Psalm 148.

We'll discuss how it went during the next lesson.

Key Points

1. The praises of G-d that we recite as the Verses of Song assist us in discovering more about G-d and becoming inspired by Him.

2. Everything in Creation is invested with spiritual content and exists for a purpose. The meditations of the Verses of Song help us train ourselves to see the world this way.

A *TECHINAH* FOR ROSH CHODESH

Techinah fun Rosh Chodesh Bentchen **(Lemberg, 1864), p. 5**

Rabbi Yaakov Gordon, trans., *Techinos* (Jerusalem: Feldheim Publishers, 2011), pp. 8–12

This *techinah* is written for recitation in the synagogue before the new month is blessed during the prayers on the Shabbat preceding the beginning of the month.

Image courtesy of the National Library of Israel.

ג

תחנה פון ראש חודש בענטשין

תחנה פון ראש חודש בענטשין

תחנה אמהות פון שרה רבקה רחל לאה

R 71 A 4306

296.319.1

LEAH HOROWITZ
18TH CENTURY

Sarah Rivkah Rachel Leah Horowitz was born in Bolechów, Poland, where her father Yaakov served as the rabbi. She was known as an accomplished Talmudic scholar, a rarity for women in her era. Leah was married twice, first to Rabbi Aryeh Leib of Dobromil, and then to Rabbi Shabetai Rappoport, the rabbi of Krasny, Russia. Leah authored a remarkable *techinah* for the Shabbat on which the new month is blessed. She wrote it in three languages: Hebrew, Aramaic, and Yiddish.

Leah Horowitz, Techinah fun Rosh Chodesh Bentchen

Master of the universe, great and awesome G-d; in Your compassion You gave us the New Months. When Yisrael was sovereign in their land, the holy Sanhedrin sanctified the months. But from the time we were exiled from our land, all that remains for us from the mitzvah of the sanctification of the New Month is our announcing and blessing of the new moon on the Shabbat before the New Month. Our Father in heaven, we lift up our hearts in prayer and make our voices heard before You, [and ask] that You return us to Yerushalayim, Your holy city, and renew our days as of old.

Your nation is like a flock of sheep without a shepherd, and many suffer from the fear of those who rise up against us—but You are a vengeful G-d Who punishes the wicked. We therefore ask of You, Master of the universe, to answer us in the merit of our Forefathers and Foremothers, You, G-d of goodness. Just as You answered them, answer us in the coming month.

[Answer us] in the merit of our Mother Sarah: Just as You did not allow Avimelech to harm her or Your righteous one, Avraham, do not allow anyone to harm her children. [Answer us] in the merit of our Mother Rivkah, by whose hand our Father Yaakov received the blessings from his father Yitzchak. May we merit that those blessings be speedily fulfilled in the nation of Yisrael, her children.

[Answer us] in the merit of our faithful Mother Rachel, for You promised her, O G-d, that in the merit of her prayers her children would be redeemed from all their suffering. When Yisrael went into exile, they passed by the gravesite of our Mother Rachel and asked their captors to allow them to pray. The exiles came to her grave and cried out to You and wept [before her], "Mother, Mother, how can you bear to see our troubles—our going from our country into exile?" Rachel then went up to G-d and cried out, "Master of the World, Your compassion is greater than the compassion of one who is only flesh and blood! I was filled with compassion for my sister Leah, when our father switched us and gave her to my intended husband Yaakov in my stead. It was very difficult for me, but I overcame my pain and had mercy on my sister so that she would not be disgraced. Therefore, You, merciful and gracious One, must surely have mercy and show grace to the children of Your people." Benevolent G-d, You answered her, "Because of you, Rachel, I will reestablish Yisrael in their land. Return to your place of rest and your children shall return to their borders." Please fulfill the promise that You promised her, speedily in our day.

And [answer us] in the merit of our Mother Leah, whose eyes became tender from crying day and night so that she would not fall to the lot of the wicked Eisav. For her sake, bring light to our eyes and ease our suffering, we, the children of Avraham, Yitzchak, and Yaakov. Generously cleanse us from our transgressions and purify us from our sins.

Bestow good on us this month and bring us joy and happiness. Our Power and Strength, turn all our bad into good in the merit of our righteous Forefathers, Avraham, Yitzchak, and Yaakov. Master of the Universe, You called us Your chosen and Your beloved. Therefore, we call to You, benevolent G-d, and plead before You that You give to us and to all of Yisrael offspring who are worthy, vital, and enduring. May they be Torah scholars and serve You with love and perfect hearts, just as the righteous ones of old served You. Amen, so may it be.

I ask of You, mighty and awesome G-d, the Eternal, Who is all powerful, merciful, and kind, the King Who is King of kings and the Master of all masters, to listen to all of our prayers and supplications. Protect me, my husband, and my children from all evil, and accept my prayer just as You accepted the prayer of Chanah, and You fulfilled the request that she asked of Your holy Name.

King of mercy, King of the world, I call to You, do not abandon us! Provide for our livelihood and all our needs from Your broad and full hands, and not from the hands of men, G-d forbid. Give us all that we need easily, and without hardship. May my husband and I merit long life and may we see our children "like olive saplings" around our table, and may they be good advocates for us in the next world.

King, the King of kings, the Holy One, Blessed is He, I call out before You, for You alone are our G-d and there is no one but You. You are the One Who feeds us and provides for all our needs, and from the time I was created and until now, You have fed me and raised me. Protect me and my husband and children from early and abnormal death, and remember us for good and for blessing each day. Listen to our prayers always and do not turn away from them. May they not return unanswered from before You, for You hearken to the prayers of those who plead before You with all their heart. Amen, and may it be Your will.

LESSON FIVE

A WORK OF TRANSCENDENCE

ACHIEVING TRUE TRANSCENDENCE IN PRAYER

We relate to G-d via His interactions with us and see G-d reflected in the miracles of nature. But can we connect in a meaningful way with G-d Himself—as He transcends the universe? This lesson reveals and explores the transcendence hardwired into the Jewish prayers, provides intense insights into our bond with G-d, and invites us to venture beyond.

I. Intimacy with G-d

Figure 5.1

Shema and Its Blessings

SECTIONS	PARAGRAPHS	THEME	ORIGINS
First blessing pp. 39–41*	*Yotzer Or* *Hame'ir La'aretz* *Titbarech* *Et Shem Hakel* *Kadosh* *Lakel Baruch*	Creation of light and darkness Angels' praise of G-d	Men of the Great Assembly
Second blessing pp. 41–42	*Ahavat Olam*	G-d's love of the Jewish people	Men of the Great Assembly
Shema pp. 42–44	*Shema* *Baruch Shem* *Ve'ahavta* *Vehayah Im Shamo'a* *Vayomer*	Belief in G-d Commitment to the Torah Exodus	Deuteronomy 6:4–9 Deuteronomy 11:13–21 Numbers 15:37–41
Third blessing pp. 44–45	*Emet Veyatziv* *Ezrat Avoteinu* *Shirah Chadashah*	G-d's faithfulness to the Jewish people Exodus	Men of the Great Assembly

*The page number references are to the Siddur Tehilat Hashem prayer book (New York: Merkos L'Inyonei Chinuch, 2004).

Text 1

FIRST BLESSING OF THE SHEMA, MORNING PRAYERS

כּוּלָּם אֲהוּבִים, כֻּלָּם בְּרוּרִים, כֻּלָּם גִּבּוֹרִים, כֻּלָּם קְדוֹשִׁים, וְכֻלָּם עֹשִׂים בְּאֵימָה וּבְיִרְאָה רְצוֹן קוֹנָם. וְכֻלָּם פּוֹתְחִים אֶת פִּיהֶם בִּקְדֻשָּׁה וּבְטָהֳרָה, בְּשִׁירָה וּבְזִמְרָה, וּמְבָרְכִים וּמְשַׁבְּחִים, וּמְפָאֲרִים וּמַעֲרִיצִים, וּמַקְדִּישִׁים וּמַמְלִיכִים.

אֶת שֵׁם הָאֵ-ל, הַמֶּלֶךְ הַגָּדוֹל הַגִּבּוֹר וְהַנּוֹרָא קָדוֹשׁ הוּא . . . כֻּלָּם כְּאֶחָד עוֹנִים בְּאֵימָה וְאוֹמְרִים בְּיִרְאָה:

קָדוֹשׁ קָדוֹשׁ קָדוֹשׁ ה׳ צְבָאוֹת.

All the angels are beloved, all are pure, all are mighty, all are holy, and all perform the will of their Maker with fear and awe. And all of them open their mouths in holiness and purity, with song and melody, and bless and adore, glorify and revere, hallow and ascribe sovereignty to:

The Name of the Almighty G-d, the great, powerful, and awe-inspiring King; holy is He. . . . Together, all exclaiming in unison, with awe, and declaring in reverence:

"Holy, holy, holy is the L-rd of hosts."

Text 2

RABBI SHNEUR ZALMAN OF LIADI, *LIKUTEI TORAH*, EMOR 32B

וְעִיקָּר הַהַשָּׂגָה הוּא זֶה אֵיךְ שֶׁהוּא יִתְבָּרֵךְ קָדוֹשׁ וּמוּבְדָּל בִּבְחִינַת אֵין עֲרוֹךְ אֵלָיו בָּרוּךְ הוּא, וּמָקוֹר הַמְשָׁכַת הַחַיּוּת מִמֶּנּוּ יִתְבָּרֵךְ לִהְיוֹת בִּבְחִינַת מְמַלֵּא כָּל עָלְמִין הוּא רַק עַל יְדֵי צִמְצוּם עָצוּם בִּבְחִינַת שַׂעֲרָה, כַּנִּזְכָּר לְעֵיל . . .

וְהִנֵּה עַל יְדֵי הִתְבּוֹנְנוּתָם וְהַשָּׂגָתָם בָּזֶה, אֲזַי הֵם מִתְלַהֲבִים וּמִתְלַהֲטִים בִּתְשׁוּקָה וְרִשְׁפֵּי אֵשׁ לְאִסְתַּכְּלָא בִּיקָרָא דְמַלְכָּא בִּבְחִינַת סוֹבֵב כָּל עָלְמִין שֶׁהוּא קָדוֹשׁ וּמוּבְדָּל. וְלָכֵן נִקְרָאִים שְׂרָפִים, עַל שֵׁם הָרִשְׁפֵּי אֵשׁ וְהַתְּשׁוּקָה הַנִּפְלָאָה.

וְזֶהוּ שֶׁאוֹמְרִים "קָדוֹשׁ" . . . שֶׁעִיקָּר תְּשׁוּקָתָם לְהַשִּׂיג בְּחִינַת סוֹבֵב כָּל עָלְמִין, הַנִּקְרָא קָדוֹשׁ.

The angels perceive the element of G-d that completely transcends them and the worlds in which they reside. For only a minimal amount of His energy, like the minimal amount of life-force found in a hair, is manifest in the worlds....

Due to the angels' acute awareness of the transcendent aspect of G-d, they burn with a fiery desire to experience this element of G-d that is not manifest in the world. Indeed, one of the schools of angels is termed *seraphim* (those that burn), referring to their burning desire to experience G-d.

This is the meaning of the praise, *kadosh*, that the angels say.... They yearn to experience the element of G-d that is *kadosh*—that transcends the worlds.

RABBI SHNEUR ZALMAN OF LIADI (ALTER REBBE)
1745–1812

Chasidic rebbe, Halachic authority, and founder of the Chabad movement. The Alter Rebbe was born in Liozna, Belarus, and was among the principal students of the Magid of Mezeritch. His numerous works include the *Tanya*, an early classic containing the fundamentals of Chabad Chasidism; and *Shulchan Aruch HaRav*, an expanded and reworked code of Jewish law.

Text 3a

RABBI YOSEF YITZCHAK SCHNEERSOHN,
KUNTRES TORAT HACHASIDUT, PP. 10–11

פַּעַם יָשְׁבוּ הַחֶבְרַיָא קַדִּישָׁא — הֵן הֵמָּה כְּבוֹד קְדוּשַּׁת תַּלְמִידֵי הָרַב הַמַּגִּיד נִשְׁמָתוֹ בְּגִנְזֵי מְרוֹמִים זַיַ"ע — וְשׂוֹחֲחוּ בֵּינֵיהֶם בְּמַעֲלַת מַדְרֵיגוֹת מַלְאֲכֵי מָרוֹם, אוֹפַנִּים וְחַיּוֹת הַקֹּדֶשׁ בְּמֶרְכָּבָה הָעֶלְיוֹנָה אֲשֶׁר בְּכָל עוֹלָם וְעוֹלָם.

אֶחָד הַתַּלְמִידִים דִּבֵּר בְּמַעֲלַת הַמַּלְאָכִים שֶׁהֵם שִׂכְלִים נִבְדָּלִים, וְכָל חַיּוּתָם הוּא דְּבַר ה', וְהַשֵּׁנִי דִּבֵּר בְּמַעֲלָתָם שֶׁל הָאוֹפַנִּים וְחַיּוֹת הַקֹּדֶשׁ אֲשֶׁר הֵם תָּמִיד בְּאַהֲבָה וְיִרְאָה שֶׁהוּא רָצוֹא וָשׁוֹב . . . וְהַשְּׁלִישִׁי מֵהַחֲבֵרִים הַקְּדוֹשִׁים מְבָאֵר בְּמַעֲלָתָם שֶׁל הַשְּׂרָפִים שֶׁהֵם עוֹד לְמַעְלָה בְּמַדְרֵיגָה, לִהְיוֹת עֲמִידָתָם הוּא בְּעוֹלָם הַבְּרִיאָה.

וְהַחֶבְרַיָא קַדִּישָׁא בְּקִנְאָתָם הַפְּלָאַת מַעֲלַת רוֹמְמוּת נְעִימוּת יְדִידוּת עֲבוֹדָתָם שֶׁל הַנֶּאֱצָלִים הָעֶלְיוֹנִים, הִתְלַהֲבוּ וְהִתְלַהֲטוּ בְּרִשְׁפֵּי אֵשׁ לַהֲבַת שַׁלְהֶבֶת גַּעֲגוּעֵי עֲבוֹדַת ה' יִתְבָּרֵךְ, הִנֵּה רוּבָּם כְּכוּלָּם מְרַחֲשִׁים בְּשִׂפְתוֹתֵיהֶם וְקוֹלָם לֹא יִשָּׁמַע, כּוּלָּם רוֹעֲדִים וְגוֹעִים בִּבְכִיָּה.

אֲחָדִים מֵהַחֶבְרַיָא קַדִּישָׁא הָיוּ פְּנֵיהֶם לְהָבִים, עֵינֵיהֶם לְטוּשׁוֹת, וְכַפֵּיהֶם פְּרוּשׂוֹת מִבְּלִי תְּנוּעָה כַּהֲלוּמֵי רַעַם, וַאֲחָדִים נִגְּנוּ בְּנִיגּוּן חֲרִישִׁי, וְלִבָּם סוֹעֵר אֲשֶׁר עוֹד מְעַט וְנַפְשָׁם תִּשְׁתַּפֵּךְ בְּחֵיק בּוֹרֵא כָּל הַנְּשָׁמוֹת.

The students of the Magid of Mezeritch, "the holy group," once sat and discussed the exalted level of the angels—the *ophanim* and *chayot hakodesh* of the supernal *merkavah* (chariot)—that reside in the spiritual worlds.

One student described the angels as purely intellectual beings, acutely aware of the word of G-d that enlivens them. Another student extolled how the *ophanim* and *chayot hakodesh* are in a perpetual emotional cycle of love and awe, yearning and

RABBI YOSEF YITZCHAK SCHNEERSOHN (RAYATZ, FRIERDIKER REBBE, PREVIOUS REBBE) 1880–1950

Chasidic rebbe, prolific writer, and Jewish activist. Rabbi Yosef Yitzchak, the 6th leader of the Chabad movement, actively promoted Jewish religious practice in Soviet Russia and was arrested for these activities. After his release from prison and exile, he settled in Warsaw, Poland, from where he fled Nazi occupation and arrived in New York in 1940. Settling in Brooklyn, Rabbi Schneersohn worked to revitalize American Jewish life. His son-in-law Rabbi Menachem Mendel Schneerson succeeded him as the leader of the Chabad movement.

returning. Yet a third student explained the unique spiritual experience of the *seraphim*, who reside in the realm of *beriah*.

Inspired by the tremendous spirituality of the Heavenly angels, the members of the holy group burned with a great desire to become closer to G-d. They whispered with their lips, their voices inaudible; they trembled and wept.

Some of them sat there, their faces alight, eyes glowing, and their arms remaining outstretched as if thunderstruck. Others hummed soft melodies, their hearts astir—their souls yearning to be reunited with their Creator.

Figure 5.2

Text 3b

RABBI YOSEF YITZCHAK SCHNEERSOHN, IBID.

בְּלִי סָפֵק — אוֹמֵר כְּבוֹד קְדוּשַּׁת אָחִי — אֲשֶׁר בְּאִם לֹא הָיָה נִכְנַס כְּבוֹד קְדוּשַּׁת מוֹרֵנוּ וְרַבֵּנוּ הָרַב הַמַּגִּיד לְבֵית הַמִּדְרָשׁ בְּשָׁעָה הַהִיא, כִּי אֲחָדִים מֵהַחֲבֵרִים הַקְּדוֹשִׁים הָיוּ כָּלִים מַמָּשׁ בִּכְלוֹת הַנֶּפֶשׁ מִגּוֹדֶל תְּשׁוּקַת צִמְאוֹנָם לְהִכָּלֵל בְּחֶבְיוֹן עוּזּוֹ יִתְבָּרֵךְ וְיִתְעַלֶּה, אֲבָל מִכֵּיוָן שֶׁנִּשְׁמְעוּ צַעֲדֵי מוֹרֵנוּ וְרַבֵּנוּ, הִנֵּה כְּרֶגַע נֵעוֹרוּ כָּל הַחֶבְרַיָּא קַדִּישָׁא מֵעוֹמֶק דְּבֵיקוּתָם הַנִּפְלָאָה וַיַּעַמְדוּ הָכֵן לְקַבֵּל פְּנֵי הַקֹּדֶשׁ

כְּשֶׁנִּכְנַס מוֹרֵנוּ וְרַבֵּנוּ, יָשַׁב בְּרֹאשׁ הַשּׁוּלְחָן וַיֹּאמַר תּוֹרָה:

"אָנֹכִי עָשִׂיתִי אֶרֶץ וְאָדָם עָלֶיהָ בָרָאתִי" (יְשַׁעְיָה מה, יב), אָנֹכִי מִי שֶׁאָנֹכִי, שֶׁהוּא נֶעֱלַם וְנִסְתָּר גַּם מִנֶּאֱצָלִים הֶיוֹתֵר עֶלְיוֹנִים, הִלְבִּישׁ עַצְמוּתוֹ יִתְבָּרֵךְ בְּכַמָּה צִמְצוּמִים לְהַאֲצִיל הַנֶּאֱצָלִים וְלִבְרוֹא הַנִּבְרָאִים, שְׂרָפִים חַיּוֹת וְאוֹפַנִּים מַלְאָכִים וְעוֹלָמוֹת עַד אֵין מִסְפָּר, וּבְצִמְצוּמִים עַד אֵין שִׁיעוּר עָשִׂיתִי אֶרֶץ הַלָּזוּ הַגַּשְׁמִית, וְאָדָם עָלֶיהָ בָרָאתִי, הָאָדָם הוּא תַּכְלִית הַהִתְהַוּוּת, וּבָרָאתִ"י, בְּגִימַטְרִיָּא תַּרְיַ"ג, הוּא תַּכְלִית הָאָדָם . . .

כְּשֶׁגָּמַר מוֹרֵנוּ וְרַבֵּנוּ אֶת הַתּוֹרָה, חָזַר לְהֵיכַל קָדְשׁוֹ. וּבְתוֹרָה זוּ הִרְגִּיעַ רוּחַ קָדְשָׁם שֶׁל הַחֶבְרַיָּא.

Had the Magid not entered the study hall at that moment, some of the students would have certainly expired from their burning desire to be subsumed in G-d's vast greatness. But upon hearing the footsteps of the Magid, the students were instantly brought back to their senses as they stood to welcome their teacher.

When the Magid entered the room, he sat down at the head of the table and began to speak:

"The verse says, 'I created the world and placed humankind upon it' (ISAIAH 45:12). This verse can be interpreted as follows:

"'I'—referring to G-d's very essence, which is beyond even the most exalted of spiritual beings—concealed Myself in order to create *seraphim, chayot hakodesh, ophanim,* and countless other angels and spiritual worlds. 'Created the world,' that is, the physical world, 'and placed humankind upon it,' humankind being the purpose of all of Creation, through their fulfillment of the Torah."...

Upon finishing this teaching, the Magid returned to his room. This teaching settled the students' fiery spirits.

Text 4a

SECOND BLESSING BEFORE SHEMA, MORNING PRAYERS

אַהֲבַת עוֹלָם אֲהַבְתָּנוּ ה' אֱלֹקֵינוּ.

חֶמְלָה גְדוֹלָה וִיתֵרָה חָמַלְתָּ עָלֵינוּ.

L-rd our G-d, You have loved us with everlasting love (*ahavat olam*).

You have bestowed upon us exceedingly abounding mercy.

Text 4b

RABBI SHNEUR ZALMAN OF LIADI, *TANYA, LIKUTEI AMARIM*, CHAPTER 49

"אַהֲבַת עוֹלָם אֲהַבְתָּנוּ ה' אֱלֹקֵינוּ".

כְּלוֹמַר, שֶׁהִנִּיחַ כָּל צְבָא מַעְלָה הַקְּדוֹשִׁים, וְהִשְׁרָה שְׁכִינָתוֹ עָלֵינוּ . . .

וְהַיְינוּ כִּי אַהֲבָה דוֹחֶקֶת הַבָּשָׂר. וְלָכֵן נִקְרָא "אַהֲבַת עוֹלָם", שֶׁהִיא בְּחִינַת צִמְצוּם אוֹרוֹ הַגָּדוֹל הַבִּלְתִּי תַּכְלִית, לְהִתְלַבֵּשׁ בִּבְחִינַת גְּבוּל הַנִּקְרָא "עוֹלָם", בַּעֲבוּר אַהֲבַת עַמּוֹ יִשְׂרָאֵל, כְּדֵי לְקָרְבָם אֵלָיו לִיכָּלֵל בְּיִחוּדוֹ וְאַחְדוּתוֹ יִתְבָּרֵךְ.

וְזֶהוּ שֶׁנֶּאֱמַר: "חֶמְלָה גְדוֹלָה וִיתֵרָה",

פֵּרוּשׁ, יְתֵרָה עַל קִרְבַת אֱלֹקִים שֶׁבְּכָל צְבָא מַעְלָה.

"L-rd our G-d, You have loved us with everlasting love (*ahavat olam*)."

[Aside from meaning *eternal*, the word *olam* can also be translated as *world*. Thus, *ahavat olam* can be translated as *worldly love*.]

The reason why G-d's love toward us is described as "worldly love" is as follows:

Due to G-d's great love of His nation, the Jewish people, He set aside the spiritual beings. Rather, G-d contracted His infinite expression in order to invest Himself in the confines of the world, and thus rest His presence on us and bring us close to His unity. Indeed, love inspires contraction.

"You have bestowed upon us exceedingly abounding mercy."

This refers to the distinct closeness G-d has granted us, which exceeds that of any of the spiritual beings.

Text 5

DEUTERONOMY 6:4, SHEMA, MORNING PRAYERS

שְׁמַע יִשְׂרָאֵל ה' אֱלֹקֵינוּ ה' אֶחָד.

Hear O Israel, the L-rd is our G-d, the L-rd is One.

Text 6

ZOHAR, VOL. 3, P. 257B

דְאִיהוּ הֲוָה קֹדֶם כָּל הֲוַיָין, וְאִיהוּ בְּתוֹךְ כָּל הֲוָיָה, וְאִיהוּ לְאַחַר כָּל הֲוָיָה.

The word *Havayah* shares the same letters as the Hebrew words that translate as "was," "is," and "will be." This represents how G-d precedes Creation, exists currently, and remains the same after Creation.

ZOHAR

The seminal work of kabbalah, Jewish mysticism. The *Zohar* is a mystical commentary on the Torah, written in Aramaic and Hebrew. According to the Arizal, the *Zohar* contains the teachings of Rabbi Shimon bar Yocha'i, who lived in the Land of Israel during the 2nd century. The *Zohar* has become one of the indispensable texts of traditional Judaism, alongside and nearly equal in stature to the Mishnah and Talmud.

Text 7

RABBI YAAKOV BEN ASHER, *ARBAAH TURIM, ORACH CHAYIM* 5

וּבְהַזְכִּירוֹ "אֱלֹקִים" יְכַוֵּין שֶׁהוּא תַּקִּיף, אַמִּיץ, אֲשֶׁר לוֹ הַיְכוֹלֶת בָּעֶלְיוֹנִים וּבַתַּחְתּוֹנִים.

כִּי "אֵ-ל" לָשׁוֹן כֹּחַ וְחוֹזֶק הוּא, כְּמוֹ: "וְאֶת אֵילֵי הָאָרֶץ לָקָח" (יְחֶזְקֵאל יז, יג).

The word *Kel* [the first two letters of *Elokim*] means power, as in the verse, "He took away the powerful ones (*eilei*) of the land" (EZEKIEL 17:13).

Therefore, when saying the name *Elokim*, one should contemplate that G-d is mighty and powerful, ruling the higher and lower worlds.

RABBI YAAKOV BEN ASHER (*TUR*, BAAL HATURIM) C. 1269–C. 1343

Halachic authority and codifier. Rabbi Yaakov was born in Germany and moved to Toledo, Spain, with his father, the noted Halachist Rabbi Asher, to escape persecution. He wrote *Arbaah Turim* ("*Tur*"), an ingeniously organized and highly influential code of Jewish law. He is considered one of the greatest authorities on Halachah.

Question for Discussion

How might the names *Havayah* and *Elokim* correlate to the manifest and transcendent aspects of G-d?

Text 8

RABBI SHNEUR ZALMAN OF LIADI,
CITED IN *HAYOM YOM*, 12 CHESHVAN

שְׁמַע יִשְׂרָאֵל - אַ אִיד דֶערְהֶערְט,

הֲוַיֶ"ה אֱלֹקֵינוּ - אַז כּוֹחֵנוּ וְחַיּוּתֵינוּ אִיז דָאס לְמַעְלָה מִן הַטֶבַע,

און - הֲוַיֶ"ה אֶחָד.

Shema Yisrael—a Jew perceives that,

Havayah Elokeinu—our strength and life is beyond nature, and

Havayah Echad—that G-d is One.

II. Reflective Love

Text 9a

DEUTERONOMY 6:5, SHEMA, MORNING PRAYERS

וְאָהַבְתָּ אֵת ה' אֱלֹקֶיךָ בְּכָל לְבָבְךָ, וּבְכָל נַפְשְׁךָ, וּבְכָל מְאֹדֶךָ.

You shall love the L-rd your G-d with all your heart, with all your soul, and with all your might.

Text 9b

MISHNAH, BERACHOT 9:5

בְּכָל לְבָבְךָ: בִּשְׁנֵי יְצָרֶיךָ, בְּיֵצֶר טוֹב וּבְיֵצֶר הָרָע.

וּבְכָל נַפְשְׁךָ: אֲפִלּוּ הוּא נוֹטֵל אֶת נַפְשְׁךָ.

וּבְכָל מְאֹדֶךָ: בְּכָל מָמוֹנְךָ.

"With all your heart": with both your positive and negative inclinations.

"With all your soul": even if it costs your life.

"With all your might": with all your possessions.

MISHNAH

The first authoritative work of Jewish law that was codified in writing. The Mishnah contains the oral traditions that were passed down from teacher to student; it supplements, clarifies, and systematizes the commandments of the Torah. Due to the continual persecution of the Jewish people, it became increasingly difficult to guarantee that these traditions would not be forgotten. Rabbi Yehudah Hanasi therefore redacted the Mishnah at the end of the 2nd century. It serves as the foundation for the Talmud.

Text 10

DEUTERONOMY 11:13-14, SHEMA, MORNING PRAYERS

וְהָיָה אִם שָׁמֹעַ תִּשְׁמְעוּ אֶל מִצְוֹתַי אֲשֶׁר אָנֹכִי מְצַוֶּה אֶתְכֶם הַיּוֹם, לְאַהֲבָה אֶת ה׳ אֱלֹקֵיכֶם, וּלְעָבְדוֹ בְּכָל לְבַבְכֶם וּבְכָל נַפְשְׁכֶם. וְנָתַתִּי מְטַר אַרְצְכֶם בְּעִתּוֹ, יוֹרֶה וּמַלְקוֹשׁ, וְאָסַפְתָּ דְגָנֶךָ וְתִירֹשְׁךָ וְיִצְהָרֶךָ.

And it will be, if you will diligently obey my commandments that I enjoin upon you this day, to love the L-rd your G-d and to serve Him with all your heart and with all your soul: I will give rain for your land at the proper time.

Text 11

MISHNAH, BERACHOT 2:1

אָמַר ר׳ יְהוֹשֻׁעַ בֶּן קָרְחָה:

לָמָּה קָדְמָה פָּרָשַׁת שְׁמַע לִוְהָיָה אִם שָׁמֹעַ?

כְּדֵי שֶׁיְּקַבֵּל עָלָיו עוֹל מַלְכוּת שָׁמַיִם תְּחִלָּה וְאַחַר כָּךְ מְקַבֵּל עָלָיו עוֹל מִצְוֹת.

Rabbi Yehoshua ben Karcha said:

"Why did the rabbis place the paragraph beginning with Shema before the paragraph beginning with *Vehayah im shamo'a*?

"It is because one must first accept the rule of G-d, and only then one can commit to the *mitzvot*."

Text 12

NUMBERS 15:41, SHEMA, MORNING PRAYERS

אֲנִי ה' אֱלֹקֵיכֶם, אֲשֶׁר הוֹצֵאתִי אֶתְכֶם מֵאֶרֶץ מִצְרַיִם לִהְיוֹת לָכֶם לֵאלֹקִים. אֲנִי ה' אֱלֹקֵיכֶם.

I am the L-rd your G-d Who brought you out of the land of Egypt to be your G-d; I, the L-rd, am your G-d.

Text 13

RABBI SHNEUR ZALMAN OF LIADI, *TANYA, LIKUTEI AMARIM*, CHAPTER 47

וְהִנֵּה בְּכָל דּוֹר וָדוֹר וְכָל יוֹם וָיוֹם, חַיָּיב אָדָם לִרְאוֹת עַצְמוֹ כְּאִלּוּ הוּא יָצָא הַיּוֹם מִמִּצְרַיִם. וְהִיא יְצִיאַת נֶפֶשׁ הָאֱלֹקִית מִמַּאֲסַר הַגּוּף . . . לִיכָּלֵל בְּיִחוּד אוֹר אֵין סוֹף בָּרוּךְ הוּא עַל יְדֵי עֵסֶק הַתּוֹרָה וְהַמִּצְוֹת בִּכְלָל. וּבִפְרַט בְּקַבָּלַת מַלְכוּת שָׁמַיִם בִּקְרִיאַת שְׁמַע, שֶׁבָּהּ מְקַבֵּל וּמַמְשִׁיךְ עָלָיו יִחוּדוֹ יִתְבָּרֵךְ בְּפֵירוּשׁ, בְּאָמְרוֹ "ה' אֱלֹקֵינוּ ה' אֶחָד".

In every generation and on every day, a person must view oneself as if they left Egypt that day. This means freeing the G-dly soul from the domination of the body . . . in order to become one with the infinite G-d. Generally put, this is done through engaging in the Torah and its *mitzvot*. More specifically, this is achieved through accepting G-d's rule when saying the Shema. When one says the words *Havayah Elokeinu*—the L-rd is our G-d—one acknowledges and experiences unity with G-d.

Exercise 5.1

Which theme of this lesson is most meaningful to you?

____

____

____

____

Takeaway Exercise

Love. Take a couple of minutes every day to reflect upon humanity's relative insignificance when contrasted with the sheer greatness and grandeur of the infinite G-d. Then, consider how fortunate you are that G-d not only notices you but also cares for you deeply and individually. Follow this up immediately with an out-loud reading of the Shema.

We'll discuss how it went during the next lesson.

Key Points

1. The Shema prayer is flanked on either side by prayers that help frame its message.

2. Angels are spiritual beings with a heightened consciousness of G-d. They perceive the transcendent aspect of G-d and yearn for it. This is the meaning of their saying *kadosh*.

3. Despite G-d's transcendence, He contracted Himself to create our finite world because He desires to connect with us. This theme is reflected in the verse of Shema Yisrael.

4. Meditating on this inspires us to love G-d and dedicate ourselves to fulfilling His will.

TECHINOT FOR **CHILDBIRTH**

Rachel Mevakah Al Baneha **(Vilna, 1910), p. 205***

The following two *techinot* beseech G-d for an easy and healthy birth. The first is worded for recitation by the expectant mother herself, while the second is intended for recitation by other women on behalf of an expectant mother in labor. These *techinot* are published in *Rachel Mevakah Al Baneha*, a collection of *techinot* printed in Vilna. The book's title page says it was edited by Rachel Esther bas Avichayil of Jerusalem, which appears to be a pseudonym.

*The Yiddish text for these *techinot* use old Yiddish terms and spelling conventions.

אָנָא ה' אֱלֹקֵי יִשְׂרָאֵל, איך בעט דיר דער גאָט פון יִשְׂרָאֵל, אז דוא זאָלסט פארנעמען מיין גיבעט, ווי דו האָסט פארנומען דאָס גיבעט פון אונזער מוטער די נְבִיאָה חַנָּה, וואָס זי האָט גיבעטין אויף איר זוהן שְׁמוּאֵל הַנָּבִיא, און איר זְכוּת זאָל מיר ביישטיין, אז איך דיין מאגד זאָל דאָס קינד וואָס איך טראָג יעצט אין די גידערים (דיין באשעפעניש) זאָל איך אויסטראָגין אין גאינצין שוואנגערהייט, עס זאָל ארויס אגיזונדע קינד,

עס זאָל זיין איין פרומער יוד, ער זאָל דיר דינען בְּכָל לֵב וָנֶפֶשׁ, ער זאָל זיין איין אוֹהֵב תּוֹרָה, און איין יְרֵא שָׁמַיִם, ווי דיין הייליגער ווילען, און ער זאָל זיין איין שיינע פלאנצונג אין דעם וידישען וויינגארטען לְתִפְאֶרֶת יִשְׂרָאֵל, אָמֵן:

I entreat You, G-d of Israel, accept my prayer, just as You accepted the prayer of our mother, Chanah the prophetess, when she prayed for her son, Samuel the prophet. May her merit assist me, so that I, Your maidservant, may bear to full term this child that I carry now in my womb—Your creation—and that a healthy child may emerge.

May he or she be a pious Jew, may they serve You with all their heart and soul, and may they be a lover of Torah and G-d-fearing, according to Your holy will. May they be a beautiful seedling in the Jewish vineyard, for the glory of the Jewish people. Amen.

אֵ-ל רַחוּם וְחַנוּן! שטארקער באשעפער, האָב רַחֲמָנוּת אויף די אִשָּׁה (פב"פ) (מען דארף דא דערמאנען דעם נאמען פון די יוֹלֶדֶת, און דעם נאָמען פון איר מוטער) אז זי זאָל האָבּן דאָס קינד בְּשָׁלוֹם,

דער זְכוּת פון אונזערע הייליגע אִמָהוֹת, שָׂרָה, רִבְקָה, רָחֵל, וְלֵאָה, און דעם זְכוּת פון אונזערע נְבִיאוֹת מִרְיָם, דְבוֹרָה, חַנָה, חוּלְדָה, און דער זְכוּת פון יָעֵל זאָלין איר בּיישטיין אין די סַכָּנָה צייט, אז זי זאָל האָבּין דאָס קינד גרינג אָן יְסוּרִים,

דען דו גאָט קאָנסט ווייזין אזא נֵס, בִּזְכוּת די צִדְקָנִיוֹת פון אונזערע עלטערין, און דאס קינד זאָל גיבָּארין ווערין איין ריינע זעלע צו דיין דינסט, איין צַדִיק, און ער זאָל עוֹסֵק זיין בַּתּוֹרָה וּבְמִצְוֹת, און אויבּע א נְקֵבָה, זאָל זי זיין איין אִשָּׁה צְנוּעָה, איין אִשָּׁה יִרְאַת ה' און זאָל האָבּין אגוטין מַזָל,

עס זאָל גיזונד זיין דיִ מוטער מיט די קינד, און זי זאָל קומען אויף דער וועלט, צוא יְשׁוּעוֹת וְנֶחָמוֹת אויף כְּלַל יִשְׂרָאֵל, אין איר צייט זאָלין יודען זוֹכֶה זיין איין ווארע גְאוּלָה אָמֵן.

Merciful and gracious G-d! Mighty Creator, have compassion on the woman [insert the name of the woman in labor and the name of her mother] that she may have this child safely.

May the merit of our holy matriarchs—Sarah, Rebecca, Rachel, and Leah—and the merit of our prophetesses—Miriam, Deborah, Hannah, and Huldah—and the merit of Jael—protect her in this time of danger so that she may have this child easily and without suffering.

For You, G-d, can perform such a miracle, through the merits of the righteous women from among our ancestors, that the child should be born a pure soul for Your service, a righteous person who will devote himself to the study of Torah and performance of *mitzvot*. And if it is a female, may she be a modest woman, a G-d-fearing woman, and may she have good fortune.

May both mother and child be healthy and may the child enter the world along with salvation and comfort for all of the Jewish people. May the Jewish people merit the true Redemption in their lifetime. Amen.

The Hidden Beauty of the Shema

By Lisa Aiken, PhD

During World War II, countless Jewish parents gave their precious children to Christian neighbors and orphanages in the hope that the latter would provide safe havens for them. The parents expected that they, or their relatives, would take these children back if they survived the war.

The few parents who did not perish in the Holocaust, and were able to reclaim their children, often faced another horror. While the parents had summoned the strength to survive the slave labor and death camps, or had hidden out for years, those who took their children were busy teaching them to love Christianity, and to hate Jews and Judaism.

To add insult to injury, many Jewish children who were taken in by Christian orphanages, convents, and the like, had no parents or close relatives left after the Holocaust. When rabbis or distant relatives finally tracked down many of these children, the priests and nuns who had been their caretakers insisted that no children from Jewish homes were in their institutions. Thus, countless Jewish children were not only stripped of their entire families, they were also stripped of their souls.

In May, 1945, Rabbi Eliezer Silver from the United States and Dayan Grunfeld from England were sent as chaplains to liberate some of the death camps. While there, they were told that many Jewish children had been placed in a monastery in Alsace-Lorraine. The rabbis went there to reclaim them.

When they approached the priest in charge, they asked that the Jewish children be released into the rabbis' care. "I'm sorry," the priest responded, "but there is no way of knowing which children here came from Jewish families. You must have documentation if you wish me to do what you ask."

Of course, the kind of documentation that the priest wanted was unobtainable at the end of the war. The rabbis asked to see the list of names of children who were in the monastery. As the rabbis read the list, they pointed to those that belonged to Jewish children.

"I'm sorry," the priest insisted, "but the names that you pointed to could be either Jewish or Gentile. Miller is a German name, and Markovich is a Russian name, and Swersky is a Polish name. You can't prove that these are Jewish children. If you can't prove which children are Jewish, and do it very quickly, you will have to leave."

LISA AIKEN, PHD

Born in Baltimore, Maryland; noted author and speaker; served as chief psychologist at Lenox Hill Hospital in New York City from 1982–1989. Among her works are *Creating Healthy Marriages*, and *Faith, Meaning, and Self-Esteem*. She currently lives in Jerusalem.

One of the rabbis had a brilliant idea. "We'd like to come back again this evening when you are putting the children to sleep." The priest reluctantly agreed.

That evening the rabbis came to the dormitory, where row upon row of little beds were arranged. The children, many of whom had been in the monastery since the war started in 1939, were going to sleep. The rabbis walked through the aisles of beds, calling out, "Shema, Yisrael, Hashem Elokeinu, Hashem Echad!" ("Hear, Jewish people, the L-rd is our G-d, the L-rd is One!")

One by one, children burst into tears and shrieked, "Mommy!" "Maman!" "Momma!" "Mamushka!" in each of their native tongues.

The priest had succeeded in teaching these precious Jewish souls about the Trinity, the New Testament, and the Christian savior. Each child knew how to say Mass. But the priest did not succeed in erasing these children's memories of their Jewish mothers—now murdered—putting them to bed every night with the Shema on their lips.

(My thanks to Miriam Swerdlov for relating this story to me.)

G-D'S ONENESS

We say in the Shema that G-d is One, meaning that He is singular, unique, and incomparable. His uniqueness includes the idea that all else exists and functions only according to His will. He, of course, exists and functions without depending on anything else. The idea of G-d's singularity encompasses the first three of Maimonides' Thirteen Principles of Faith:

> *1. I believe with complete faith that the Creator, blessed is His Name, creates and guides all creations, and He alone made, makes and will make all things.*

This principle states that G-d has no "assistants" nor partners when He runs the world. This contrasts with pagan beliefs that many forces run the world and Christian beliefs that G-d is part of a trinity. This principle also includes the idea that the world only exists because of G-d's constant will for it to be sustained.

> *2. I believe with complete faith that the Creator, blessed is His Name, is unique, that there is no uniqueness like His in any way, and that He alone is our G-d who was, is, and always will be.*

G-d cannot be divided into component parts because He is a total unity that is indivisible.

> *3. I believe, with complete faith, that the Creator, blessed is His Name, has no body and is not affected by physical events, and He has absolutely no physical likeness.*

The idea of G-d's unity reminds us that our world's many creations do not function and exist independently. They all operate under G-d's providence. One of the Shema's main functions is to underscore this unity.

During Creation, the world expanded to the extent that G-d exclaimed, "If I create one more physical thing, the world will conceal Me so much that people won't be able to find Me. Enough concealment!" G-d wanted our world to operate via natural laws of cause and effect that would conceal His "directing the show" behind the scenes. At the same time, He wanted people to find Him. Some concealment was necessary to challenge us to use our free will to find and obey G-d. But He wanted us to grow from the challenges of the physical world, not assume that natural forces are in charge and that He is absent. Believing that the physical world is ultimate reality, and ignoring G-d's presence and will, negates the world's entire purpose.

The Almighty hides within the physical world and wants us to look for Him there. All life and blessing filters down here through Him, although we sometimes believe that other forces, such as nature, luck, fate, or people, ultimately make things happen. The more we believe that He is the only force that rules us, the less energy we waste compromising ourselves and trying to placate and control other forces. For example, if we believe that our efforts alone control our financial destiny and security, we might lie, act unethically, or compromise ourselves trying to get whatever financial benefits we can. If we believe that doctors restore our health, we look to them alone when we are sick and leave G-d out of the picture. If we think that we are fully responsible for our achievements, we try to accomplish goals on our own without asking for G-d's help.

The blessings that we receive actually depend upon how connected we are to our Source. The more we bond with and rely only upon Him, the more blessing we receive, and the less secondary forces distract us. Since "a servant can only serve one master," tying ourselves to extraneous forces makes us less available for a relationship with the Almighty. While He wants us to do our utmost to take care of our health, earn a living, and get what we need within the constraints of the physical world, we need always remember that G-d is the only *ultimate* Source. Finding a balance between having faith in Him while doing what we must to live in a material world is an ongoing, lifelong challenge.

When we get distracted by this world's superficiality, we think that it is ultimate reality. That prevents us from noticing the divine Presence behind the scenes. The more He seems absent, the more people tend to do negative things that fill the apparent void. That only makes Him even more hidden.

We can only see and appreciate G-d's unity and uniqueness by constantly searching for it. That is why the Hebrew word for "world" is *olam*. It derives from the word *he'elem* meaning "concealed." G-d designed a world that conceals His presence so that we can be rewarded for looking for Him. Searching for and finding Him lets us discover a hidden world of spiritual treasures that we aren't aware of otherwise.

HISTORICAL BACKGROUND OF THE SHEMA

The Midrash (homiletical explanation of the Torah) gives two historical sources for the first two verses of the Shema prayer: "Hear, Israel, the L-rd is our G-d, the L-rd is One," and "Blessed is the Name of His glorious kingdom forever and ever."

One midrash describes our forefather Jacob being on his deathbed, surrounded by his children. He prophetically saw his descendants suffering so terribly that they questioned G-d's ways. He wanted to ensure that they would withstand the challenges and tribulations of exile while retaining their faith, by revealing to his sons the events that would lead to the coming of the Messiah. He was not going to tell them when the Messiah would arrive, nor could he, because the Jews' behavior will determine when the Messiah arrives. Rather, Jacob wanted to tell his children how the darkest times in their history would contribute to a good end. Unfortunately, he lost his prophetic vision and divine inspiration a moment before he could do this.

Jacob wondered if his children's blemished faith had caused G-d to prevent him from revealing how Jewish suffering would eventually lead to future goodness. If so, his sons must have unresolved theological questions that Jacob could help put to rest. Since his children were going to be the pillars of the Jewish nation, if they thought that G-d was unfair or unjust, how would their descendants fare millennia later? The latter would be so far removed from people like Jacob that their doubts would topple them spiritually.

This prompted Jacob to ask his sons, "Do you have any complaints about G-d?"

His children unanimously responded, "Hear, Israel (one of Jacob's names), the L-rd (who is compassionate) is our G-d (who metes out justice), the (compassionate) L-rd is One." Thus, they stated their belief that one loving G-d executes justice and runs the world.

Jacob was ecstatic when he heard their response. It reassured him that he would leave behind twelve sons who had perfect faith in G-d and who would be a strong foundation for the Jewish nation. He joyfully responded, "Blessed is the Name of His glorious kingdom forever and ever."

This midrash says that the Jewish people subsequently got the mitzvah of saying the Shema in the merit of Jacob's sons' response. The tribes' strong faith was also indelibly etched into the spiritual persona (collective unconscious) of the Jewish people forever. Our ancestors enabled every one of their descendants to believe that everything ultimately has a good purpose.

Throughout history, Jews suffered torture and martyrdom while declaring their faith in G-d as they said the Shema. For example, Rabbi Akiva died with the Shema on his lips as he bled from wounds inflicted by the Romans. During the Crusades and the Inquisition, Christians tortured and martyred hundreds of thousands of Jews who refused to renounce their religion and who expired while saying the Shema. The same happened when countless Jews were murdered by Nazis and Nazi sympathizers. This type of Jewish fortitude was possible because Jacob's children said the Shema around his deathbed.

A second midrashic explanation traces the Shema's roots to the giving of the Ten Commandments. G-d told the Israelites the First Commandment, "I am the L-rd, your G-d, who brought you out of the land of Egypt, out of the house of slaves." They responded, "Hear, Israel." Then He uttered the Second Commandment, "You shall have no other gods before Me." The Jews replied, "The L-rd is our G-d, the L-rd is One." When the Almighty uttered each successive commandment, the Jews responded with corresponding verses from the Shema. In this way, the Shema formed part of the Jews' acceptance of the Ten Commandments. According to this midrash, the Israelites' response merited G-d's commanding them and their descendants to recite the Shema.

These two midrashic explanations as to why we say the Shema apparently contradict each other. One says that we say the Shema because of Jacob's sons' faith, while the other attributes it to what the Israelites said when they received the Torah.

When two *midrashim* seem to contradict each other, it means that they are addressing different aspects of the same idea. One of the above *midrashim* refers to the aspect of the Shema which Jacob and his children emphasized: our faith that G-d directs everything and, notwithstanding the pain and suffering that surrounds us, that we will ultimately realize His total goodness. We proclaim this faith when what we know—that G-d is totally good—and what we see and experience—that the world is full of pain and evil—are not congruent.

But the Shema has a second aspect to it. It expresses our Torah knowledge, which the Jews had when they received the Torah at Mount Sinai. When we accepted the Torah, we were simultaneously given the ability to understand its wisdom and absorb its deepest levels of truth. We can relate to G-d's uniqueness and unity because of the knowledge that Torah study gives, not because we have blind, non-rational belief.

THE CLARITY OF TORAH

Torah is the best means for finding our inner selves. Its wisdom, truth, and energy can pierce the surface camouflages of G-d and let us discover what life is really about. Even if the rest of the world believes that their views of reality are true, Torah tells us that there is a spiritual system that is much more real than the purely physical world around us. Even when the physical world conceals G-d's singularity, our connection to Torah allows us to still see it.

When Jacob's sons surrounded his deathbed, they told him that they didn't understand G-d's ways, but believed in Him anyway. When the Jews received the Torah at Mount Sinai, they had clear knowledge and perceptions about G-d. They knew without a shadow of a doubt that He existed and was revealing absolute truth to them via the Torah. Their responding to each of the Ten Commandments with verses from the Shema meant that they saw G-d's unity through Torah. At that moment, they did not have to *believe* in G-d's unity—they *knew* it from their experience.

Throughout Jewish history, millions of Jews remained loyal to Judaism despite their lack of Jewish education because they inherited their faith from Jacob's children. Jews who are disconnected from Torah knowledge may still know the truth about G-d's existence and our obligation to be loyal to Him. When that happens, it is because they have blind faith, not because they understand the Almighty's ways.

Connecting to Torah gives us a certainty about how to live, despite what the rest of the world believes. A Jew who is strongly bound to Torah will survive the worst crises, while a Jew who is removed from Torah may or may not. Studying Torah always links us to what is happening behind the scenes and keeps us from despairing when we see only life's surface. This aspect of the Shema is rooted in the clarity and wisdom of Torah.

Because the Israelites in Egypt lacked this, they did not listen to Moses when he told them that they would soon go free. The Torah says that their "shortness of spirit and suffering from hard work" prevented them from believing him. "Shortness of spirit" means that they were not connected to Torah. When that happens, Jews do not appreciate the reality that underlies the superficial world and can easily be overwhelmed by its difficulties and burdens.

When we pray the morning or evening services, we precede the Shema with a blessing about G-d's tremendous love for the Jews. We ask Him to inspire us and give us the wisdom to understand the Torah, to do what it asks of us, to understand its secrets, and to be excited by it.

Shortly after rising every morning, we are supposed to thank the Almighty for the privilege of being able to study Torah before we begin learning it that day. If we forget to say that blessing, we can fulfill our obligation to say it by reciting the prayer before the Shema asking G-d to help us learn Torah.

We precede the Shema by yearning to learn Torah because we can only truthfully say, "Hear, Israel, the L-rd is our G-d, the L-rd is One" if we know Torah well. This verse expresses that we know G-d as clearly as the Israelites did at Mount Sinai. When the world around us seems full of injustice, and it is hard to believe that our lives are being guided by a divine Hand, only plumbing the depths of Torah and internalizing its message that G-d is running a purposeful world allows us to truly believe that He is One.

A midrash helps us understand how G-d can love and care for us when we feel that He has abandoned us. It describes a king who married his fiancée after exchanging many love letters and promising to give her many gifts once they got married. Shortly after the wedding, though, she became promiscuous. Her disloyalty angered her husband and he abandoned her. Many months passed and people told the queen that her husband would never come back. They advised her to marry someone else. They were so persuasive that she almost followed their advice. She cried, thinking that they might be right, and sequestered herself in her chambers. She read his love letters, reviewed his promises, and reminisced about their wonderful times together. She finally concluded that her husband would inevitably return.

When her husband finally did come back after a very long time, the first thing he asked was, "How did you have the strength to wait for me for so many years?"

She responded, "I honestly don't know. But every time that I was ready to break down and give up hope, I took out all of your letters. I read about all of the things that we had shared, and something convinced me that deep, deep down, we still shared an enduring love."

And so it is with G-d and us. He wed the Jews, then we strayed from the way that we had agreed to live. We devoted ourselves to many pursuits besides G-d, so He eventually "left." The nations of the world came to us and said, "Your G-d left. He hasn't been around for years. You might as well forget about Him ever coming back. Come and join us. You'll prosper, have a good time, and be accepted by the world."

Our connection to Torah is the only thing that guarantees that our love relationship with G-d never ends, no matter what the illusions of life suggest. Throughout history, Jews reached their breaking point and were about to renounce their belief in, and commitment to, G-d. But by entering our house of learning and prayer and reading the Torah, something always convinced us that G-d would come back.

G-d will openly return to us when the Messiah comes. The first thing He will ask is, "How did you have the strength to wait for Me for so many years?"

We will respond, "Had we not revived ourselves by studying Torah whenever we verged on giving up, we would not have made it. Its messages convinced us of Your undying love for us."

The Hidden Beauty of the Shema
(Brooklyn: Judaica Press, 2004), pp. 17-19, 38-40, 44-50

LESSON SIX

A WORK OF SYNTHESIS

SYNTHESIZING DIVINITY AND MATERIALITY IN THE AMIDAH

Materialism and spirituality appear in conflict, but the centerpiece of Jewish prayer—the Amidah that crowns each service—is the apex of both Divine bonding and pleas for material needs. This lesson revolutionizes our view of material-spiritual dissonance and offers a profound and fresh appreciation for prayer, G-d, and life on planet Earth.

I. The Ladder

Text 1

RABBI SHALOM DOVBER SCHNEERSOHN,
SEFER HAMAAMARIM 5680, P. 153

שְׁמוֹנָה עֶשְׂרֵה הוּא בִּיטּוּל אֲמִיתִּי וְהִתְכַּלְּלוּת בְּאוֹר אֵין סוֹף בָּרוּךְ הוּא מַמָּשׁ הַסּוֹבֵב כָּל עָלְמִין כו'. . . וְאֵינָהּ עוֹלָה בְּשֵׁם אַהֲבָה כְּלַל, רַק בְּחִינַת בִּיטּוּל בִּמְצִיאוּת לְגַמְרֵי, וְהַיְינוּ בְּחִינַת הִשְׁתַּפְּכוּת נַפְשׁוֹ אֶל חֵיק אָבִיהָ מַמָּשׁ לִהְיוֹת כְּאַיִן וְאֶפֶס מַמָּשׁ.

The Amidah is the experience of true surrender and immersion in the endless light of G-d that envelops all of existence.... This cannot be called love; rather, it is a sense of complete surrender. The soul melts into its Heavenly Father and feels literally as naught.

RABBI SHALOM DOVBER SCHNEERSOHN (RASHAB) 1860–1920

Chasidic rebbe. Rabbi Shalom Dovber became the 5th leader of the Chabad movement upon the passing of his father, Rabbi Shmuel Schneersohn. He established the Lubavitch network of *yeshivot* called Tomchei Temimim. He authored many volumes of Chasidic discourses and is renowned for his lucid and thorough explanations of kabbalistic concepts.

Question for Discussion

Can prayer be meaningful for people who do not experience this feeling of total surrender during the Amidah? If yes, in what way?

Question for Discussion

Imagine yourself standing before a king. What emotions does this evoke within you?

Text 2a

PSALMS 51:17

ה' שְׂפָתַי תִּפְתָּח וּפִי יַגִּיד תְּהִלָּתֶךָ.

G-d, open my lips, and may my mouth speak your praises.

PSALMS

Biblical book. The book of Psalms contains 150 chapters expressing praise for G-d, faith in G-d, and laments over tragedies. The primary author of the psalms was King David, who lived in the 9th century BCE. Psalms also contains material from earlier figures. The feelings and circumstances expressed in the psalms resonate throughout the generations, and they have become an important part of communal and personal prayer.

Text 2b

RABBI YOSEF YITZCHAK SCHNEERSOHN,
SEFER HAMAAMARIM 5682, P. 221

בִּתְפִלַּת שְׁמוֹנֶה עֶשְׂרֵה, דְאָז הוּא כְּעוֹמֵד לִפְנֵי הַמֶּלֶךְ וּמִתְבַּטֵּל בִּמְהוּתוֹ, הִנֵּה הַתְחָלַת הַדִּיבּוּר הוּא "ה' שְׂפָתַי תִּפְתָּח". וְהוּא לְפִי שֶׁאֵינוֹ יָכוֹל לְדַבֵּר כְּלָל בְּכֹחַ עַצְמוֹ, לִהְיוֹתוֹ בִּלְתִּי מַרְגִּישׁ אֶת עַצְמוֹ כְּלָל בִּבְחִינַת יֵשׁ וּמְצִיאוּת דָּבָר, שֶׁיּוּכַל לְדַבֵּר וּלְשַׁבֵּחַ. וְאֵין מִילִּין בִּלְשׁוֹנִי כְּלָל.

The experience of the Amidah is akin to the complete surrender that one feels when standing before a king. We feel unable to utter a word because any form of speaking, including words of praise, requires a degree of self-awareness. Bereft of the ability to speak, we ask G-d to open our lips.

RABBI YOSEF YITZCHAK SCHNEERSOHN (RAYATZ, FRIERDIKER REBBE, PREVIOUS REBBE)
1880–1950

Chasidic rebbe, prolific writer, and Jewish activist. Rabbi Yosef Yitzchak, the 6th leader of the Chabad movement, actively promoted Jewish religious practice in Soviet Russia and was arrested for these activities. After his release from prison and exile, he settled in Warsaw, Poland, from where he fled Nazi occupation and arrived in New York in 1940. Settling in Brooklyn, Rabbi Schneersohn worked to revitalize American Jewish life. His son-in-law Rabbi Menachem Mendel Schneerson succeeded him as the leader of the Chabad movement.

Figure 6.1

Basic Laws and Customs of the Amidah

1	Stand upright.
2	Pray silently.
3	At certain points, bend at the knees and bow from the waist.

Text 3

TALMUD, BERACHOT 31A

כַּמָּה הִלְכְתָא גַבְרְוָותָא אִיכָּא לְמִשְׁמַע מֵהַנֵי קְרָאֵי דְחַנָּה: "וְחַנָּה הִיא מְדַבֶּרֶת עַל לִבָּהּ" (שְׁמוּאֵל א, א, יג) - מִכָּאן לַמִּתְפַּלֵּל צָרִיךְ שֶׁיְּכַוֵּין לִבּוֹ. "רַק שְׂפָתֶיהָ נָּעוֹת" (שָׁם) - מִכָּאן לַמִּתְפַּלֵּל שֶׁיַּחְתּוֹךְ בִּשְׂפָתָיו. "וְקוֹלָהּ לֹא יִשָּׁמֵעַ" (שָׁם) - מִכָּאן שֶׁאָסוּר לְהַגְבִּיהַּ קוֹלוֹ בִּתְפִלָּתוֹ.

We infer many laws of prayer from the story of Chanah. "And Chanah spoke in her heart" (I SAMUEL 1:13): from this we learn that we must concentrate during prayer. "Only her lips were moving" (IBID.): this teaches us that the words of prayer must be articulated orally. "And her voice was not heard" (IBID.): from this we learn that it is forbidden to pray loudly.

BABYLONIAN TALMUD

A literary work of monumental proportions that draws upon the legal, spiritual, intellectual, ethical, and historical traditions of Judaism. The 37 tractates of the Babylonian Talmud contain the teachings of the Jewish sages from the period after the destruction of the 2nd Temple through the 5th century CE. It has served as the primary vehicle for the transmission of the Oral Law and the education of Jews over the centuries; it is the entry point for all subsequent legal, ethical, and theological Jewish scholarship.

II. The Blessings

Figure 6.2

		SUMMARY OF BLESSING	NOTES ON THE ORDER
PRAISING G-D	1.	We praise G-d as great, powerful, and awesome. We also describe His benevolence toward His children.	This blessing comes first because it describes G-d's benevolence, which is key to the granting of blessings.
	2.	We praise Almighty G-d for rainfall, supporting the fallen, healing the ill, and reviving the dead.	G-d protects us because He loves us. It follows that after praising G-d for His benevolence and love, we praise G-d for His might and protection.
	3.	We praise G-d's transcendence.	Here we transition from talking about things G-d does in the world to talking about His transcendence.
REQUESTS FOR OUR NEEDS	4.	We ask G-d to grant us wisdom, knowledge, and understanding.	This is the first in a series of thirteen requests. We begin with a request for knowledge because the ability to distinguish between right and wrong, and between good and bad, is the most important value.
	5.	We ask G-d to accept our repentance.	With wisdom, we recognize our sins and wish to repent.
	6.	We ask G-d to forgive our sins.	Having repented, we ask G-d to forgive our sins.
	7.	We ask G-d to save us from our daily adversaries, troubles, and distresses.	Having been forgiven, we are worthy of being protected.
	8.	We ask G-d to heal us and our loved ones from illness.	Having been forgiven, we are worthy of healing.
	9.	We ask G-d to provide for us and sustain us.	Having been forgiven, we are worthy of sustenance.

Section	#	SUMMARY OF BLESSING	NOTES ON THE ORDER
REQUESTS FOR OUR NEEDS *cont.*	10.	We ask G-d to gather all Jews who are scattered across the globe and bring them to Israel.	Here we transition from personal requests to requests on behalf of the collective Jewish people.
	11.	We ask G-d to restore the Jewish High Court, which governed and taught the Torah from the Temple Mount.	After Mashiach leads the Jews back to Israel, the Jewish High Court will be restored.
	12.	We ask G-d to eradicate sectarians who cause suffering to the Jewish people.	After Mashiach comes and Jewish governance is reestablished, we will no longer suffer at the hands of those who wish us harm.
	13.	We ask G-d to reward and never disappoint those who place their trust in Him.	When wickedness ceases, the star of the righteous will shine properly.
	14.	We ask G-d to rebuild Jerusalem and restore the seat of David's kingdom.	The righteous will shine most prominently in Jerusalem, which will be rebuilt in its full glory when Mashiach comes.
	15.	We ask G-d to bring the Mashiach, whose coming we await every day.	After we pray for the restoration of the seat of David's kingdom, we ask G-d that Mashiach, a descendant of King David, not tarry.
	16.	We ask G-d to listen to and accept all our prayers.	This is a general prayer that wraps up the request portion of the Amidah. It asks G-d to grant all our requests.
THANKING G-D	17.	We ask G-d to accept us, the people of Israel, and our prayers.	This blessing serves to introduce the following one. It also serves as a general reiteration of all our previous prayers.
	18.	We acknowledge and thank G-d for the many miracles that He performs for us daily.	This is the blessing of gratitude. In order to highlight its importance, it is preceded and followed by a blessing.
	19.	We ask G-d to bless us with peace.	We follow the prayer of gratitude with a plea for peace. It is a worthy ending because peace is the vehicle for all blessings.

III. The Nature of Needs

Question for Discussion

Why do you think we focus on our needs during the Amidah, a time that should be focused entirely and exclusively on G-d?

Exercise 6.1

Write down three important things that you need or would like to have that you consider G-d-oriented.

1

2

3

Write down three important things that you need or would like to have that you consider self-oriented.

1

2

3

Text 4

THE REBBE, RABBI MENACHEM MENDEL SCHNEERSON,
LIKUTEI SICHOT 19, P. 294

אִין בַּקָשַׁת צְרָכָיו . . . אִיז נִיט אַרַיינְגֶעמִישְׁט אַ הֶרְגֵשׁ פוּן מְצִיאוּת הָאָדָם, וַוייל עֶר בֶּעט זֵיי נָאר פַאר דֶעם אוֹיבֶּערְשְׁטְנ'ס וֶועגְן. וְאַדְרַבָּה - דָאס קוּמְט דַוְקָא מִצַד דֶעם תַּכְלִית הַבִּיטּוּל.

Our requests . . . are not marked by a sense of self, because we ask for them exclusively for G-d's sake. In fact, our requests stem specifically from an absence of self-awareness and an utter focus on G-d.

RABBI MENACHEM MENDEL SCHNEERSON 1902–1994

The towering Jewish leader of the 20th century, known as "the Lubavitcher Rebbe," or simply as "the Rebbe." Born in southern Ukraine, the Rebbe escaped Nazi-occupied Europe, arriving in the U.S. in June 1941. The Rebbe inspired and guided the revival of traditional Judaism after the European devastation, impacting virtually every Jewish community the world over. The Rebbe often emphasized that the performance of just one additional good deed could usher in the era of Mashiach. The Rebbe's scholarly talks and writings have been printed in more than 200 volumes.

Text 5

THE REBBE, RABBI MENACHEM MENDEL SCHNEERSON,
IBID., P. 296

דָאס וָואס אַ אִיד בֶּעט . . . אַז דֶער אוֹיבֶּערְשְׁטֶער זָאל אִים גֶעבְּן צְרָכָיו הַגַשְׁמִיִּים וְהָרוּחָנִיִּים, אִיז [אַף עַל פִּי אַז בְּחִיצוֹנִיוּת אִיז עֶס מִצַד דֶערוֹיף וָואס אִים זַיינֶען נוֹגֵעַ עִנְיָנִים פוּן בָּנֵי חַיֵי וּמְזוֹנֵי, אוּן זַיין מְצִיאוּת, אִיז אָבֶּער] דֶער אֱמֶת אוּן פְּנִימִיּוּת פוּן דֶער שְׁפִיכַת הַנֶפֶשׁ - דֶער "הוּנְגֶער" פוּן נְשָׁמָה צוּ אוֹיסְפִירְן דִי כַּוָונָה הָעֶלְיוֹנָה צוּ מַאכְן פוּן דִי דְבָרִים גַשְׁמִיִּים אַ דִירָה לוֹ יִתְבָּרֵךְ.

On the surface, we plead with G-d . . . to provide for our physical and spiritual needs because we want those things for ourselves and because our health, children, and sustenance are important to us. Nevertheless, the inner truth is that these pleas are outpourings of the soul's yearning to fulfill G-d's wish that we make a home for Him through our physical possessions.

Exercise 6.2

Reread the items you listed in Exercise 6.1 as G-d-oriented and the items you listed as self-oriented, and consider whether you want to change any of your entries in light of what we just learned.

IV. Gratitude

Text 6

MODIM, EIGHTEENTH BLESSING OF THE AMIDAH

מוֹדִים אֲנַחְנוּ לָךְ, שָׁאַתָּה הוּא ה' אֱלֹקֵינוּ וֵאלֹקֵי אֲבוֹתֵינוּ לְעוֹלָם וָעֶד. צוּר חַיֵּינוּ, מָגֵן יִשְׁעֵנוּ, אַתָּה הוּא לְדוֹר וָדוֹר. נוֹדֶה לְךָ וּנְסַפֵּר תְּהִלָּתֶךָ, עַל חַיֵּינוּ הַמְּסוּרִים בְּיָדֶךָ, וְעַל נִשְׁמוֹתֵינוּ הַפְּקוּדוֹת לָךְ, וְעַל נִסֶּיךָ שֶׁבְּכָל יוֹם עִמָּנוּ, וְעַל נִפְלְאוֹתֶיךָ וְטוֹבוֹתֶיךָ שֶׁבְּכָל עֵת, עֶרֶב וָבֹקֶר וְצָהֳרָיִם.

We thankfully acknowledge that You are our G-d and the G-d of our forefathers forever. You are the strength of our life and the shield of our salvation in every generation. We thank You and recount Your praises—evening, morning, and noon—for our lives that are committed into Your hand, for our souls that are entrusted to You, for Your miracles that are with us daily, and for Your continual wonders and kindnesses.

Question for Discussion

Is there one phrase that jumps out at you and resonates with you in a personal way?

Takeaway Exercise

Choose one of the thirteen requests-focused blessings in the Shemoneh Esreh prayer that is particularly meaningful to you. Identify the G-d-oriented purpose this particular request may have and focus on asking G-d for this blessing for its G-d-oriented purpose.

We'll discuss how it went in the next class.

Key Points

1. The Amidah is the highest rung on the ladder of prayer. It is a time of complete focus on G-d and total emotional surrender.

2. Although it is primarily the soul that experiences this utter surrender, our objective is to tap into this feeling in our conscious minds as well. Reminding ourselves every day that we are standing before G-d allows us to expand our capacity for this kind of emotional surrender.

3. The Amidah contains praises of G-d and words of gratitude to G-d, but the heart of the Amidah is the section in which we make requests of G-d. In this section, we pray for our personal needs as well as our collective needs.

4. Deep down, our desire for personal needs—such as health, success, and prosperity—is an expression of our soul's desire to fulfill the purpose of creation. Thus, we pray for our needs during the Amidah even though our focus is completely on G-d.

TECHINOT FOR
SENDING CHILDREN TO SCHOOL

Rachel Mevakah Al Baneha **(Vilna, 1910), p. 207***

The following two *techinot* are written for recitation upon sending one's child to *cheder*, a school for religious Jewish instruction. They are published in *Rachel Mevakah Al Baneha*, a collection of *techinot* printed in Vilna. The book's title page says it was edited by Rachel Esther bas Avichayil of Jerusalem, which appears to be a pseudonym.

*The Yiddish text for these *techinot* use old Yiddish terms and spelling conventions.

בּוֹרֵא הָעוֹלָמוֹת!

Creator of the worlds!

מִיט גרויס חָכְמָה האָסטוּ בּעשאפין דיא וועלט וויא מיר וויסין, אונ דעם יֵצֶר הָרָע ער זאָל מאכען זינדיג דעם מענשין, פאר אַ רְפוּאָה האָסטוּ בּעשאפען די הייליגע תּוֹרָה, דארום האָבּין מיר אונזר זאָהן אָפּגעגעבּין צו לערנען תּוֹרָה,

We know that You created the world with great wisdom. You also created the negative inclination to entice a person to transgress, and, as a remedy for this, You created the holy Torah. Therefore, we have sent our son to study Torah.

בּעט איך דיר גאָט, שטארק זיין הארץ ער זאָל פלייסיג לערנען, ער זאָל היטען דיינע מִצְו ת און אונזערע עֵצוֹת, פיהר אים בְּדֶרֶךְ הַתּוֹרָה וְהַמִּצְוָה, מיר זאָלען דער לעבּין זעהן, אז ער וועט זיין אגרויסער מופלָג בַּתּוֹרָה און איין ערליכער יוּד, אָמֵן.

I beseech You, G-d, strengthen his heart so that he may study diligently, observe Your *mitzvot*, and heed our advice. Lead him in the path of Torah and *mitzvot*. May we live to see him become a great Torah scholar and a sincere Jew. Amen.

רִבּוֹנוֹ שֶׁל עוֹלָם! דו האָסט גיבּאָטען אין דער הייליגר תּוֹרָה דאָס עלטערין זאָלין לערנען תּוֹרָה מיט זייערע קינדער, דארום אזוי וויא מיר האָבּין קיין צייט ניט צוא לערנען מיט אונזער זאָהן, האָבּין מיר געדונגען אַ מְלַמֵּד פר אים,

Master of the universe! You have commanded in the holy Torah that parents should teach their children Torah. However, since we do not have the time to teach our son ourselves, we have hired a teacher for him.

דארוּם בּעט איך דיך גאָט נעם אָן אונזער געלד וויא מיר אליין וואָלטען מיט אים געלערינט, דער זְכוּת פון דר תּוֹרָה זאָל אויף אונז מגין זיין אז מיר זאָלין האָבּין פון אים נַחַת, אָמֵן.

Therefore, I beseech You, G-d, to accept our money as if we ourselves were teaching him. May the merit of the Torah protect us so that we may have much *nachas* from him. Amen.

ADDITIONAL READING

Personalizing Our Prayer Experience

By Rabbi Aryeh Ben David

Blessed are You, L-rd, our G-d
and the G-d of our Fathers,
the G-d of Abraham, the G-d
of Isaac, and the G-d of Jacob.

—Prayer book, opening words of the Amida prayer.

The peak moment of Jewish prayer, the standing, silent prayer (the *Amida*), teaches us the primacy of personalizing the prayer experience.

The *Amida* begins with the phrase "Our G-d and the G-d of our Fathers." These are two radically different experiences of the Divine.

"Our G-d" reflects the G-d of personal experience, the G-d of our lifetime. "Our G-d" refers to our personal and private relationship with G-d, which is unmediated by anyone else. No one else can create this for us. No one else can teach it to us. It is intimate and uniquely ours. This close, individual connection with G-d is sometimes referred to as a "vertical experience," a direct encounter with the beyond. The rabbis say that at Mount Sinai everyone heard a different voice—each person's relationship with G-d was unique.

"The G-d of our Fathers" is totally different. "The G-d of our Fathers" reflects the G-d of history. It is the G-d of Abraham, Isaac and Jacob. But it is not only the G-d of these three forefathers. It can also be understood to include all the people that preceded us. Everyone experiences G-d differently. This is the path that others have walked and that we can learn from. This experience of G-d is not accessed directly, nor is it the product of personal experience. Rather, it is learned through texts, stories, and a tradition conveyed by others. This indirect, mediated connection with G-d is sometimes referred to as a "horizontal experience," which is passed on through people, rather than through a direct experience with the transcendent.

We might have thought that the *Amida* would have begun with "the G-d of our Fathers" and then afterward mention "Our G-d." Their experience chronologically preceded our own. Nevertheless, we begin the *Amida* with "Our G-d." "Our G-d" precedes "the G-d of our Fathers."

Why?

First, we need to establish our own relationship with G-d. We need the "vertical" before the "horizontal." Only after this personal connection has been created can the teachings of "the G-d of our Fathers" resonate within us. The experience that

—

RABBI ARYEH BEN DAVID

Rabbi Aryeh Ben David lives in Efrat, Israel. A lifelong educator, his passion is helping students engage with their spiritual heritage on a personal level. He blogs extensively, lectures internationally on the subject, and has authored two books. He is the founder of Ayeka, a center that develops and teaches pedagogical methods for bringing Jewish wisdom from the mind to the heart.

others have had with G-d is meaningful only when we have already established our own experience of the holy.

Once, in the classroom, I asked if my students had ever been in love. One shook his head, saying "Never been." I said to him, "I love my wife very much. Do you have any idea how much I love my wife?" He answered, "No, not really, but it sounds nice." Since he had never been in love, he really had no idea what I was talking about. Then I asked a different student who *had* been in love before, "Do you have any idea how much I love my wife?" He nodded in confirmation and said, "Sure, I'm in love right now." Even though our experiences were probably completely different, he nevertheless could identify with my feelings, and we were able to carry on a discussion from a common platform.

Only after someone has undergone a similar experience is it possible to fully identify and integrate the lessons from someone else's life. Otherwise, their experience will remain on a superficial level—that is, purely as intellectual information that does not affect a person deeply.

This is why "Our G-d" has to precede "the G-d of our Fathers." Only *after* we have had our own direct experience with G-d can we then benefit from someone else's experience of the Divine. Only *after* we have had our very own uniquely personal and distinct "spiritual" experience can we identify with, and take in, the experience of someone else.

This is one of the reasons why the words of the prayer book often do not resonate with people. They are the words of "our Fathers." They will only resonate with us after we have formed our own personal relationship with G-d.

THE G-DFILE

To develop your relationship with G-d, you have to click up your G-dfile. To click it up, you first have to write it.

What is a "G-dfile"? The G-dfile encompasses your relationship with G-d. It includes moments of overwhelming joy and of deep despair, of loving closeness and of painful distance. It consists of times when we are in dialogue with G-d and our belief is intact, and of times when we sorely feel an absence. Imagine now that all of the dimensions of this multifaceted relationship have been transcribed to a computer file entitled "The G-dfile."

Why might this metaphor be helpful? So often I have observed the frustration and disappointment of family members, friends and students—and certainly within myself as well—when the spiritual "lift" we expect at certain moments simply does not happen. Much of this frustration can be attributed to our mistaken expectations. We cannot expect to feel spiritually uplifted simply because of the uniqueness of the moment; we need to prepare ourselves in advance.

A personal example: When my wife and I were married in Jerusalem, my grandmother came to Israel for the first time for the wedding. She had been raised in a marginally connected Jewish home, and Judaism was not central to her life. We went to the Western Wall together, where she said: "Aryeh, I'm here at the Wall for the first time, and it is not doing anything for me. I don't feel anything special."

Why didn't the Wall do anything for my grandmother? I believe it is because she had not written her "Western Wall file" during her life. She had not come to Israel prepared for this potentially inspiring moment. Had she learned about this religiously significant and historical site and contemplated its meaning deeply, her visit might have been transformed into an overwhelmingly powerful experience:

Another example from routine, everyday life.

I am busy at work. In the middle of the day, I decide to call home to check in with my wife. Is it possible for us to have a brief, yet meaningful, interaction during a two or three-minute phone call? What of any consequence could possibly be expressed in these few minutes? The truth is that the amount of time is irrelevant. Even the briefest conversation offers the potential for a deep connection that is unrelated to the specific words that we will say. The conversation can be extremely meaningful and significant because over the past 25 years I have been developing and deepening my relationship with my wife, writing the "wife-file." The phone call itself will never *create* the beauty and depth of the relationship, but it can *maintain* it. This fleeting conversation is a chance to click on the wife file in the computer of my life, briefly calling up our shared history and reinforcing our commitment to a shared future.

Clearly, the conversation will only be as meaningful as the extent of the "file." I cannot create a relationship during a two-minute phone call, but I can build on the 20-year relationship that has already been developed and sustained. This history will imbue meaning to the conversation. "I love you, Sandra." Four short words carry with them all the connections, experiences and emotions built in our 20-year history.

If you take a break from your computer for a few minutes, the screen saver appears. Eventually you return to the computer, tap on the mouse, and the file that you were working on reappears on the screen. The file that appears is only as long or short, meaningful or shallow as what you had written before. When you click on the mouse, you never expect the tap to create the contents of the file. It only calls up whatever already exists.

Walking into a synagogue is like tapping on the mouse. It brings up a file. If you have written an extensive file, then all the emotions connected to that file will be evoked. If you have written only a small file, you can only expect to draw on the little that is already there.

Many of us walk into a synagogue with the expectation that a spiritual experience will descend upon us, regardless of how much or little we have written in our own personal G-dfile. We expect that the setting, prayer book, or maybe even the singing will elicit spiritual feelings. But in truth, neither the synagogue nor the prayer book can create a spiritual connection.

During the time of formal prayer, it is practically impossible to *create* a relationship with G-d. The synagogue can only serve to remind you of a relationship that already exists. Praying in a synagogue can certainly eclipse many of life's distractions, and help focus a relationship with G-d, but it is very unlikely that it will actually create the relationship. When no G-dfile has been written, and thus no file appears, frustration and disillusionment set in. The process is not magical. A file in which nothing has been written will produce just that—nothing. It is not the computer's fault. It is not the fault of the synagogue or the prayer book: they are simply tools designed to help us bring up the G-dfile. Just as in any relationship, it takes effort to build a relationship with G-d—effort that takes place in many settings besides the synagogue. Only you can write your own G-dfile.

OVERCOMING OBSTACLES TO WRITING YOUR G-DFILE

We may find that in our path to writing a G-dfile, we encounter obstacles along the way, both internal and external.

INTERNAL OBSTACLE #1: THE SPIRITUAL STEREOTYPE

One common obstacle is the pervasive stereotype of the "spiritual type." Often I ask groups of students, "What do spiritual people do? What do they look like? What do spiritual people eat?" I inevitably receive the same answers: "They are mellow," says one. "They meditate a lot," says another. Others will say, "They do yoga, they sing, they dance; they are probably vegetarian or vegan; they wear flowing clothes, probably white." Then I ask the group, "How many of you fit into these categories?" Rarely does a hand go up.

"What is the goal of becoming more spiritual?" I persist. Again, the answers usually include such stereotypical notions as, "Being at peace with oneself, achieving nirvana, calmness and serenity. An inner glow."

Unfortunately, this characterization is terribly limiting. And since most people do not match this limited image, they believe that they themselves lack spirituality. These preconceived notions discourage most from ever trying to pursue a more spiritual path. I cannot begin to count the number of people who have told me, "I am simply not a spiritual person. I am not the spiritual type."

OVERCOMING THE OBSTACLE: BREAKING THE STEREOTYPE

I often ask people if they think they have a soul. They almost always respond affirmatively. "Well," I continue, "what does this soul do? What does it occupy itself with? Does it 'just sit there,' or is it active in any manner? Have you ever felt your soul communicating something to you? Have you ever had a spiritual moment?"

Invariably, one person begins to open up, and others begin to nod in agreement.

At the closing circle of one of our retreats, we invited everyone to talk for a few minutes about where they were spiritually. One elderly man had barely opened his mouth during our three days together. We hadn't expected him to say anything, so we were surprised when he began to talk and continued for over 20 minutes. Suddenly he stopped talking, and began to shake and cry. With tears welling up in his eyes, he whispered that all of his life he felt he had been on the outside of Judaism looking in. Now, for the first time, he felt as if someone had opened a door to let him in.

Who had locked this man out? Who created this "inside" and "outside" perception? Unfortunately, most of the time we do it to ourselves.

With an unrealistic stereotype of the "spiritual person" firmly embedded in our minds, we close the door to spirituality and lock ourselves out. The essential step in overcoming this obstacle, and placing ourselves back inside, is telling oneself, "I have a soul. I am a spiritual person."

INTERNAL OBSTACLE #2: FEAR OF CHANGE

Countering the desire within each of us for growth is an equally strong voice saying, "You're okay as you are, don't mess up your life. Who knows where change will lead? Why bother?"

According to the Talmud, we were all created with a drive that tricks us into complacency. We have a subconscious drive that urges us to remain static, to resist growth.

Sometimes when we see people after a long absence we observe that they haven't changed. Are they stable? Or are they stuck? One of the most difficult moments for students who return home after a year in Israel occurs when a relative or friend looks disapprovingly at them and remarks, "You've changed," subtly implying that change is a negative development reflecting a lack of stability.

At various stages in my life, an internal voice urged me to resist any kind of change. I convinced myself that more than anything, I needed to regain a sense of stability. I would often worry and feel uncertain about what a possible new stage might demand of me. Sometimes I simply lacked the energy and emotional strength to consider change and self-growth. For many years, I was aware that I had reached an impasse, and that I was spiritually stuck, yet I found myself incapable of overcoming this block. I was trapped in the daily routine of going through the motions.

OVERCOMING THE OBSTACLE: FINDING THE WILL TO CHANGE

There is no single way to overcome this obstacle. Each person has his or her own personal demons. Personally, my desire to grow finally outweighed my drive to resist change. A spiritual block is like a black cloud that depletes joy and passion.

The crucial step in overcoming this obstacle requires asking ourselves three questions:

- Am I stuck?
- What exactly am I afraid of?
- What is holding me back?

EXTERNAL OBSTACLE #1: THE SYNAGOGUE—WHERE IS MY VOICE?

Did you ever feel like walking out of your synagogue?

Why is it that attending synagogue can be such a frustrating, and often empty, experience? Did you ever feel that it just was not working for you? You look around; everyone else is uttering the words, going through the motions. But the words of the prayer book are not your words; the pace of the service is not your pace. You're feeling lonely, alienated, out of it, and the feeling intensifies with each passing moment. Maybe you're wondering, "Am I the only one who feels like this? What's the matter with me?"

Perhaps you are asking yourself, "What am I supposed to be feeling at this moment? What is supposed to be happening now? Should I be asking for something? Should I be crying? Am I supposed to be feeling spiritual? Am I hoping for a mystical breakthrough? I know how to recite the words of the prayer book, but then what? What am I doing here? Where is my personal voice in all of this? There's no time or room for me to discover how I really feel about all of this. And, most painfully and poignantly of all, what is my voice supposed to be?"

At certain points in my life, the daily routine of praying in synagogue helped me build the stability of my faith. I enjoyed the connection with my friends in synagogue, the camaraderie before and after *davenning* (prayer) and the singing. But did the actual moment of prayer have any impact on my life? Was it meaningful?

I came to realize that for me—then—the answer was no.

Not only did my prayers lack meaning, but they often left me feeling deeply dissatisfied and frustrated, regardless of how many different synagogues I attended.

OVERCOMING THE OBSTACLE: FINDING YOUR OWN VOICE

Serious prayer should involve more than just the recitation of liturgical, or even informal, words. Prayer should be an authentically personal experience. It is not *someone's* prayer; it is *your* prayer. The Talmud refers to prayer as "the work of the heart." Prayer should reach the depths of your being and touch your heart.

The prayer book is supposed to be the springboard for this "work of the heart." Sometimes, however, the words of the prayer book take over, usurping your personal meditations. You follow the lines of the prayer book without personalizing them, without adding words or thoughts. You are not transformed. In fact, there is no "you" there.

You need to somehow find a place for yourself in the prayer book, to insert your own words, emotions and needs that you are feeling precisely at that moment. You need to bring yourself into the prayer experience.

Is this possible? Can you find room for yourself in the midst of an organized prayer service and fixed liturgy? Human beings are forever changing, but the prayer book does not: If the prayer book does not change, how can your own personal experience of prayer evolve to reflect your needs?

The rabbis themselves stressed the need to add personal prayers during the *Amida*, the silent standing prayer. During the "Listen to our voice" (*Shema Koleinu*) section of the *Amida*, one is encouraged to add personal thoughts. At the end of the *Amida*, and even during each blessing of the *Amida*, the rabbis encouraged the inclusion of personal insertions.

The essential step in overcoming this obstacle is saying to yourself, "I have a voice. I am allowed to add my personal prayers to the words of the prayer book. What personal words do I want to include?"

EXTERNAL OBSTACLE #2: PUBLIC NATURE OF PRAYER IN PLACES OF WORSHIP

A second obstacle in creating one's own G-dfile is the focus of religious education on the "externals" of prayer, often at the expense of the "internals." Instead of concentrating on developing a rich internal life, and tapping into our spiritual beings, there has been a preoccupation with mastering the mechanics and technique of prayer.

I recognized this phenomenon while working with my students. They were talented young adults from all over the world. For many of them, this was their first serious encounter with Judaism. They began to learn about Jewish ideas and gradually incorporated more religious observances into their lives. They inevitably began to think about joining a Jewish community and wondered how they would fit in. How would they manage socially in this new milieu? Would it be awkward? Would they stand out? Would they feel self-conscious?

In their desire to integrate into Jewish communities, they pushed themselves to learn the essentials of Jewish public life: how to say the prayers, when to stand and when to bow. Some even learned how to lead the prayers. These were the easy things to teach and to learn.

Because of the public nature of places of worship, students became consumed with learning about the more visible and social dimensions of prayer. They often avoided the deeper question of how to use prayer to express their relationship with G-d.

OVERCOMING THE OBSTACLE: FINDING YOUR PRIVATE SPACE IN PLACES OF WORSHIP

Prayer comes in a number of forms. Certain forms center on the individual experience, a solitary figure sitting in solitude, in meditation, in supreme aloneness.

In community-centered prayer, the individual is swallowed up in the group experience. I remember being spellbound watching a Christian "revival" that culminated in a community singing of Halleluyah. In the frenetic energy of the congregation, the individuals seemed to merge into one communal being.

Which of these paradigms of prayer most reflects Judaism's approach—a solitary experience or a communal one? Actually, neither. Rather, the moment of encountering G-d in Jewish prayer reflects the fusion of these two models.

Although the *Shema* is probably the most well-known Jewish prayer, the central and most important moment in Jewish prayer is the silent standing prayer, the *Amida*. The *Shema* always precedes the *Amida*.

At the beginning of the *Amida*, one takes three steps backward, followed by three steps forward. Although one is now standing physically in the same spot, on a spiritual level, one moves into an entirely different place when entering the "*Amida* space." Despite being surrounded by others, the person praying is in a very private space—a space which draws upon the spiritual energy and mood of those around us, but that leaves us utterly alone at the ultimate moment of prayer. Students often refer to it as "the encounter" or "the zone" of standing in the presence of G-d.

Unfortunately, the social and communal nature of the synagogue and prayer often eclipse this precious moment. Extra effort is necessary to regain this sense and sanctity of private, solitary space. The rabbis of the Talmud instruct that one should not take any notice of any interruption—not even the entry of a king into the room or the sensing of a snake wrapped around one's legs. At this moment of silent prayer, one is entering a spiritual twilight zone, and nothing else exists but our relationship with G-d.

> *Three steps backward, three steps forward. You are alone with yourself: What are you thinking?*

Once you enter your "three steps forward" space, you enter sacred space, beyond time. You may find it helpful to pause, take several deep breaths, and repeat to yourself: "Three steps backward, three steps forward. I just entered into a different zone of being."

The rest of the congregation may be rushing forward with their own prayers, but you can and should take as long as you want during your private silent prayer. This is your time with G-d and everything else will simply have to wait.

After having taken three steps backward and three steps forward, what is supposed to happen now?

This moment cannot be captured through the words of the Jewish prayer book. It may be beyond all words. It is your opportunity to connect to the deepest part within yourself, to something greater than yourself. This is an experience that cannot be dictated for you by others, a moment of self-definition that only you can create for yourself. Only you will ever know what has transpired during this interval. Will this moment be meaningful? Or will it be empty?

Three steps backward, three steps forward. What kind of space have you entered? That depends on how you prepared yourself for this moment. The community cannot be held responsible for the depth, or lack of depth, of this spiritual moment. You have total control over the quality of the private space that you create during prayer. The important step in overcoming this obstacle is asking yourself, "Have I entered into a sacred space? What has changed within me? What does this open up within me?"

The G-dfile: 10 Approaches to Personalizing Prayer (Jerusalem: Devora Publishing, 2007), pp. 3–10, 25–33

LESSON SEVEN

A WORK OF ALLIANCE

FINDING MEANING IN COMMUNAL PRAYER

Prayer is a deeply personal journey that includes reflection and contemplation. Why does Judaism insist on communal services, when solitude seems more conducive? This lesson investigates the role and power of communal prayer, reveals how it is essential in order to achieve the ultimate goals of prayer, and charts a path to balancing the personal with the collective.

I. Communities That Pray Together

Text 1

RABBI YOSEF CARO, SHULCHAN ARUCH, *ORACH CHAYIM* 90:9

יִשְׁתַּדֵּל אָדָם לְהִתְפַּלֵּל בְּבֵית הַכְּנֶסֶת עִם הַצִּבּוּר.

One should endeavor to pray in a synagogue together with a congregation.

SHULCHAN ARUCH
1565

Code of Jewish law. Shulchan Aruch—meaning the "set table"—is a comprehensive code, published in 1565, of all practical Jewish law, written by Rabbi Yosef Caro, a refugee from Spain then living in Safed, Israel. Rabbi Caro's work represented the Halachic tradition and customs of Spanish Jewry, and Rabbi Moshe Isserlis of Cracow, Poland, wrote the *Mapah*—meaning "tablecloth"—glosses presenting the Ashkenazi tradition. The unified Shulchan Aruch has been accepted by communities across the Jewish world as the most authoritative work of Jewish law.

Exercise 7.1

List some of the advantages and disadvantages of praying alone and praying with a group.

	ADVANTAGES	DISADVANTAGES
PRAYING ALONE		
PRAYING WITH A GROUP		

Text 2a

TALMUD, YEVAMOT 49B

אָמַר רָבָא, מֵידָן דַּיְינֵיה וְקַטְלֵיה.

אָמַר לֵיה . . . מֹשֶׁה רַבָּךְ אָמַר: "מִי . . . כַּה' אֱלֹקֵינוּ בְּכָל קָרְאֵנוּ אֵלָיו" (דְבָרִים ד, ז), וְאַתְּ אָמַרְתְּ: "דִרְשׁוּ ה' בְּהִמָּצְאוֹ" (יְשַׁעְיָה נה, ו).

Rava said: "Manasseh judged Isaiah and then killed him."

Manasseh said to Isaiah, . . . "Moses, your master, said, 'Who is like our G-d, Who is near to us whenever we call upon Him?' (DEUTERONOMY 4:7). But you said, 'Seek G-d while He may be found [call upon Him while He is near]' (ISAIAH 55:6)."

BABYLONIAN TALMUD

A literary work of monumental proportions that draws upon the legal, spiritual, intellectual, ethical, and historical traditions of Judaism. The 37 tractates of the Babylonian Talmud contain the teachings of the Jewish sages from the period after the destruction of the 2nd Temple through the 5th century CE. It has served as the primary vehicle for the transmission of the Oral Law and the education of Jews over the centuries; it is the entry point for all subsequent legal, ethical, and theological Jewish scholarship.

Text 2b

TALMUD, IBID.

מִכָּל מָקוֹם קָשׁוּ קְרָאֵי אַהֲדָדֵי . . .

דִּרְשׁוּ ה' בְּהִמָּצְאוֹ, הָא בְּיָחִיד הָא בְּצִבּוּר.

וְיָחִיד אֵימַת? אָמַר רַב נַחְמָן אָמַר רַבָּה בַּר אֲבוּהָ: אֵלּוּ עֲשָׂרָה יָמִים שֶׁבֵּין רֹאשׁ הַשָּׁנָה לְיוֹם הַכִּפּוּרִים.

In any case, these verses do in fact appear to contradict each other. . . .

[The Talmud responds:] Isaiah's prophecy, "Seek G-d *while* He may be found," was said with regard to the individual. Whereas the verse, "whenever we call upon Him," is stated with regard to a community.

And when is G-d found near the individual? Rabbi Nachman said in the name of Rabah bar Avuha, "These are the ten days between Rosh Hashanah and Yom Kippur."

II. Of the People, by the People, for the People

Text 3

RABBI YEHUDAH HALEVI, *KUZARI* 3:17–19

וּמָשָׁל מִי שֶׁהִתְפַּלֵּל לְצוֹרֶךְ עַצְמוֹ, כְּמָשָׁל מִי שֶׁהִשְׁתַּדֵּל לְחַזֵּק אֶת בֵּיתוֹ לְבַדּוֹ וְלֹא רָצָה לְהִכָּנֵס עִם אַנְשֵׁי הַמְּדִינָה בְּהֶעָזְרָם עַל חִזּוּק חוֹמוֹתָם, הוּא מוֹצִיא הַרְבֵּה וְעוֹמֵד עַל הַסַּכָּנָה, וַאֲשֶׁר יִכָּנֵס בְּמַה שֶּׁנִּכְנָסִים בּוֹ הַצִּבּוּר, מוֹצִיא מְעַט וְעוֹמֵד בְּבִטְחָה, כִּי מַה שֶּׁמְּקַצֵּר מִמֶּנּוּ אֶחָד מַשְׁלִימוֹ אַחֵר, וְתָקוּם הַמְּדִינָה בְּתַכְלִית מַה שֶּׁיֵּשׁ בִּיכוֹלֶת, וְיִהְיוּ אֲנָשֶׁיהָ מַגִּיעִים כֻּלָּם אֶל בִּרְכָתָהּ בְּהוֹצָאָה מוּעֶטֶת . . .

שֶׁמְּעַט הוּא שֶׁתִּשְׁלַם תְּפִלָּה לְיָחִיד מִבְּלִי שְׁגָגָה וּפְשִׁיעָה. וּמִפְּנֵי כֵּן קָבְעוּ לָנוּ שֶׁיִּתְפַּלֵּל הַיָּחִיד תְּפִלַּת הַצִּבּוּר . . . כְּדֵי שֶׁיַּשְׁלִים קְצָתָם מַה שֶּׁיֶּחְסַר בִּקְצָתָם בִּשְׁגָגָה אוֹ בִּפְשִׁיעָה, וְיִסְתַּדֵּר מֵהַכֹּל תְּפִלָּה שְׁלֵמָה בְּכַוָּנָה זַכָּה וְתָחוּל הַבְּרָכָה עַל הַכֹּל . . .

כִּי הַיָּחִיד בִּכְלַל הַצִּבּוּר כְּאֵבֶר הָאֶחָד בִּכְלַל הַגּוּף. אִילוּ הָיָה מַקְפִּיד הַזְּרוֹעַ עַל דָּמוֹ כְּשֶׁהוּצְרַךְ אֶל הַהֲקָזָה, הָיָה נִפְסָד הַגּוּף כּוּלוֹ וְנִפְסָד הַזְּרוֹעַ בְּהֶפְסֵדוֹ.

Praying on our own can be compared to attempting to fortify our home by ourselves rather than joining the people of the city in reinforcing the city walls. It is more expensive and less effective, whereas joining the people of the city is less expensive and more effective. When we act as a group, what one lacks, the other completes, resulting in much better security at a much lower cost. . . .

RABBI YEHUDAH HALEVI
C. 1075–1141

Noted author, physician, and poet. Rabbi Yehudah Halevi is best known as the author of the *Kuzari*, a philosophical work presenting the principles of Jewish belief in the form of a dialogue between the king of the Khazars and representatives of Judaism, Christianity, and Islam. In addition to the *Kuzari*, he wrote thousands of poems, of which only a few hundred survive today.

> It is uncommon for an individual's prayer to be complete without any inadvertent or negligent deficiency. This is why they established that the individual should join in congregational prayer. . . . In this way, people will complement each other's prayer, thus producing a complete prayer with pure intent, resulting in blessing for all. . . .
>
> An individual in a community is like a limb in a body. If an arm would resist giving its blood when necessary, the entire body would deteriorate, and the arm would also suffer.

Text 4

THE REBBE, RABBI MENACHEM MENDEL SCHNEERSON, *SEFER HAMAAMARIM MELUKAT* (*TORAT MENACHEM* EDITION) 2, P. 77

צִבּוּר רָאשֵׁי תֵּיבוֹת: צַדִּיקִים בֵּינוֹנִים וּרְשָׁעִים. שֶׁכָּל ג' סוּגִים אֵלּוּ הֵם מְצִיאוּת אַחַת.

The Hebrew word *tzibur*, congregation, can be seen as an acronym for *tzadikim*, *beinonim*, and *resha'im*—the righteous, intermediate, and wicked people. These three types combine to form a single unit.

RABBI MENACHEM MENDEL SCHNEERSON 1902–1994

The towering Jewish leader of the 20th century, known as "the Lubavitcher Rebbe," or simply as "the Rebbe." Born in southern Ukraine, the Rebbe escaped Nazi-occupied Europe, arriving in the U.S. in June 1941. The Rebbe inspired and guided the revival of traditional Judaism after the European devastation, impacting virtually every Jewish community the world over. The Rebbe often emphasized that the performance of just one additional good deed could usher in the era of Mashiach. The Rebbe's scholarly talks and writings have been printed in more than 200 volumes.

Text 5

TALMUD, BERACHOT 7B–8A

אָמַר לֵיהּ רַבִּי יִצְחָק לְרַב נַחְמָן: מַאי טַעֲמָא לֹא אָתֵי מַר לְבֵי כְּנִישְׁתָּא לְצַלּוּיֵי? אָמַר לֵיהּ: לֹא יָכִילְנָא . . .

וְלֵימָא לֵיהּ מַר לִשְׁלוּחָא דְצִבּוּרָא בְּעִידְנָא דְמַצְלֵי צִבּוּרָא לֵיתֵי וְלוֹדְעֵיהּ לְמַר.

אָמַר לֵיהּ: מַאי כּוּלֵי הַאי? אָמַר לֵיהּ: דְאָמַר רַבִּי יוֹחָנָן מִשּׁוּם רַבִּי שִׁמְעוֹן בֶּן יוֹחָאי, מַאי דִכְתִיב: "וַאֲנִי תְפִלָּתִי לְךָ ה' עֵת רָצוֹן" (תְּהִילִים סט, יד)? אֵימָתַי עֵת רָצוֹן, בְּשָׁעָה שֶׁהַצִּבּוּר מִתְפַּלְלִין . . .

רַבִּי נָתָן אוֹמֵר: מִנַּיִן שֶׁאֵין הַקָּדוֹשׁ בָּרוּךְ הוּא מוֹאֵס בִּתְפִלָּתָן שֶׁל רַבִּים? שֶׁנֶּאֱמַר: "הֵן אֵ-ל כַּבִּיר וְלֹא יִמְאָס" (אִיּוֹב לו, ה).

Rabbi Yitzchak said to Rabbi Nachman, "Why did Your Honor not come to the synagogue to pray?" Rabbi Nachman replied, "I was weak and unable to attend."...

Rabbi Yitzchak suggested another option, "Your Honor should ask the congregation to notify you when they are praying so that you can pray at home simultaneously."

Rabbi Nachman asked, "Why go to such lengths?" Rabbi Yitzchak answered him that Rabbi Yochanan said, in the name of Rabbi Shimon ben Yocha'i, "The verse states, 'May my prayer to You, G-d, be in a time of favor' (PSALMS 69:14). When is it a time of favor? When the congregation prays."...

Rabbi Natan says, "How do we know that G-d does not spurn the prayer of the masses? Because the verse says, 'The mighty [i.e., the masses], G-d will not spurn' (JOB 36:5)."

Text 6

RABBI YOSEF YITZCHAK SCHNEERSOHN,
SEFER HAMAAMARIM 5688, PP. 148-152

אָמְרוּ רַבּוֹתֵינוּ זִכְרוֹנָם לִבְרָכָה, תְּפִלַּת רַבִּים אֵינָהּ נִמְאֶסֶת, שֶׁנֶּאֱמַר: "הֵן אֵ-ל כַּבִּיר וְלֹא יִמְאָס". שֶׁהָרַבִּים בִּתְפִילָּתָם מַמְשִׁיכִים י"ג מִדּוֹת הָרַחֲמִים.

Our sages taught, "The prayer of the masses will never be spurned, as is implied by the verse, 'The mighty [i.e., the masses], G-d will not spurn' (JOB 36:5). This is because communal prayer channels the Thirteen Attributes of Mercy."

RABBI YOSEF YITZCHAK SCHNEERSOHN (RAYATZ, FRIERDIKER REBBE, PREVIOUS REBBE) 1880–1950

Chasidic rebbe, prolific writer, and Jewish activist. Rabbi Yosef Yitzchak, the 6th leader of the Chabad movement, actively promoted Jewish religious practice in Soviet Russia and was arrested for these activities. After his release from prison and exile, he settled in Warsaw, Poland, from where he fled Nazi occupation and arrived in New York in 1940. Settling in Brooklyn, Rabbi Schneersohn worked to revitalize American Jewish life. His son-in-law Rabbi Menachem Mendel Schneerson succeeded him as the leader of the Chabad movement.

Text 7

EXODUS 34:6-7

ה' ה' אֵ-ל רַחוּם וְחַנּוּן, אֶרֶךְ אַפַּיִם וְרַב חֶסֶד וֶאֱמֶת. נֹצֵר חֶסֶד לָאֲלָפִים, נֹשֵׂא עָוֹן וָפֶשַׁע וְחַטָּאָה וְנַקֵּה.

G-d, G-d, benevolent G-d, compassionate and gracious, slow to anger and abounding in kindness and truth. He preserves kindness for two thousand generations, forgiving iniquity, transgression, and sin, and He cleanses.

III. The Glue That Holds Us Together

Text 8

RABBI CHAIM VITAL, *PERI ETZ CHAYIM, SHAAR HAKAVANOT, DERUSHEI BIRCHOT HASHACHAR*

קוֹדֶם שֶׁהָאָדָם יְסַדֵּר תְּפִילָּתוֹ בְּבֵית הַכְּנֶסֶת . . . צָרִיךְ שֶׁיְּקַבֵּל עָלָיו מִצְוַת וְאָהַבְתָּ לְרֵעֲךָ כָּמוֹךָ. וִיכַוֵּין לֶאֱהוֹב כָּל אֶחָד מִבְּנֵי יִשְׂרָאֵל כְּנַפְשׁוֹ, כִּי עַל יְדֵי זֶה תַּעֲלֶה תְּפִילָּתוֹ כְּלוּלָה מִכָּל תְּפִילוֹת יִשְׂרָאֵל, וְתוּכַל לַעֲלוֹת לְמַעְלָה וְלַעֲשׂוֹת פְּרִי.

Before beginning to pray in the synagogue ... we must undertake to fulfill the commandment of "love your fellow as yourself." ... Thereby, our prayers will ascend and merge with the prayers of all Jewish people and bear fruit.

RABBI CHAIM VITAL
C. 1542–1620

Lurianic kabbalist. Rabbi Vital was born in Israel, lived in Safed and Jerusalem, and later lived in Damascus. He was authorized by his teacher, Rabbi Yitzchak Luria, the Arizal, to record his teachings. Acting on this mandate, Vital began arranging his master's teachings in written form, and his many works constitute the foundation of the Lurianic school of Jewish mysticism. His most famous work is *Etz Chayim*.

Text 9

HAREINI MEKABEL, RECITED BEFORE THE MORNING PRAYERS (IN PRAYER BOOKS THAT FOLLOW THE TRADITION OF ARIZAL)

נָכוֹן לוֹמַר קוֹדֶם הַתְּפִילָּה: הֲרֵינִי מְקַבֵּל עָלַי מִצְוַת עֲשֵׂה שֶׁל וְאָהַבְתָּ לְרֵעֲךָ כָּמוֹךָ.

It is proper to make the following statement before prayer: "I hereby undertake to fulfill the positive commandment to love your fellow as yourself."

Text 10

RABBI YOSEF YITZCHAK SCHNEERSOHN, *SEFER HASICHOT* 5700, PP. 156–157

מָאנְטָאג, י"ב תַּמּוּז, אִין טָאג פוּן מַיין בַּר מִצְוָה . . . אַ זֵייגֶער זֶעקְס הָאט מֶען זִיךְ גֶעוַואשְׁן צוּ דֶער סְעוּדַת מִצְוָה. הוֹד כְּבוֹד קְדֻשַּׁת אֲדוֹנִי אָבִי מוֹרִי וְרַבִּי הָרַב הַקָּדוֹשׁ אִיז גֶעוֶוען זֵייעֶר אוֹיפְגֶעלֵייגְט . . . אוּן מִיט דֶעם סִגְנוֹן הָאט הוֹד כְּבוֹד קְדֻשַּׁת אֲדוֹנִי אָבִי מוֹרִי וְרַבִּי הָרַב הַקָּדוֹשׁ בַּא דֶער סְעוּדָה פוּן מַיין בַּר מִצְוָה מִיךְ אָנְגֶערוּפְן בַּיים נָאמֶען אוּן גֶעזָאגְט: יוֹסֵף יִצְחָק, פְרֶעג עֶפֶּעס.

הָאבּ אִיךְ גֶעפְרֶעגְט בַּא הוֹד כְּבוֹד קְדוּשַּׁת אֲדוֹנִי אָבִי מוֹרִי וְרַבִּי הָרַב הַקָּדוֹשׁ: אִין סִידוּר שְׁטֵייט נָכוֹן לוֹמַר קוֹדֶם הַתְּפִילָּה הֲרֵינִי מְקַבֵּל עָלַי מִצְוַת עֲשֵׂה שֶׁל וְאָהַבְתָּ לְרֵעֲךָ כָּמוֹךָ, אִיז פַארְוָואס שְׁטֵייט דָאס דַּוְקָא קוֹדֶם הַתְּפִילָּה. אוּן אוֹיבּ אַהֲבַת יִשְׂרָאֵל דַארְף זַיין תֵּיכֶף בַּבֹּקֶר, הָאט מֶען דָאס בַּאדַארְפְט קוֹבֵעַ זַיין צוּזַאמֶען מִיט בִּרְכוֹת הַשַּׁחַר.

הָאט הוֹד כְּבוֹד קְדוּשַּׁת אֲדוֹנִי אָבִי מוֹרִי וְרַבִּי הָרַב הַקָּדוֹשׁ מִיר גֶעעֶנְטְפֶערְט: וֶוען אַ טַאטֶע הָאט אַ סַךְ קִינְדֶער אִיז דֶער עִיקָּר הַתַּעֲנוּג זַיינֶער וֶוען עֶר זֶעט אַז אַלֶע זַיינֶען זֵיי בְּאַחְדוּת אוּן הָאבְּן זִיךְ אֵיינֶער דֶעם אַנְדֶערְן לִיבּ. תְּפִילָּה אִיז דָאךְ בַּקָּשַׁת צְרָכִים

רוּחָנִיִּים, אִיז קוֹדֶם הַבַּקָּשָׁה דַארְף מֶען מַאכְן אַ נַחַת רוּחַ לְאָבִינוּ שֶׁבַּשָּׁמַיִם, אוּן דֶערִיבֶּער הָאט מֶען קוֹבֵעַ גֶעוֶוען דֶעם לְקַבֵּל מִצְוַת עֲשֵׂה פוּן אַהֲבַת יִשְׂרָאֵל קוֹדֶם הַתְּפִילָּה דַוְקָא.

On Monday, the twelfth of the month of Tamuz, the day of my bar mitzvah . . . at about six o'clock, my father washed his hands for the festive *mitzvah*. His cheerful spirits were apparent. . . . He called me by name: "Yosef Yitzchak, ask something."

I asked, "It is written in the siddur that it is proper to say before the Morning Prayer, 'I hereby undertake to fulfill the positive commandment to love your fellow as yourself.' Why does this instruction appear as a preface to the prayer? After all, since the obligation to love our fellow is incumbent upon us from the beginning of the day, shouldn't the instruction have been inserted in the Morning Blessings that are recited first thing in the morning?"

My father answered, "When a father has many children, he derives the greatest pleasure from seeing their unity and love for each other. Prayer is a request for one's needs, both material and spiritual. Before making a request, we must grant our Father in Heaven pleasurable *nachas* [satisfaction]. This is why the instruction to undertake the *mitzvah* to love our fellow appears as a preface to the prayer."

Text 11

RABBI YOSEF YITZCHAK SCHNEERSOHN,
SEFER HASICHOT 5709, P. 319

אַמָאלִיגֶע חַסִידִים פְלֶעגְן מַאכֶען יֶעדֶען טָאג אַ קְנֵייטְשׁ אִין סִידוּר, הַיינְט הָאבּ אִיךְ גֶעדַאוֶוענְט בִּיז דָא.

עֶר פְלֶעגְט כַּמוּבָן גוֹמֵר זַיין דֶעם גַאנְצֶען דַאוְונֶען, נָאר "גֶעדַאוֶוענְט" הָאט עֶר נָאר בִּיז דַאנֶען. מָארְגֶען פְלֶעגְט עֶר דַאוְונֶען נָאךְ אַ שְׁטִיקֶעלֶע אוּן דָארְט מַאכְן דֶעם קְנֵייטְשׁ אִין סִידוּר.

There were Chasidim in the past who would fold an ear of a page in the siddur every day, indicating, "Today I prayed until this point."

Of course, they would complete the prayers in their entirety. But their deep, contemplative prayer was only until that point. The next day, they would continue their contemplative prayer where they left off and meditate on another part of the prayers. They would then make another fold where they concluded.

IV. Course Conclusion

Exercise 7.2

At the beginning of Lesson One, we each wrote down what we hoped to gain from this course. At this point, let's return to page 2 and take a minute to reflect on whether our goals were met.

If you are willing to share those thoughts, please do so.

Text 12

RABBI YITZCHAK BEN SHESHET, *RESPONSA* 157

רַבִּי שִׁמְשׁוֹן מִקִינוּן זִכְרוֹנוֹ לִבְרָכָה, שֶׁהָיָה רַב גָדוֹל מִכָּל בְּנֵי דוֹרוֹ . . . הָיָה אוֹמֵר: אֲנִי מִתְפַּלֵל לְדַעַת זֶה הַתִּינוֹק.

Rabbi Shimshon of Chinon, of blessed memory, who was the greatest rabbi in his generation . . . would often say, "I pray with the thoughts of a child."

RABBI YITZCHAK BEN SHESHET (RIVASH)
1326–1408

Halachist. Rivash studied under Rabbeinu Nisim of Gerona (Ran) in Barcelona and served as rabbi there and in other important Jewish communities in Spain. Because of the eruption of anti-Jewish riots in 1391, he fled to North Africa and settled in Algiers. He was the first to address the Halachic status of Marranos. Rivash's Halachic responsa are his most important work; they contain sources no longer extant and served, in part, as a basis for the Code of Jewish Law.

Takeaway Exercise

Collective Experience. This Shabbat, join your fellow Jews for a group prayer. As you pray, be mindful not only of the personal energies you invest in your prayers but also the powerful collective energy emerging from the group. Sense your own inner voice amplified by the energies of the people around you, and then hear your own contribution echo within the collective prayer, greatly strengthening its combined potential.

Key Points

1 Joining others and praying together as a congregation is a major theme in Jewish life, and for good reason: it dramatically enhances our prayers.

2 Communal prayer works like teamwork, and everyone—from the wicked to the righteous and all in between—has something to contribute to the group effort.

3 Praying together makes our prayers most acceptable on High, and our unity brings G-d *nachas*.

4 A critical part of the prayers is verbally and truly accepting the *mitzvah* to love every Jew as you start to pray.

5 You can pray at your own pace and still be a part of the community's prayer.

Appendix A

Text 13

RABBI YAAKOV BEN YOSEF REISCHER,
RESPONSA SHEVUT YAAKOV 2:25

דְּכוּלֵי עַלְמָא מוֹדוּ, דְּקוֹדֶם שֶׁנִּקְבַּר הַמֵּת, דְּכֵיוָן שֶׁפָּטוּר מִן הַתְּפִילָה, דְּאֵינוֹ מִצְטָרֵף כְּלַל לְמִנְיָן עֲשָׂרָה.

The Halachic consensus is that a mourner whose next of kin has yet to be buried is not counted in a *minyan* because he is exempt from prayer.

RABBI YAAKOV BEN YOSEF REISCHER
C. 1670–1733

Renowned rabbi, Halachic authority, and author. He served on rabbinical courts in Prague, Ansbach, Worms, and Metz. He was accepted by contemporary rabbis as the ultimate authority on Halachic issues, and problems were addressed to him from all over the Diaspora and Israel. His most famous works are *Chok Yaakov*, an exposition on the section of the Shulchan Aruch pertaining to the laws of Passover; and his responsa collection *Shevut Yaakov*.

Appendix B

Text 14

TALMUD, BERACHOT 28B

וּכְשֶׁאַתֶּם מִתְפַּלְּלִים - דְּעוּ לִפְנֵי מִי אַתֶּם עוֹמְדִים.

When you pray, know before Whom you stand.

A *TECHINAH* FOR
ROSH HASHANAH

"Techinah Imahot Min Rosh Chodesh Elul,"
***Techinot Ubakashot* (Vilna, 1850), pp. 58–59**

The following *techinah* was written to be recited in the synagogue on Rosh Hashanah, while the ark is open and the Torah scrolls are being brought out. The prayer beseeches G-d for mercy and forgiveness on this Day of Judgment and then turns to each of the four matriarchs and asks them to advocate on our behalf as well. Drawing from the life experiences of the matriarchs, the author gives special reasons why they should intercede on our behalf.

SERIL RAPPOPORT
18TH CENTURY

Seril Rappoport was born in Dubno, Ukraine, where her father, Rabbi Yaakov of Dubno, known as the Dubner Magid, served as a famous preacher and ethicist. She married Rabbi Mordechai Rappoport, and they lived in the Ukrainian village of Novyi Oleksynets, where Mordechai served as the rabbi. Seril wrote the popular "Techinah Imahot Min Rosh Chodesh Elul" (*Techinah* of the Matriarchs for the Beginning of the Month of Elul) which contains *techinot* to be recited during the month of Elul and Rosh Hashanah.

Seril Rappoport, Techinah Imahot Min Rosh Chodesh Elul*

רבש"ע פאטר דר בארמיגר דר בארם זיך איבר אונז נעם אן אונזר גיבעט דען דו האסט גיהייסן דיין פאלק ישראל זאלין שופר בלאזין זייא זאלין פאר מישן דעם שטן אז ער זאל אויף אונז ניט קענן מקטרג זיין. דו האסט גיהייסין דיין פאלק ישראל בלאזן תקיעה שברים תרועה.

דיא ערסטע איז תקיעה דען תקיעה מאכט מען זייער גלאט אונ איין גבויגן. אזו טוען מיר זיך איין בייגין פר דיר אונ בעטן פאטר דער בארמיגר אז דער שטן זאל אויף אונז ניט מקטרג זיין. די אנדערע בלאזט מען שברים איז טייטש צו בראכין דרום טוען מיר צו ברעכן אונזרע הערצר אזו וויא אין תהלים שטייט (לב נשבר כו') איין צו בראכין הארץ טוט גאט ניט פאר שמעהן אונ מיר זיינען אויף זיך מקבל אז מיר וועלין צו ברעכן דעם יצר הרע. דאש דריטי איז תרועה איז טייטש גישריי אונ קלאג דרום טוא זיך דר בארימן איבר אונז פר מיש דעם שטן וואס איז אויף אונז מקטרג אז ער זאל ניט מקטרג זיין אונ עש זאל חס וחלילה ניט נגזר ווערין אין אונזרע הייזר איין קלאג אונ גשריי אונ זאלסט ניט אוועק נעמן אונזרי קליינע קינדר אונ דר בארעם זיך אין אונזר משפט דען דו טוסט היינט אנטפלעקין דאס משפט.

Master of the universe, merciful Father, have mercy on us, accept our plea. You have commanded Your people Israel to blow the shofar to confuse the Satan, so that he will not be able to accuse us. You have commanded Your people Israel to blow the sounds of *teki'ah*, *shevarim*, and *teru'ah*.

The first is *teki'ah*. *Teki'ah* is sounded smoothly and curved. Thus, we bow before You and pray, merciful Father, that the Satan should not be able to accuse us. The next is *shevarim*, which means *to break*. Therefore we break our hearts, just as the verse in Psalms (51:19) states, "G-d does not reject a broken heart." We also undertake to break our negative inclination. The third is *teru'ah*, which means *cry and lament*. Therefore, have mercy upon us and confuse the Satan who accuses us, so that he will not be able to accuse us anymore. May no lamentation and outcry be decreed in our home, G-d forbid. Do not take away our little children. Have mercy in judging us, for today You reveal our sentence.

*The Yiddish text for this *techinah* uses old Yiddish terms and spelling conventions.

רבש"ע ווען איך בין שוין יוא שולדיג צום משפט זאל דאך דיין מדת הרחמים גובר זיין דעם מדת הדין און פר גיב אונז אונזערי זינד דען צווישן דייני י"ג מדות איז די ערשטע (רחום וחנון) איז דאך גיוויש דיין (מדה) פון (רחמים) זייער גרויש און בפרט איצונד מיט דעם קול פון שופר דען דו האסט אין דיין הייליגע תורה אן גשריבן אז עס קומט ר"ה זאל מען בלאזן מיט אשופר דאש איז איין סימן אלע קנעכט אין א"י זאלן פרייא ארויס גיין פון זייערי הערין.

פאטר דער בארמיגר זיינן מיר אזו וויא דיינע קינדר גירעכינט דר בארעם זיך וויא איין פאטר איבר זייני קינדר אויב חלילה מיר האבן מיט אונזרי ביטערי עבירות גורם גיווען אז מיר זיינען נאר גירעכינט וויא איין קנעכט זאלין מיר דאך מיט דעם קול פון שופר ארויס פרייא פון דעם משפט אלע אונזרע זינד זאלסטו אוועק בלאזן מיט דעם קול פון שופר און מיט דעם וואס מיר טוען ניין מאל שופר בלאזן זאל אונז בייא שטיין בייא דעם משפט דר זכות פון די פיר אמהות און דר זכות פון די דרייא אבות און זכות פון משה ואהרן דען זיי זיינען אויך ניין.

צום ערשטן בעטן מיר אונזער מוטער שרה אז זיא זאל פאר אונז בעטין בשעת משפט אז מיר זאלין פרייא ארויש גיין פון דעם משפט דען השי"ת ב"ה האט איר מוסיף גיוועזין דעם ה' פון (שם הוי"ה ברוך שמו) מוזטו אויך האבין דיא מדה פון רחמים. דרום דער בארעם דיך אונזר מוטער אויף דיינע קינדער. אוב בפרט צו בעטן פר אונזערי קינדר זייא זאלין זיך ניט אפ שיידן פון אונז דו ווייסט דאך וואול אז עש איז זייער ביטר אז מען נעמט

Master of the universe, if I am indeed guilty in Your judgment, let Your attribute of mercy overpower Your attribute of justice and forgive us for our sins. For among Your thirteen attributes, compassion and mercy are the first. Therefore, Your attribute of mercy is certainly very great, especially now with the sounding of the shofar. For You have written in Your holy Torah that when the new year comes, we should sound the shofar as a sign for all of the servants in Israel to be freed from their masters.

Merciful Father, if we are like Your children, have mercy upon us, like a father does on his children. If, G-d forbid, we have, through our bitter sins, acted in such a way that we should be considered mere servants, may we still be set free from Your judgment with the sound of the shofar. Blow away all of our sins with the blowing of the shofar. As we blow the shofar nine times, so may the merit of the four matriarchs, the merit of the three patriarchs, and the merit of Moses and Aaron—the nine of them together—protect us in this time of judgment.

First, we beseech our mother Sarah that she pray for us at this hour of judgment, so that we may be judged innocent. Since G-d, blessed be He, added the letter *hei* from His name to Sarah's, she must also have the

אוועק איין קינד פון דר מוטר וויא עס איז דיר גיוועזן אז מען האט אוועק גינומן דיין זון יצחק פון דיר האט דיר באנק גיטאן און היינט האסטו צייט צו בעטן דען מען טוט איצונד בלאזן מיט איין (שופר של איל) כדי ער זאל גידיינקען דעם זכות פון יצחק וואס ער האט זיך גילאזט בינדן וויא איין שאף צו דר עקידה. דרום ווערט דר שטן צו מישט און קאן איצונד אויף אונז ניט מקטרג זיין דרום האסטו איצונד צייט פר אונז צו בעטין אז עס זאל מתעורר ווערין אויף אונז דיא מדה פון רחמים.

אויך טוא איך בעטין פון אונזר מוטר רבקה זיא זאל בעטן פר אירע קינדר און זאל בעטן פאר אונזר פאטר און מוטר אז זייא זאלין זיך ח"ו ניט אפ שיידין פון אונז דען דוא ווייסט וואול וויא עש טוט באנק נאך פאטר און מוטר דען אז אליעזר דר קנעכט האט דיך אוועק גינומען פון דיין פאטר און מוטר צוא דיין מאן יצחק האשטו אויך זייער גיוויינט. דרום ווייסטו וויא עס איז שלעכט אן איין פאטר און מוטר דרום בעט פר אונזער פאטר און מוטר אז זייא זאלן האבן (שנות חיים) יארן פון לעבן (שנת טובה) איין גוט יאר אז איך מיט מיין מאן און קינדר זאלן האבן פרנסה.

אויך טוען מיר בעטן אונזר מוטר רחל אז דוא זאלסט פר אונז בעטען אז מיר זאלן איין (כתיבה וחתימה טובה) האבין און מיר זאלין קיין מאל קיין צער ניט האבין מיר ווייסין וואול אז דו קאנסט קיין צער ניט הערן דען אז מען האט דיין ליבן זון יוסף גפירט קיין מצרים האבין אים די ישמעאלים גרויש צער אן גטאן איז ער גיפאלין אויף דיין קבר און האט אן גיהייבין צו וויינן מוטר דער בארם דיך

attribute of mercy. Have mercy, our mother, on your children. Make a special plea that our children not be separated from us. You know full well how bitter it is when a child is taken away from its mother, as happened to you when your son Isaac was taken away from you and you yearned for him. Today is the appropriate time for you to pray, when a shofar made from a ram's horn is sounded, so that the merit of Isaac, who allowed himself to be bound like a sheep, is remembered. Thereby the Satan will become confused and will not be able to accuse us. Therefore, now is the time for you to plead for us that the attribute of mercy will be roused on our behalf.

I also beseech our mother Rebecca to pray for her children and for our father and mother, that they should not, G-d forbid, be separated from us. You know very well what it is like to yearn for one's father and mother, for when Eliezer the servant took you away from your father and mother and brought you to your husband Isaac, you also wept profusely. So you know how painful it is to be without a father and a mother. Therefore, pray for our father and mother that they may have further years of life and a year of goodness, and that I, my husband, and my children may earn a decent living.

איבר דיין קינד וויא קאנסטו צו זעהן מיין צער אזו ליב האסטו מיך גיהאט און היינט בין איך אזו פאר פינצטערט און קיינר דר בארעמט זיך ניט איבר מיר אזו האסטו ניט גקענט צו הערן דעם צער פון דיין קינד האסטו אים גיענטפרט מיין ליב קינד איך הער דיין גיוויין און דיין ביטער גשרייט. איך וועל מיך תמיד דר בארימן און בעטן פר אייך און וועל הערן אייער צער דרום דער בארם דיך אויף אונזער צער און אנגשט און ציטערנש פר דעם משפט און בעט פר אונז עס זאל אונז אן גשריבין ווערן איין גוט יאר אז מיר זאלן קיין מאל קיין צער ניט האבין אמן.

אויך טוען מיר בעטן אונזר מוטר לאה אז זיא זאל אוין בעטן פאר אונז דען איצונדערט קענט איר פר אונז אלע בעטן דען היינט איז דער ערשטר טאג פון עשרת ימי תשובה דאס איז שוין דיא לעצטע צייט דען איך ווייש אז איך האב וויא פיל צייט אוועק גלאזין און האב קייו תשובה ניט גיטאן.

We also beseech our mother Rachel: Pray for us that we may be inscribed and sealed for a good year and that we may never know any sorrow. We know full well that you cannot bear to hear of any sorrow, for when your beloved son Joseph was taken away to Egypt, the Ishmaelites caused him great anguish. He fell upon your grave and began to cry, "Mother! Have pity upon your child! How can you bear to see my anguish? You loved me so much, and now I am so unhappy, and no one has mercy on me." You could not bear to hear the anguish of your child, and you answered him: "My dear child, I hear your weeping and your bitter cry. I will always have mercy on you and will pray for you and will hear your anguish." Therefore, have mercy on our sorrow and anguish and trembling before the judgment, and pray that a good year be inscribed for us so that we may never know sorrow. Amen.

We also beseech our mother Leah to pray for us. May you all pray for us now, for today is the first day of the ten days of repentance, and this is our last chance. I know that I have wasted so much time without repenting.

Thirteen Attributes of Divine Mercy

After the debacle of the Sin of the Golden Calf and G-d's favorable reaction to Moses's intercession, Moses asked G-d to reveal His glory to him. In response, G-d delivered a proclamation regarding His great mercy, and told Moses that this proclamation of the "Thirteen Attributes of Mercy" is a key to Divine forgiveness.

Presented here is the Torah passage that records the thirteen attributes of Divine mercy, with subsequent explanations regarding the functioning of these Divine elements.

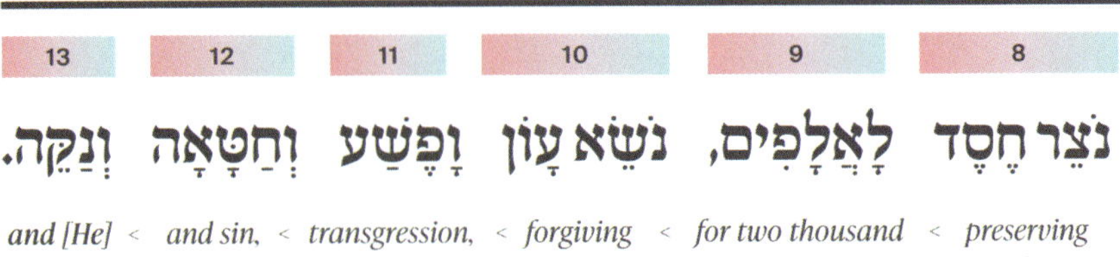

Based on *Shaar Hakavanot, Derushei Vayaavor, Derush 3*

The Source of Mercy

Rabbi Shneur Zalman of Liadi, *Likutei Torah, Derushim LeShabbat Shuvah*, p. 67d

The Thirteen Attributes of Mercy are rooted in G-d's Desire. They therefore stand beyond all of the spiritual worlds, and beyond the standard Divine attributes known as the *sefirot*. For when we seek repentance for past transgressions, the Divine attributes that are revealed within the created worlds are insufficient to help us achieve repair. The spiritual worlds are part of a logically structured system; the first of all of the Divine attributes expressed in the worlds is *chochmah*, wisdom. Now, from the standpoint of logic, once the damage of a transgression has been inflicted, there is no way to erase it and wipe the slate clean. Cleansing can only arrive as a result of something beyond the logical system, and this is where the Thirteen Attributes of Mercy enter the picture. Rooted in G-d's simple desire, there are no barriers to constrain their application; they can cleanse us from any transgression, no matter how severe.

Repentance

Rabbi Shneur Zalman of Liadi, ibid.

In order to reach and activate the Thirteen Attributes of Mercy, we need to tap into a corresponding feature within our own soul. It is not enough to merely appreciate intellectually the error of our ways and to regret them. We must also return to G-d from the very depths of our soul, based on the knowledge that we have a G-dly core that cannot bear to be separated from our Divine Source. When we step beyond our intellectual and emotional attributes, and awaken the purest desire for G-d that lies at our core, G-d will respond in kind and grant us suprarational forgiveness and cleansing from the place of His greatest desire.

		1	2	3	4	5	6	7
וַיַּעֲבֹר ה' עַל פָּנָיו וַיִּקְרָא:	ה' ה'	אֵ־ל	רַחוּם	וְחַנּוּן,	אֶרֶךְ	אַפַּיִם	וְרַב חֶסֶד	וֶאֱמֶת.
G-d passed before him and proclaimed:	G-d G-d	L-rd	merciful	and gracious	slow	to anger,	and abundant in kindness	and truth;

Humility

Rabbi Shmuel Schneersohn, *Likutei Torah: Torat Shmuel* 5637:2, p. 930

The actual Thirteen Attributes of Mercy are limitless. They can express themselves in any place and at any time. On our end, however, we need to be capable of receiving and assimilating their light. When we enter a state of *bitul*—humble submission and self-negation—we are capable of receiving this vast, unlimited light from beyond the spiritual cosmic system.

Communal Prayer

Rabbi Shmuel Schneersohn, ibid. 5627, p. 373

The Thirteen Attributes of Mercy can also be effectively invoked through the community gathering to pray together. G-d pledged that He will never reject our communal prayers (Job 36:5; Talmud, Berachot 8b); He is always fully accessible when we assemble to unite in prayer.

The High Holy Days

Rabbi Shneur Zalman of Liadi, *Likutei Torah*, *Nitzavim* 51a

The ten days that begin with Rosh Hashanah and end with Yom Kippur are known as the "Ten Days of Repentance." Regarding this auspicious time, we are told to "seek out G-d when He is present, call out to Him when He is near" (Isaiah 55:6; Talmud, Rosh Hashanah 18a). For the Thirteen Attributes of Mercy are revealed throughout these ten days, and they facilitate our repentance and atonement. True, the Thirteen Attributes of Mercy can be accessed all year round via heartfelt repentance. Nevertheless, it requires great effort on our end to evoke this coveted Divine response. By contrast, during the Ten Days of Repentance, the Thirteen Attributes of Mercy are revealed and we can access them with less effort on our part. For that reason, we recite the Thirteen Attributes of Mercy repeatedly during our prayers on Rosh Hashanah and Yom Kippur.

The Call of the Shofar

Rabbi Shneur Zalman of Liadi, *Likutei Torah*, *Ki Tavo* 43d

The Thirteen Attributes of Mercy are rooted in G-d's deepest desire, and we can evoke them through arousing our own deep desire for closeness to G-d. Over the course of our day-to-day lives we are engaged in the pursuit of mundane needs and desires, which causes the profound spiritual desire that breathes at our core to be lulled into slumber. The sound of the shofar on Rosh Hashanah is intended to serve as a wakeup call, arousing our truest desire from its hibernation. Our freshly awakened boundless passion for G-d activates G-d's own limitless attributes of mercy in response, providing us with forgiveness and a clean slate for the new year.

My Beloved *Mechitzah*

By Joelle Keene

I didn't know these lovebirds, but they were obviously just that, standing at Sabbath morning services amid a sea of men and women with his arm around her waist, she leaning into his shoulder and the two of them swaying gently back and forth to the sound of the prayers. How nice, I thought, that they're learning Torah together. Where it will take them no one can say, but they're together on a great and splendid journey.

Since then, my own journey, begun in part in that same room, has led me to a place where I could not possibly stand in prayer with my husband's arm around my waist. Praying might just be the most important thing we humans do, setting the stage for all of the rest of our behavior, but it is not the easiest. For most of us it takes tremendous concentration, a great erasing of everything outside and at the same time a bringing of everything we are into one small moment framed by a particular piece of ancient text. The problem is that love is so powerful—especially love for a spouse, but even premonitions of love like crush and curiosity—that in any given moment, prayer cannot compete.

Perhaps that's why Judaism promotes something called the *mechitzah*, surely the most widely maligned—I would say misunderstood—of any institution in Judaism today. A *mechitzah*, literally "separation," is a screen or other barrier in a traditional synagogue that separates women from men during worship; in this separation, some say, the women are demeaned. The religious idea is that men should not be able to see women while they're praying, for if they do, their prayer will not be heard. To me, that's not demeaning; it's a statement of obvious fact. It's hard enough to pray when you're alone.

Try this exercise: Imagine that you need to speak with G-d. Imagine that you need something very, very badly, and that G-d really is all-powerful and the only One Who can grant it to you. Or imagine that you've done something terribly wrong and need some great forgiveness, or that your first child has just been born and you want to offer thanks. Close your eyes. Find the words. Now try, really try, to send them up to heaven.

Could you do this while cuddling with your spouse? Could you do it while ogling the latest beauty to join the synagogue, or that guy you

JOELLE KEENE

Mother of three, currently teaches music and journalism at Shalhevet High School in Los Angeles. Joelle previously worked as an award-winning newspaper reporter for the *Los Angeles Herald Examiner* and *The Seattle Times*. Additionally, she was a music critic, and served as associate editor of *OLAM Magazine*.

see each Saturday who's so cute it makes you laugh? Maybe you could—everyone's different—but I strive mightily just to sense G-d's listening when I pray.

Sometimes I picture great tree limbs, an overarching Father seeing every word and deed, or see myself as human clay addressing Him who formed it. Or I conjure up an awesome, holy Throne bathed in rays of light, considering with mercy my so tiny, distant plea. Yet with all these tools and more, still it's hard. We need all the help we can get.

And so we have a curtain—to center us perhaps, to make a place that forms a space where we can pray. There are as many kinds of *mechitzahs* as there are synagogues—I've seen sleek wood carved in modern shapes, and balconies where height is the *mechitzah*, and gathered lace on curtain rods that roll.

But all *mechitzahs* hold us back from one another and group our prayers by gender rising heavenward. Perhaps this helps G-d hear us, too; perhaps we sound clearer, are more ourselves, unmediated by our opposites. Judaism loves categories and celebrates them every way—night and day, milk and meat, Sabbath versus holidays and ordinary days—and gender's no exception.

The men's section is front and center because men have more ritual commandments in the synagogue, while women are responsible for bringing Torah into the home. Synagogue becomes one place where we can be with our own gender, something not without a pleasure all on its own.

So you can say the *mechitzah* exists to keep women out, that the genders are identical and all else is cultural conceit. For many of us, though, the *mechitzah* opens a door in, perhaps into a more concentrated experience of who we are and certainly into the presence of G-d where holiness and much direction lie. In prayer, we reach outside our earthly yearnings and search for something different, something that ennobles us, sets our sights high and improves us from the inside out. In love, we find an outlet for those improvements, for our goodness, kindness, generosity. Love is arguably our most G-d-like activity, and also our greatest earthly reward; in its physical expression, it is said to bring G-d's presence to rest on us directly. Each paves the way for the other; I'm a better wife for praying, and drawn closer to G-d through the love my marriage brings. Each creates a chasm we can cross.

And so I wonder again about those Sabbath lovebirds, trying to make their yearnings heard above the din of daily life, studying Torah and singing psalms, arms linked, perhaps journeying down paths deep into wisdom.

There's no one way to pray, and none of us can say for sure whose prayers are heard. But perhaps their love has grown so much that they can't sit together in services anymore, or their love for G-d has grown in such a way that they don't want to. Maybe it would take more than a curtain to keep them apart—and perhaps just a curtain to link them.

THE HOW OF JEWISH PRAYER

Jewish prayer is a powerful and highly calibrated tool to connect, communicate, petition, and discover G-d. But for many today, it is a lost art, due partly to unfamiliarity with its language, structure, setting, and texts. "The How of Jewish Prayer" is a game-changing step-by-step guide to daily prayer, congregational prayer, and the prayer book.

I. Introduction to Prayer

A. *Nusach*—Prayer Rite

The prayer book that we know today evolved over millennia, drawing from the experiences and contributions of multiple Jewish communities. The process was launched in the third century BCE, when the Jewish leader known as Ezra the Scribe, in partnership with a venerable body of sages referred to as the Men of the Great Assembly, established the basic structure of standardized prayers. Future sages and communities continued to build on this initial framework for centuries thereafter. Many of our prayers are selected readings from ancient biblical sources; other contributions, such as *lechah dodi*, the poetic-mystical prayer chanted on Friday night to welcome the Shabbat, were penned as recently as the sixteenth century.

As the Jewish nation spread further in exile, diverse liturgical customs and textual nuances took hold in various communities, countries, and continents. Several, but not all, of these colorful variations are extant today. The two most widely adopted varieties today are Ashkenaz, rooted in the ancient tradition of Germanic Jewry, and Sefard, based on the ancient tradition of Spanish Jewry. Despite the various liturgical styles and disparities between Jewish prayer texts, the core elements and order of the prayers, as articulated in the Talmud, are identical across all traditions.[1]

When faced with a choice of liturgical style (*nusach*), it is generally appropriate to pray in the *nusach* that has remained in one's family tradition for centuries. If this information has been lost or cannot be identified, one should consult a rabbi about choosing an appropriate *nusach*.

---

1. See *Responsa Maharshdam*, *Orach Chayim* 35.

Before presenting a brief overview of the standard prayers and their appropriate order, it is important to note that most of what is said below pertains across all traditions, but some of the information is not true for every *nusach*. In these cases, the information presented here is based specifically on the Chabad custom, which is rooted in the mystical teachings of one of Jewish history's foremost and revered mystics, Rabbi Yitzchak Luria (sixteenth century), referred to as the Arizal (hence the identification of the style as *nusach Ari*).

All references to the prayer book are taken from *Siddur Tehilat Hashem* (New York: Merkos L'Inyonei Chinuch, 2004).

B. Three Daily Prayers

According to Jewish law and custom, Jews open their hearts in prayer three times a day: Shacharit in the morning, Minchah in the afternoon, and Arvit (Maariv) in the evening.

Ancient tradition traces the origin of these three daily prayers, although not their precise content, to the earliest dawn of Jewish history: Abraham established Shacharit, Isaac established Minchah, and Jacob established Arvit.[2] After the destruction of the Second Temple, these three daily prayers assumed an entire new significance and degree of obligation, whereby the Jewish people adopted them as substitutes for the daily offerings that were brought in the Temple.[3]

The three prayers can be located in the prayer book as follows:

- Shacharit, the weekday morning service, begins on page 27 and ends on page 81. Shacharit for Shabbat can be found on pages 181–221.

2. Talmud, Berachot 26b.
3. Ibid.

- Minchah, the weekday afternoon service, begins on page 101 and ends on page 117. Minchah for Shabbat can be found on pages 253–269.
- Arvit, the weekday evening service, begins on page 118 and ends on page 135. Arvit for Friday night can be found on pages 154–176.

One who is unable to recite the entire Shacharit should recite the following three segments as a minimum: the Blessings of Gratitude (pp. 6–7), the Shema and its blessings (pp. 39–45), and the Amidah (for weekdays, pp. 45–54; for Shabbat, pp. 211–217). If praying three times a day is unachievable, one should recite as many of the daily prayers as personal circumstances permit.

C. Where

Praying together with a congregation is the optimum choice by far, and should be attained whenever possible. Our sages revealed that congregational prayer is more glorifying to G-d than individual prayer[4] and that G-d accepts the congregation's prayers irrespective of whether its members are deserving.[5]

It is best for the congregation to include a *minyan*—a quorum of at least ten Jewish men aged thirteen or older—because our sages taught that G-d is particularly present in the presence of a *minyan*.[6]

If attending a *minyan* is not a viable option, one should schedule one's prayers to coincide with the *minyan*'s prayer at the synagogue. If that is not feasible, it is preferable to pray alone in the synagogue despite the lack of a congregational service because (a) it is appropriate to pray in a sacred location, and (b) prayers recited

4. *Shulchan Aruch HaRav, Orach Chayim* 90:10.
5. Ibid., and 52:1.
6. *Ethics of the Fathers* 3:6.

in a synagogue are received more favorably by G-d.[7] If that is not an option, one may pray at home or any location that is conducive to focused concentration.

Unstable surfaces or wide-open spaces are not recommended for prayer because the need to maintain balance or vigilance is likely to disturb one's concentration.[8] The best place for undistracted prayer is in front of a plain wall.[9]

One should designate a permanent, personal place at home or at the synagogue for daily prayer.[10] Praying in an established location each day turns the spiritual exercise of prayer, and the sincere bond with G-d that it enables, into a permanent feature of our minds, hearts, and lives.[11] It also makes it obvious to spectators that one is praying, and they will recognize the need to avoid disturbances or interruptions.[12]

D. Language of Prayer

It is best to pray in Hebrew. Hebrew is the unique language of the Jewish people, the native expression of the Jewish soul, and the sacred tongue in which the Torah was written. Furthermore, the majority of our prayers were composed in this language, and they are far more accurate, potent, and rich in their original. In addition, the sages who composed these prayers encoded in their subtle choices of Hebrew words, letters, and vowels various esoteric intentions that are key to the soul of prayer and are entirely lost in translation.

---

7. *Shulchan Aruch HaRav, Orach Chayim* 90:10; *Kitzur Shulchan Aruch* 12:7.
8. *Shulchan Aruch HaRav, Orach Chayim* 90:1, 5.
9. Shulchan Aruch, *Orach Chayim* 90:21.
10. Shulchan Aruch, *Orach Chayim* 90:19.
11. Maharal, *Netiv Haavodah*, chapter 4.
12. *Shulchan Aruch HaRav, Orach Chayim* 90:18.

That said, it is crucial to the function of the prayers to understand their plain meaning. This concern outweighs the benefits of praying in Hebrew, so one who does not understand Hebrew should rightfully pray in a familiar language. Nevertheless, it is preferable to aim for the best of both options: to recite the prayers in a language that is understood while taking additional time to study the meaning of the Hebrew prayers, enabling a gradual transition to Hebrew.[13]

There is another option for one who wishes to pray in Hebrew specifically, despite not understanding the meaning of the prayers: to maintain an overall meditation while praying by reflecting on the greatness of G-d and the comparative insignificant stature of the human being, and also to picture the degree of undistracted focus appropriate at an intimate audience with a mortal monarch, and then consider the far greater focus required when standing in prayer before the King of all kings, the Creator of the universe.[14] At the same time, it is appropriate to petition G-d to accept one's prayers as if they were offered with all the appropriate understandings, intentions, and meditations.[15]

E. Preparation for Prayer

Jewish tradition offers several activities as appropriate preparations for prayer:

1. *Proper attire:* The standards of attire for prayer are largely determined by what is commonly considered acceptable at highly formal interviews in one's culture and region.[16] Nevertheless, the requisite for modest attire overrides cultural norms, and this includes a head covering for men.[17]

---

13. *Shulchan Aruch HaRav, Orach Chayim* 101:5.
14. *Shulchan Aruch HaRav, Orach Chayim* 98:1.
15. Rabbi Yosef Yitzchak Schneersohn, *Igrot Kodesh* 3:144.
16. Shulchan Aruch, *Orach Chayim* 91:5.
17. Ibid., 91:3.

2. *Ritual washing of the hands:* Fill a washing cup with water. Pour it over the right hand from wrist to fingers, and then proceed to do the same over the left hand. Repeat this procedure three times. Those who are left-handed simply reverse the order, and begin with the left hand.[18] If one washed the hands ritually earlier in the morning, it is sufficient to simply rinse the hands under running water before prayer.

3. *Donate to charity:*[19] This can be a nominal amount, but it should be given before praying (except on Shabbat and Jewish festivals, when handling money and making transactions is prohibited).

4. *Mental focus:* To enhance concentration during prayer, it is necessary to spend several minutes beforehand in quiet reflection, in order to remove distracting thoughts that might result from previous activities, and to focus the mind and settle the emotions in readiness to focus on G-d and converse with Him in prayer.[20]

5. Men don a *talit* (prayer shawl) before Shacharit and wear it for the duration of the service. On weekdays, men also don *tefilin* (phylacteries) for Shacharit. A man who is unable to recite Shacharit, or who cannot do so with *tefilin*, should make an effort to wear *tefilin* briefly at any point later in the day and recite the Shema while wearing them.

F. Verbalizing Prayer

A prayer in the heart is a healthy start, but one's personal obligation to pray has not been satisfied until the words are verbalized. Prayer must be *from* the heart but should not *remain* in the heart. In order

18. *Kitzur Shulchan Aruch* 2:3.
19. Talmud, Bava Batra 10a.
20. Shulchan Aruch, *Orach Chayim* 93:1–3 and 98:1.

for the experience to embrace not just the soul but also the physical body and human condition, it must find tangible expression.[21] Preferably, the words should be audibly vocalized; however, there is no need to raise one's voice. The exception is the Amidah prayer, which should be verbalized in an undertone so that the words are audible only to the one uttering them.

G. Standing and Sitting

It is customary to stand for certain prayers and sit for others. We stand for prayers in which we address G-d directly, such as the Amidah, or to highlight the significance of specific prayers. Most prayer books indicate the prayers for which it is considered appropriate to stand. In a congregational setting, we also stand to honor the Torah as it is carried to and from the ark.

21. *Tanya, Likutei Amarim*, chapter 37.

II. Daily Prayer, Step-by-Step

A. Morning

1. Modeh Ani—"I Offer Thanks"

We collapse into bed at night, weary and weak from a long day, but as the sun climbs back into the skies, we arise rejuvenated and refreshed. It is most appropriate to offer our sincerest thanks to our Creator at the start of each day for the precious gift of life, and our sages therefore minted a powerful, single-sentence prayer to be recited immediately upon awakening.[22] (In the siddur, it appears on p. 5.) Some have the custom to recite this prayer while sitting up in bed with the head bowed toward the chest, and with the fingertips held against each other.[23]

2. Morning Blessings and Preliminary Readings

Our morning prayers begin with a series of brief blessings to thank G-d for many elements of daily life that might otherwise be taken for granted (pp. 6–9), such as the ability to see, sit up, stand upright, and walk. We also thank G-d for providing us with clothes, shoes, and so forth, as well as the privilege of being Jewish and having been given the Torah and its sacred laws.

3. *Korbanot*—The Sacrificial Offerings

The subsequent section in the prayer book describes the sacrificial and incense offerings in the Holy Temple (pp. 17–24). Before entering this topic, however, we declare our love for our fellow Jews (p. 12);[24] we then read a biblical passage that describes Abraham's

---

22. *Kitzur Shulchan Aruch* 1:2.
23. *Sefer Haminhagim, Minhagei Chabad*, p. 1.
24. *Igrot Kodesh Rayatz* 3, p. 143.

binding of Isaac (pp. 13–14), followed by the Shema declaration that is Judaism's ultimate proclamation of faith in G-d (p. 16).

After reading a description of the daily offerings (pp. 17–21), we read the thirteen principles that govern the derivation of Jewish law from Torah passages, as formulated by the ancient sage Rabbi Ishmael.

In a congregational prayer with a minyan, the leader recites *Kaddish Derabbanan* (p. 26) after the teaching of Rabbi Ishmael. For more information about Kaddish, see below.

B. Shacharit—The Morning Prayer

1. *Hodu*—"Offer Praise"

The formal start of the Shacharit prayer is the passage that begins *hodu*, "Offer praise to the L-rd" (pp. 27–29). This section is a collage of verses culled from diverse biblical sources, all of which offer praise to G-d and describe the Creator's providence over our people.

On Shabbat, several additional prayers are inserted into this section (pp. 184–191).

2. *Pesukei Dezimrah*—Verses of Sing

This section (pp. 30–38) is built of entire paragraphs and chapters from biblical texts that descriptively sing G-d's praises. It is designed to awaken feelings of admiration, gratitude, awe, and love for G-d. This section is introduced with a poetic blessing and signs out with another, as described below.

Baruch she'amar ("Blessed is He Who spoke") (p. 30). This blessing sets the tone for *pesukei dezimrah*. It is customary for men to recite it while grasping the front two *tzitzit* (fringes of the *talit*) in the left hand.[25] Some run the *tzitzit* lightly over the eyes and then kiss them at the conclusion of *Baruch She'amar*.[26]

There are two parts to *pesukei dezimrah*. Its first half is primarily comprised of Psalms 145–150. Our sages taught that one who recites Psalm 145 three times daily is assured of a share in the World to Come. This psalm includes the verse, "You open Your hand and satisfy the needs of every living thing," which testifies to G-d's providence over creation, a central message of *pesukei dezimrah*.[27] Psalm 145 is followed by Psalms 146–150 because each chapter in this series begins and ends with the words "praise the L-rd," which is the ultimate goal of this stage of our morning prayers.[28]

The second half of *pesukei dezimrah* is comprised of selections from Chronicles, Nehemiah, and Exodus that praise G-d for creation and for the miracles He performed for us during the Exodus and at the Sea of Reeds.

The grand finale of this section is *yishtabach* ("may Your Name be praised forever") (p. 38), a blessing filled with expressions of praise derived from the preceding passages.[29] On Shabbat, an additional prayer, *nishmat* ("the soul of every living being"), is inserted before *yishtabach* (pp. 199–201).

---

25. *Shulchan Aruch HaRav, Orach Chayim* 51:2.
26. *Sefer Haminhagim, Minhagei Chabad*, p. 9.
27. *Shulchan Aruch HaRav, Orach Chayim* 51:8.
28. Ibid., 51:1.
29. Ibid.

In a congregational prayer with a minyan, *yishtabach* is followed by "half Kaddish" (p. 38), which is in turn followed by *barchu* (p. 39). These will be explained further below.

3. *Birchot Keri'at Shema*—Blessings Surrounding the Shema

The next step in our ladder of prayer is the Shema that is preceded by two blessings and trailed by a third blessing (pp. 39–45):

The initial blessing preceding the Shema mentions the enormity and brilliance of G-d's creation[30] and contains the *kedushah*—a prayer that describes the loving and reverential prayers offered by the angels in Heaven. On Shabbat, the first blessing is modified and expanded (pp. 203–205).

The second blessing describes G-d's eternal love for us and our profound devotion to Him. During this blessing, men gather the four *tzitzit* of the *talit* and grasp them in the left hand (those who are left-handed gather them into their right hand).

4. Shema

The Shema consists of three distinct portions from the Torah. The first (Deuteronomy 6:4–9) is a declaration of our faith in G-d's unity and our love for G-d. The second (Deuteronomy 11:13–21) describes the rewards earned by the observance of the Divine commandments and the consequences that result from disobeying them. The third (Numbers 15:37–41) defines the *mitzvah* of *tzitzit* and the imperative to recall our Exodus from Egypt.

---

30. During the first blessing (p. 39), it is customary for men who are wearing *tefilin* to touch the hand-*tefilin* at the words *yotzer or* ("Who forms light"), and to touch the head-*tefilin* while reciting *uvorei choshech* ("and creates darkness") (*Kaf Hachayim, Orach Chayim* 59:2).

The opening verse of the Shema is traditionally recited aloud to enhance concentration. It is customary to cover the eyes with the right hand while reciting this verse, to avoid distractions. Those who are left-handed cover their eyes with the left hand. Our sages taught that the final word, *echad* ("one"), should be extended long enough to reflect on the idea that G-d is King over everything that exists in every direction—east, west, north, south, above, and below.[31]

Before continuing the biblical passage, we insert a non-biblical phrase (*baruch Shem* ["blessed be the Name"]). The Talmud teaches that when our forefather Jacob's twelve sons, the progenitors of the tribes of Israel, declared their faith in G-d by reciting the Shema, Jacob expressed his happiness by reciting this passage in response.[32] *Baruch Shem* is recited quietly to distinguish it from the Shema itself, to avoid confusing passages of biblical and non-biblical origin.[33]

The third paragraph of the Shema (p. 43) contains the biblical commandment of *tzitzit*. Before reciting this paragraph, it is customary for men to transfer the *tzitzit* that they are holding in their left hand to their right hand. Those who are left-handed do the opposite. The strings of the *tzitzit* are then kissed each time the word *tzitzit* is read—and once more at the word *emet* ("truth"), which is appended to the conclusion of the Shema (p. 44).[34]

---

31. *Shulchan Aruch HaRav, Orach Chayim* 61:5-7.
32. Talmud, Pesachim 56a.
33 *Shulchan Aruch HaRav, Orach Chayim* 61:13.
34. See Talmud, Berachot 14a.

When praying in private, before adding the word *emet* ("truth"), the last three words of the Shema are repeated. These are the words *Ado-nai Elo-heichem emet*, thereby bringing the total of the words of the Shema to 248, corresponding to the number of positive commandments in the Torah. When praying with a minyan, this is not necessary because the *chazan* repeats these three words on behalf of the congregation.

In the *Ashkenaz* custom, when praying without a minyan, one recites three alternate words *before* the Shema.

5. Final Blessing of *Birchot Keriat Shema*

The Shema is followed by a blessing of praise for the wondrous miracles that G-d performed during the Exodus and at the Sea of Reeds (pp. 44–45), in fulfillment of our obligation to praise G-d each morning for the miracles He performs.[35] The blessing concludes with a declaration of our faith that G-d is our redeemer.

6. Amidah

The Amidah begins on page 45 and concludes on page 54. On Shabbat, it begins on page 211 and concludes on page 217.[36]

This most important prayer, the pinnacle of our morning devotion, is recited standing upright, feet together, preferably in front of a wall, and facing in the direction of Jerusalem.[37] The tradition of facing Jerusalem dates back to King Solomon, who taught that all the prayers in the world make their way to the Temple Mount and from there ascend to G-d.[38]

Before beginning, it is customary to take three steps forward to demonstrate that we are approaching G-d in direct, personal prayer.[39] When standing in front of a table or wall, take three steps back and then three steps forward.

It is ancient tradition to take a number of bows during the Amidah as follows: At the very start of the initial blessing, we bend the knees at the word *baruch* ("blessed"), then bow forward from the waist at the word *Atah* ("You"), and then stand erect once more before continuing. This procedure is repeated at the end of the first blessing as well. It is repeated once more at the conclusion of the eighteenth blessing. In addition, at the start of the eighteenth blessing, at the

---

35. Psalms 92:3; Rashi, Berachot 12a.
36. The Amidah for festivals appears on pages 331–337.
37. Shulchan Aruch, *Orach Chayim* 90:21 and 94:1.
38. Ibid., 94:1.
39. *Shulchan Aruch HaRav* 95:2.

words *modim anachnu Lach she'Atah Hu* ("we thankfully acknowledge that You"), we bow from the waist.[40]

After completing the Amidah, we take three steps backward (moving the left foot first as a symbol of reluctance to depart from G-d's presence). We do so with the head bowed toward the chest, as if departing humbly from a king. After taking three steps, we straighten our posture and bow the head to the left, to the right, and forward as we recite the phrase *Oseh shalom* ("He Who makes peace"). Finally, we take three steps forward to our original position. Some have a custom of rising slightly on their toes to express a desire to draw closer to G-d.

On Shabbat and festivals, only the first three blessings of the Amidah and its final blessing remain the same. The entire middle section of the Amidah is replaced so that instead of reciting a series of thirteen blessings, we offer a single blessing that depicts the nature and theme of the occasion.

In a congregational prayer with a minyan, the leader repeats the Amidah aloud once the congregation has concluded their muted prayers. The congregation listens attentively, responds *amen* at the conclusion of each blessing, and participates in the recital of *kedushah*. This will be explained further below.

7. Special Inserts into the Amidah

Havdalah: On Saturday nights, a prayer to mark the end of Shabbat, known as Havdalah ("distinction"), is inserted into the fourth blessing (p. 125) to distinguish between Shabbat and the weekdays. It is included in the prayer for knowledge because our sages taught

40. Shulchan Aruch, *Orach Chayim* 113:1 and 121:1.

that knowledge is a prerequisite to our ability to make appropriate distinctions.[41]

Fast Days: The ninth day of the month of Av (a day known as Tishah Be'Av) marks the destruction of the Holy Temples. On this day, an urgent prayer for the rebuilding of Jerusalem and the Holy Temple is inserted into the fourteenth blessing (p. 106).

On all fast days, a plea for G-d to transform our tragedies into joyous occasions is inserted into the sixteenth blessing (p. 108).

Festivals: On Rosh Chodesh (the start of each Jewish month) and the intermediate days of the Passover and Shavuot festivals, a passage beginning *Elokeinu . . . yaaleh veyavo* ("our G-d . . . may there ascend") is inserted into the seventeenth blessing (p. 108). This prayer asks G-d to remember us for good, provide for us, and protect us on this auspicious day.

Several additional prayers are inserted into the Amidah during the first ten days of the Jewish year, from the start of Rosh Hashanah until the conclusion of Yom Kippur (pp. 46–47, 49, 52–53).

Seasons: The texts of the second and ninth blessings of the Amidah (pp. 46 and 48) are slightly modified to account for the changes of the natural seasons. Each of these prayers has a summer and a winter phase. The shift to the summer version is introduced on the first day of Passover. The shift to the winter version is completed in two steps: the blessing on p. 46 is modified on the festival of Shemini Atzeret, while the modification on p. 48 is made on the fifth of December.

---

41. Jerusalem Talmud, Berachot 5:2.

8. *Tachanun*—Supplications

On weekdays, the Amidah is immediately followed by *tachanun* (pp. 54–55, 59–60), in which we seek forgiveness from G-d.[42] On Monday and Thursday mornings, additional supplications are recited (pp. 56–59). None of these are recited on Shabbat, Jewish festivals, or days of special joy in the Jewish calendar or communal/personal experience.

> In a congregational prayer with a minyan, the "half Kaddish" (p. 60) is recited after *tachanun*. On Monday and Thursday mornings, this is followed by a brief Torah reading (pp. 61–65). These are explained further below.

9. *Kedushah* and the Song of the Day

The next section (pp. 66–68) is a combination of passages culled from a variety of sources. We repeat Psalm 145 (p. 66) and the *kedushah* (pp. 67–68)—in which we echo the loving and reverential prayers sung by the angels. This entire section is omitted on Shabbat.

> In a congregational prayer with a minyan, the complete Kaddish (p. 69) is recited after the completion of this section.

---

42. When *tachanun* is recited with a minyan, the congregation chants the thirteen attributes of G-d's name (p. 55) in unison. When *tachanun* is recited without a minyan, these attributes are omitted. (These attributes are not chanted in the Ashkenazic tradition.) After this point, one sits and reads the rest of the *tachanun*. When *tachanun* is recited in a house where a Torah scroll is present, we lower the head onto the left arm while reciting *tachanun*. One who is wearing *tefilin* on the left arm lowers the head onto the right arm.

Our next prayer is the Song of the Day (pp. 71–75). A different psalm is recited for each day of the week. These were the psalms chanted by the choir of Levites each day in the Holy Temple.

> In a congregational prayer with a minyan, the Mourners' Kaddish is recited at this point (p. 77).

On Shabbat, the order of prayers following the Amidah is modified so that we immediately recite the Song of the Day for Shabbat (pp. 218–219), followed by a second Amidah referred to as Musaf ("additional"—pp. 230–246).[43]

In a congregational prayer with a *minyan* on Shabbat, the entire weekly Torah portion is read before Musaf (see pp. 222–230).

10. Conclusion

The next prayer (pp. 78–79 in the weekday prayers) is a hymn of praise, followed by a description of the incense offering that was brought in the Holy Temple.

In a congregational prayer with a *minyan*, *Rabbanan Kaddish* is recited at this point (p. 79).

Our morning prayers conclude with *aleinu* (p. 88), a famous prayer that many congregations sing to a widely familiar tune. This is an ancient prayer regarding G-d's sovereignty and our subservience to G-d's kingship, authored by Joshua as he led the Jews into Israel some 3,300 years ago.[44]

---

43. The Musaf Amidah for Rosh Chodesh appears on pp. 313–320. The Musaf Amidah for Rosh Chodesh that coincides with Shabbat appears on pp. 320–326. The Musaf Amidah for festivals is on pp. 340–350.
44. *Teshuvot Hage'onim, Shaarei Teshuvah* 44. See also *Kol Bo*, chapter 16.

This final prayer is recited while standing. As we reach the words *vaanachnu kore'im* ("but we bend the knee"), we bend at the knees. At the word *umishtachavim* ("bow down"), we bow from the waist. We then stand erect for the rest of the prayer.

> In a congregational prayer with a minyan, the Mourners' Kaddish is recited at this point (p. 81).

C. Minchah–Afternoon Prayer

It is preferable to recite the afternoon service (pp. 101–117) in the later part of the day. It is comprised of Psalm 145, the Amidah, supplications for forgiveness, and *aleinu*.

D. Arvit–Evening Prayer

The evening prayer (pp. 118–135) may be recited after nightfall, preferably before midnight. It consists of the Shema and its surrounding blessings (two before the Shema and another two subsequent to the Shema), followed by the Amidah and *aleinu*. Although the themes of the blessings surrounding the Shema in the evening prayer are similar to those surrounding the Shema in the morning prayer, their texts are by no means identical.

III. Congregational Prayer

A. Chazan—Leader

When a *minyan* gathers for communal prayer, one of those present is chosen to serve as the prayer leader (referred to as the *chazan*) for that prayer service. The *chazan* stands at the front of the group and chants aloud the beginning and end of each prayer. The *chazan* also leads entire congregational portions such as the repetition of the Amidah, Kaddish, *kedushah*, and *barchu*. On Shabbat and Jewish festivals, when the congregation is less hurried due to the prohibition against working on those days, the *chazan* often incorporates melodies into the service, and the congregation joins together in song.

B. Chazarat Hashatz—Repetition of the Amidah

When praying with a *minyan*, the *chazan* repeats the entire Amidah aloud after the congregation has completed their silent reading of same text. Listening to this repetition and answering *amen* after each blessing allows those who cannot pray on their own to fulfill their obligation.[45] It is imperative that the congregants pay attention to the *chazan*'s prayers; chatting or even studying Torah are prohibited during the repetition.[46]

As the *chazan* pronounces G-d's name toward the end of each blessing, the congregation honors G-d by responding: *baruch Hu uvaruch Shemo* ("blessed is He and blessed is His name"). As the *chazan* concludes each blessing, the congregation responds with *amen*, thereby affirming their belief that the words of the prayer are

---

45. Shulchan Aruch, *Orach Chayim* 124:1.
46. Ibid., 124:4.

true. *Amen* also expresses the congregation's confidence that G-d will receive their prayers and grant their petitions.[47]

C. Kedushah

This prayer echoes the reverential prayers of the angels in Heaven, as described by the prophets. During the *chazan*'s repetition of the Amidah, this prayer is inserted immediately after the conclusion of the third blessing.

While reciting or singing these praises with the *chazan*, we strive to emulate the immense joy and reverence experienced by the Heavenly angels as they recite these same phrases.[48] At the start of each stanza, we raise our eyes Heavenward and rise lightly on our toes. This is done to mimic the angels' constant spiritual rise[49] and to indicate our desire to draw higher and closer to G-d.[50]

D. Barchu—"Bless G-d"

With this prayer, the *chazan* invites the congregation to bless G-d aloud, in unison. The *chazan* bows from the waist and proclaims: *barchu et Ado-nai Hamevorach* ("Bless G-d Who is blessed!") The congregation responds by similarly bowing from the waist and exclaiming: *barchu et Ado-nai Hamevorach le'olam va'ed* ("Blessed be G-d Who is blessed forever!") The *chazan* bows a second time and echoes the congregation's response.

This brief but powerful prayer summons us to pause and consider the tremendous significance of the prayer that we are about to

---

47. *Shulchan Aruch HaRav* 124:9.
48. *Anaf Yosef* on *kedushah* in the name of *Yaaros Devash*.
49. *Magen Avraham, Orach Chayim* 125:2.
50. *Shulchan Aruch HaRav, Orach Chayim* 125:3.

begin—the morning and evening Shema and its blessings. (An identical exchange is conducted before reading from the Torah.[51])

E. Torah Reading

When praying with a *minyan* on Mondays and Thursdays, as well as on Shabbat mornings and afternoons, the Torah scroll is removed from its ark and a portion is read.

The Torah is divided into large portions, and on each subsequent Shabbat morning, a successive portion is read so that the entire Torah is completed in the course of a year. Far briefer selections are read on Shabbat afternoons and on Monday and Thursday mornings. On those occasions, a number of opening verses from the upcoming Shabbat portion are read in advance.

The Torah is read on additional days, including Rosh Chodesh, fast days, Jewish festivals, and the High Holidays. On these dates, the selections are directly related to the theme of the day.

As the Torah is being read, each congregant should follow in a printed copy of the Torah. It is important to refrain from conversation during the reading.

After the reading, the scroll is raised high and held open for all to see. It is then lowered, closed, dressed in its mantel, and returned respectfully to its ark.

On Shabbat, Jewish festivals, and other special occasions, the last person summoned to the Torah reading chants the *haftarah*—a reading from the prophets—subsequent to the Torah reading.

---

51. Rabbi Nissan Mindel, *My Prayer* (Brooklyn, N.Y.: Merkos L'Inyonei Chinuch, 2000), p. 139.

F. Kaddish

Kaddish is a moving declaration of faith in G-d that petitions G-d to fully reveal His presence on earth. It is most familiar as the special prayer recited by mourners during the first eleven months following the passing of a parent. It is also recited annually on a *yahrzeit*—anniversary of a loved one's passing. The Mourners' Kaddish is recited at various points of the prayer service, as well as at a gravesite, at the conclusion of a funeral or unveiling, provided that ten Jewish men are present. With this prayer, mourners express their faith in the ultimate truth and justice of G-d's judgment, and they thereby continue the sacred mission of the deceased.

Nevertheless, the Kaddish is not restricted to mourners. At a number of junctures in the prayer services, the *chazan* recites the Kaddish.

Whenever it is recited, the congregation responds with *amen* in the appropriate places. The third *amen* (second in the Ashkenazic tradition) is followed by the words: *yehe Shme rabbah mevorach le'alam ule'almei almaya yitbarech* ("May His great Name be blessed forever and to all eternity!"). These words are recited aloud. Our sages taught that reciting these words aloud and with complete concentration can overturn the severest of Heaven's decrees.[52]

There are four variations of Kaddish:

a. *The Half Kaddish* is recited by the *chazan* at specific points in the service. These serve to distinguish the various sections of the prayers.

b. *The Complete Kaddish* is recited by the *chazan* upon concluding the Amidah, for it includes a prayer that G-d grant all of our petitions, and the Amidah is replete with petitions.

52. *Shulchan Aruch HaRav, Orach Chayim* 69:2.

c. *Rabbanan Kaddish* ("the Kaddish for the rabbis") includes an additional prayer for Torah students and scholars. It is recited after a passage of rabbinical teachings (Mishnah or Talmud) is studied or recited in the presence of a minyan.

d. *The Mourners' Kaddish*, as described earlier.

Afterword

Life skills are not acquired overnight, and the art of sincere and successful prayer is certainly no different. Rather, it must be approached, practiced, and perfected one step at a time. Add fresh insights and directions at a gradual pace into your prayer routine, and keep practicing. The more frequently you pray, the more familiar you will be with the nuanced customs and laws. Soon enough, it will all become routine, allowing you to advance to the next stage of inspiration and bonding with G-d, for prayer is a ladder that allows you to climb continuously higher into the Heavens, rung after rung, bringing ever greater attachment and blessings down to its feet, which are firmly planted on earth.

Acknowledgments

The initial production of this curriculum coincided with the horrific news of October 7, 2023. No work has ever embodied more heartfelt pleas to G-d on behalf of our beloved family, nation, and country. There is no one worthier of acknowledgment than our brothers and sisters in our Holy Land. To the IDF, wounded warriors, and hostages; widows, orphans, dearest heroes and heroines—all holy and pure souls: Thousands of Jewish women around the world continue to be united in prayer in your merit. May G-d protect, defend, redeem, heal, and bring true and lasting peace to our loved ones. Be strengthened and be strong. Victory is ours. *Am Yisrael Chai!*

My heart aches for our collective loss and suffering. Yet I must publicly acknowledge the incredible blessings I have been granted. Thank you G-d for allowing me to fuse a life's mission and a labor of love. This is how the heart's ache turns to song.

Extreme appreciation is owed to the course authors **Rabbi Yosi Wolf, Rabbi Baruch Shalom Davidson, Rabbi Lazer Gurkow,** and **Rabbi Shmuel Super**, for their wisdom, dedication, and skillful ability in bringing this project to fruition. Profound recognition goes to the course editor, **Rabbi Mordechai Dinerman**, for his notable curricular contribution to this body of work; and to **Rabbi Yaakov Paley**, for his magical pen. I am deeply grateful to our curriculum coordinator, **Mrs. Rivki Mockin**, whose book production sensibilities are commendable. To all of them I say: Thank you for so generously sharing your expertise. It has been a true pleasure and joy to collaborate with you every step of the way. The Rosh Chodesh Society is indeed exceedingly blessed.

Mrs. Malky Bitton, **Mrs. Shula Bryski**, **Mrs. Rochel Holzkenner**, **Mrs. Leah Rosenfeld**, and **Mrs. Yehudis Wolvovsky** graciously agreed to lend their know-how and experience—from reviewing curricula, to aiding in general course development, and to piloting the course so that others may benefit. We acknowledge their pedagogic and instructional skills and thank them on behalf of the entire Rosh Chodesh Society.

We laud our talented teams who have expended numerous hours to bring our books and materials to production with innovative vision and attention to the finest detail. **Mrs. Rachel Musicante** and **Mrs. Ya'akovah Weber** meticulously copyedited and proofread the textbooks. **Rabbi Motti Klein** is responsible for the professional layout. And we thank **Mrs. Sara Rosenblum**, for overseeing—and **Mrs. Chana Zajac** for creating—the charmingly enchanting illustrations. The artfulness, brilliant creativity, and proficiency of our design team—**Mrs. Chaya Mushka Kanner** and **Mrs. Estie Klein**—are exemplary.

Thank you to our gifted multimedia team for producing the animated PowerPoint presentations—a wonderful asset to each lesson. Having the good fortune to work on our videos with **Moshe** and **Getzy Raskin** of Swish Media, who are simply so good at all things video, is a blessing I'm sure many would wish for.

Many thanks to **Rabbi Mendel Sirota** and his team for directing the printing and publishing of our books, as well as ensuring their proper and timely shipping.

Kudos to **Mrs. Chana'le Dechter**, an administrator and singlehanded project manager par excellence. She is much more than her title can ever tell you, and my appreciation for her knows no bounds. Her wise contributions, in so many areas, are immeasurable.

I pay tribute to **Mrs. Shaina B. Mintz** for everything she does—all day, every day—to ensure that all the moving parts are aligned to perfection.

This is the first Rosh Chodesh Society course being launched since the passing of **Rabbi Moshe Kotlarsky**, OBM, our beloved mentor and friend, chairman of the Rohr Jewish Learning Institute, and vice chairman of Merkos L'inyonei Chinuch—Lubavitch World Headquarters. The Rosh Chodesh Society is forever enormously grateful for his unyielding and ceaseless encouragement. May the merit of the Torah study by Jewish women worldwide serve to honor Rabbi Kotlarsky's legacy, continuing to be a source of *nachas* to him on high, as it always was during his lifetime.

We are fortuitously blessed with the unwavering support of JLI's principal benefactors, **Mr. and Mrs. George and Pamela Rohr**, who have staunchly spearheaded and invested in the growth of the organization with an unparalleled commitment. Their dedication is evident and alive within the tens of thousands of Jewish students studying Torah around the globe. May their merit stand them—and all of us—in good stead, and may they reap bountiful blessings all the days of their long, happy, and healthy lives.

Heartfelt acclamation to **Mr. and Mrs. Yitzchak and Julie Gniwisch** and family for their steadfast support and resolute belief in us, always. May the goodness they bring to the world be returned to them ten thousandfold.

JLI's devoted executive board—**Rabbi Chaim Block**; **Rabbi Hesh Epstein**; **Rabbi Ronnie Fine**; **Rabbi Yosef Gansburg**; **Rabbi Shmuel Kaplan**, chairman of the Rosh Chodesh Society; **Rabbi**

Yisrael Rice; and **Rabbi Avrohom Sternberg**—give countless hours, deep commitment, and selfless dedication to the development and growth of JLI.

The constant progress of JLI is a testament to the visionary leadership of our director, **Rabbi Efraim Mintz**, who is never content with the status quo, boldly encourages unbridled innovation and forward thinking, and embodies successful accomplishment. You are an example to many. On this auspicious day, I thank you publicly, both personally and professionally, for this benevolent, outstanding, and truly wonderful opportunity. Directing the Rosh Chodesh Society is the calling of my heart and the journey of my soul. It is a gift that keeps on giving eternal blessings. May all who read this be equally blessed. Your merit is great. Thank you for sharing it with me.

The Rosh Chodesh Society, JLI's women's division, was launched on the anniversary of the first *yahrtzeit*s of **Rabbi Gavriel Noach and Rebbetzin Rivkah Holtzberg,** ***H"YD***, devoted Chabad emissaries to Mumbai, India. May the merit of the countless Jewish women who are engaged in these Torah studies serve as a testament to the heroic lives the Holtzbergs led and continue to perpetuate their noble deeds.

On behalf of all the individuals who play a role in the Rosh Chodesh Society, particularly our affiliates out there on the front lines fulfilling their positions, I offer up a prayer to Almighty G-d: may He actualize the hope of the Jewish nation, as repeatedly expressed by the Lubavitcher Rebbe, of righteous memory, and may we very soon experience the world as it will be, filled with the knowledge of G-d as the waters cover the sea. May we greet Mashiach today. Amen.

Shluchos! It is solely thanks to you that we will merit the fulfillment of our mandate, "No Jewish Woman Will Be Left Behind." We could never do it without you. Thank you for allowing us to partner with you. You are the heart and soul of the Jewish nation. Indeed, this is the ultimate acknowledgment.

Shaindy Jacobson
Director, Rosh Chodesh Society
Brooklyn, New York
Chai (18) Elul, 5784

The Rohr
JEWISH LEARNING INSTITUTE

An affiliate of **MERKOS L'INYONEI CHINUCH**

The Educational Arm of the **Chabad Lubavitch Movement**
832 Eastern Parkway, Brooklyn, NY 11213

FACULTY

UNITED STATES

BIRMINGHAM, AL
Mrs. Frumie Posner
Chabad of Alabama
205.276.1307
Frumieposner@gmail.com

LITTLE ROCK, AR
Mrs. Estie Ciment
Lubavitch of Arkansas
501.221.7940
Estie@arjewishcenter.com

NORTHWEST AR
Mrs. Dobie Greisman
Chabad of Northwest Arkansas
479.464.7999
dobi@jewishnwa.org

CHANDLER, AZ
Mrs. Shternie Deitsch
Chabad of the East Valley
480.855.4333
mycmommy@gmail.com

FOUNTAIN HILLS, AZ
Mrs. Tzipi Lipskier
Chabad of Fountain Hills
480.795.6292
tzipi@jewishfountainhills.com

ORO VALLEY, AZ
Mrs. Mushkie Zimmerman
Chabad of Oro Valley
347.526.5967
mushkie@jewishorovalley.com

PARADISE VALLEY, AZ
Mrs. Chaya Levertov
Chabad of Paradise Valley
305.479.9686
chaya@jewishparadisevalley.com

PEORIA, AZ
Mrs. Chana Lew
Chabad West Valley
480.227.0620
lewchana@gmail.com

PHOENIX, AZ
Mrs. Tziporah Levertov
Chabad Women Circle
602.793.5435
Chabadwomen@gmail.com

PHOENIX, AZ
Mrs. Leah Levertov
Chabad Lubavitch of North Phoenix
480.563.4898
mendyl@chabadaz.org

TUCSON, AZ
Mrs. Feigie Ceitlin
Chabad Lubavitch of Tucson
520.869.4971
FeigieCeitlin@gmail.com

ARCATA, CA
Mrs. Mushkie Cowen
Chabad of Humboldt
412.390.6481
mushkiecowen@gmail.com

BAKERSFIELD, CA
Mrs. Esther Malka Schlanger
Chabad of Bakersfield
661.835.8381
estherm@bak.rr.com

BERKELEY, CA
Mrs. Miriam Chaya Ferris
Chabad of the East Bay
510.684.5292
miriamferris@gmail.com

BEVERLY HILLS, CA
Mrs. Devorah Leah Illulian
One Lev Women's Circle
310.927.3362
dltraxler@gmail.com

BRENTWOOD, CA
Mrs. Mashie Goldshmid
Chabad of the Delta
718.812.1425
mashie@JewishDelta.com

BURBANK, CA
Mrs. Chayale Kornfeld
Chabad of Burbank
818.749.1592
chayalekornfeld@gmail.com

CALABASAS, CA
Mrs. Shaina Friedman
Chabad of Calabasas
818.222.3838
shaini@jewishcalabasas.com

DANVILLE, CA
Mrs. Mushky Raitman
Chabad of Danville & S. Ramon
925.272.9672
chabaddsr@gmail.com

ENCINO, CA
Mrs. Chana Herzog
Chabad of Encino
818.784.9986
JLI@chabadofthevalley.com

FOLSOM, CA
Mrs. Goldie Grossbaum
Chabad Folsom
916.608.9811
info@jewishfolsom.org

FREMONT, CA
Mrs. Chaya Fuss
Chabad of Fremont
510.300.4090
chaya@chabadfremont.com

FRESNO, CA
Mrs. Chanie Zirkind
Chabad of Fresno
559.432.2770
chabadfresno@sbcglobal.net

GLENDALE, CA
Mrs. Shterny Backman
Chabad of Glendale
818.240.2750
shterny@chabadcenter.org

GRANITE BAY, CA
Mrs. Malkie Korik
Chabad of Roseville
916.500.4522
rabbi@jewishroseville.com

GRASS VALLEY, CA
Mrs. Chyena Yusewitz
Chabad of Grass Valley
530.404.0020
chyena@jewishgv.com

HUNTINGTON BEACH, CA
Mrs. Susha Alperowitz
Chabad of West Orange County
714.846.2285
chabadhb@verizon.net

IRVINE, CA
Mrs. Binie Tenenbaum
Chabad of Irvine
949.786.5000
binie@chabadirvine.org

LA JOLLA, CA
Mrs. Esther Ezagui
Chabad of La Jolla
619.977.8340
Jwclajolla@gmail.com

LAGUNA NIGUEL, CA
Mrs. Kreinie Paltiel
Chabad of Laguna Niguel
949.831.7701
Kreinie@ChabadLagunaNiguel.com

LONG BEACH, CA
Mrs. Amina Newman
Congregation Lubavitch
562.596.1681
info@longbeachshul.com

LOS ALTOS, CA
Mrs. Nechama Schusterman
Chabad Los Altos
650.858.6990
nechama@bayareafc.org

LOS ANGELES, CA
Mrs. Chanie Levin
Chabad Pico - Bais Bezalel
323.377.7727
admin@chabadpico.com

LOS ANGELES, CA
Mrs. Channa Hecht
Chabad Jewish Center of Brentwood
310.826.4453
channa@chabadbw.com

LOS ANGELES, CA
Mrs. Dvonye Korf
Chabad of Greater Los Feliz
323.660.5177
rabbi@chabadlosfeliz.org

LOS ANGELES, CA
Mrs. Miriam Rav-Noy
Friendship Circle LA
310.280.0955
Miriam@fcla.org

LOS ANGELES, CA
Mrs. Runya Wagner
Chabad Jewish Student Center at USC
213.748.5884
runya@usc.edu

LOS ANGELES, CA
Mrs. Shterny Gurary
Chabad Jewish Center of Hancock Park
323.939.5138
rabbi@jewishhp.com

LOS ANGELES, CA
Mrs. Rachey Simons
YJP Los Angeles
310.595.5490
mendel@yjplosangeles.com

MALIBU, CA
Mrs. Sarah Cunin
Chabad of Malibu
310.456.6588
sarah@ganmalibu.com

MILL VALLEY, CA
Mrs. Chana Scop
Chabad of Mill Valley
415.419.7296
chanascop@gmail.com

NEWBURY PARK, CA
Mrs. Tzippy Schneerson
Chabad of Newbury Park
805.499.7051
sschneerson@gmail.com

NEWHALL, CA
Mrs. Frumi Marozov
Chabad of SCV
6616445734
frumim@gmail.com

OAKLAND, CA
Mrs. Shulamis Labkowski
Chabad of Oakland
510.545.6770
info@jewishoakland.org

OCEANSIDE, CA
Mrs. Nechama Greenberg
Chabad Jewish Center Oceanside
760.806.7765
info@jewishoceanside.com

PACIFIC PALISADES, CA
Mrs. Zisi Cunin
Chabad of Pacific Palisades
310.454.7783
info@chabadpalisades.com

PALO ALTO, CA
Mrs. Devory Levin
Chabad Palo Alto
650.561.6013
devory@chabadpaloalto.com

PASADENA, CA
Mrs. Chana Hanoka
Chabad of Pasadena
626.564.8820
hanoka@sbcglobal.net

PLEASANTON, CA
Mrs. Fruma Resnick
Chabad of the Tri-Valley
925.846.0700
Fruma@JewishTriValley.com

POWAY, CA
Mrs. Shterna Goldstein
Chabad of Poway
858.208.6613
shterna@chabadpoway.com

RANCHO MIRAGE, CA
Mrs. Chaya Posner
Chabad of Rancho Mirage
760.272.1923
chaya@chabadrm.com

RANCHO S. FE, CA
Mrs. Devorah Raskin
Chabad Jewish Center of RSF
858.756.7571
Devorah@jewishrsf.com

REDONDO BEACH, CA
Mrs. Sara Mintz
Chabad Jewish Community Center
310.214.4999
laya0208@gmail.com

REDWOOD CITY, CA
Mrs. Ella Potash
Chabad MidPen
650.232.0995
Ella@chabadmidpen.com

SACRAMENTO, CA
Mrs. Dinie Cohen
Chabad of Sacramento
916.455.1400
chabadsac@aol.com

S. BARBARA, CA
Mrs. Devorah Loschak
Chabad of S. Barbara
805.324.3584
dloschak@gmail.com

S. CLARA, CA
Mrs. Elana Rosenberg
Chabad S. Clara
408.718.9074
elana@jewishsantaclara.com

S. DIEGO, CA
Mrs. Leah Fradkin
S. Diego Chabad Headquarters
858.547.0076
lfradkin@chasd.org

S. DIEGO, CA
Mrs. Nechama Dina Carlebach
Chabad of Downtown
619.289.8770
info@ChabadDowntown.com

S. FRANCISCO, CA
Mrs. Chani Zarchi
Congregation Chevra Thilim
415.752.2866
chani@sfshul.org

S. FRANCISCO, CA
Mrs. Sara Hecht
RTC-Chabad
415.386.8123
office@rtchabad.org

S. FRANCISCO, CA
Mrs. Mattie Pil
Schneerson Center
415.933.4310
mattieplot@gmail.com

S. MONICA, CA
Mrs. Sara Levitansky
Bais Chabad of Simcha Monica
310.829.5620
soriandisaac@gmail.com

S. MONICA, CA
Mrs. Rivka Rabinowitz
Chabad Living Torah Center
310.394.5699
rabbi@livingtorahcenter.com

S. ROSA, CA
Mrs. Altie Wolvovsky
Chabad Jewish Center
707.577.0277
rabbi@jewishsonoma.com

SEAL BEACH, CA
Mrs. Bluma Marcus
Chabad of Cypress
714.828.1851
shmuelmarcus@yahoo.com

SHERMAN OAKS, CA
Mrs. Ruth Weiss
Chabad of Sherman Oaks
818.789.0850
weissruty@gmail.com

SIMI VALLEY, CA
Mrs. Bassie Gurary
Chabad of Simi Valley
805.577.0573
bassie@chabadsimi.org

SOUTH LAKE TAHOE, CA
Mrs. Shaina Richler
Chabad Jewish Center
530.539.4363
Shaina@JewishTahoe.com

STOCKTON, CA
Mrs. Nechamie Brod
Chabad of Stockton
209.471.2154
nechamie@gmail.com

TEMECULA, CA
Mrs. Dina Hurwitz
Chabad Jewish Center Temecula Valley
951.813.1401
jewishtemecula@gmail.com

THOUSAND OAKS, CA
Mrs. Shula Bryski
Chabad of Thousand Oaks
805.370.5770
shula@jewishto.org

TOLUCA LAKE, CA
Mrs. Michal Carlebach
Chabad of Toluca Lake
818.308.4118
chabadtl@gmail.com

VACAVILLE, CA
Mrs. Aidel Zaklos
Chabad of Solano County
707.592.5300
rabbi@jewishsolano.com

VENTURA, CA
Mrs. Sarah Miriam Latowicz
Chabad of Ventura
805.658.7441
chabadventura@aol.com

WALNUT CREEK, CA
Mrs. Chaya Berkowitz
Chabad of Contra Costa
925.351.3875
chaya@jewishcontracosta.com

DENVER, CO
Mrs. Elka Popack
Chabad Lubavitch of Colorado
303.780.0537
elkapopack@gmail.com

DENVER, CO
Mrs. Rivka Sirota
WCRJ
720.233.9503
rivkasirota@gmail.com

LONE TREE, CO
Mrs. Hindy Mintz
Chabad Jewish Center - South Metro Denver
303.694.9119
Hindy@DenverJewishCenter.com

WESTMINSTER, CO
Mrs. Leah Brackman
Chabad of NW Metro Denver
303.429.5177
Leahbrackman9@gmail.com

FAIRFIELD, CT
Mrs. Miriam Landa
Chabad of Fairfield
203.373.7551
miriam@chabadff.com

GLASTONBURY, CT
Mrs. Yehudis Wolvovsky
Chabad Jewish Center
860.833.6451
yehudis@chabader.com

GREENWICH, CT
Mrs. Maryashie Deren
Chabad Lubavitch of Greenwich
203.629.9059
info@chabadgreenwich.org

GUILFORD, CT
Mrs. Rochel Baila Yaffe
Chabad of the Shoreline
203.533.7495
chabad@snet.net

HAMDEN, CT
Mrs. Chaya Hecht
Chabad of Hamden
203.684.6424
info@JewishHamden.org

MILFORD, CT
Mrs. Chanie Wilhelm
Chabad Jewish Center of Milford
203.878.4569
chanie@jewishmilford.com

ORANGE, CT
Mrs. Bluma Hecht
Chabad of Orange
203.795.5261
blumahecht@gmail.com

RIDGEFIELD, CT
Mrs. Chana Deitsch
Chabad of Ridgefield
203.438.4421
ChabadRidgefield@aol.com

STAMFORD, CT
Mrs. Vivi Deren
Chabad of Stamford
203.253.0006
morahvivi@chabadstamford.org

WEST HARTFORD, CT
Mrs. Shayna Gopin
Chabad House of Greater Hartford
860.232.1116
info@chabadhartford.com

WILMINGTON, DE
Mrs. Rochel Flikshtein
Chabad of Delaware
302.529.9900
Office@ChabadDE.com

AVENTURA, FL
Mrs. Raizel Rosenblum
Aventura Chabad Lubavitch
305.933.0770
raizelrosenblum@gmail.com

BOCA RATON, FL
Mrs. Ahuva New
Chabad of East Boca Raton
561.417.7797
Office@chabadbocabeaches.com

BOCA RATON, FL
Mrs. Chanie Bukiet
Chabad of West Boca Raton
561.487.2934
cbukiet@bellsouth.net

BOCA RATON, FL
Mrs. Rivkah Denburg
Chabad of Central Boca Raton
561.526.5738
rivkahden@gmail.com

BONITA SPRINGS, FL
Mrs. Luba Greenberg
Chabad of Bonita Springs & Estero
239.949.6900
jli@jewishbonita.com

BOYNTON BEACH, FL
Mrs. Dina Ciment
Chabad of Greater Boynton Beach
561.732.4633
ciments@gmail.com

BOYNTON BEACH, FL
Mrs. Shaina Raichik
Chabad of West Boynton
561.740.8738
shainyraichik@gmail.com

BRADENTON, FL
Mrs. Chanie Bukiet
Chabad of Bradenton and Lakewood Ranch
941.752.3030
Chanie@chabadofbradenton.com

CLEARWATER, FL
Mrs. Miriam Hodakov
Chabad of Clearwater
727.265.2770
miriamhodakov@gmail.com

CORAL SPRINGS, FL
Mrs. Chaya Mushka Yaras
Chabad of Coral Springs
9548674684
chayamushkaf@gmail.com

CUTLER BAY, FL
Mrs. Mindy Wolff
Chabad of Cutler Bay and Homestead
305.307.9108
ymwolff@gmail.com

FORT LAUDERDALE, FL
Mrs. Penina Lipszyc
Mrs. Gitty Fayershteyn
Chabad Lubavitch of Greater Fort Lauderdale
917.757.9615
gittylipszyc@gmail.com

FORT LAUDERDALE, FL
Mrs. Rochel Holzkenner
Chabad of Las Olas
954.224.7162
rochelholzkenner@gmail.com

HOLLYWOOD, FL
Mrs. Sheina Kudan
Chabad Ocean Drive
954.457.8080
sheina@chabadoceandrive.com

JUPITER, FL
Mrs. Sarah Barash
Chabad Jewish Center of Jupiter
561.222.4083
sarah@jewishjupiter.com

KEY BISCAYNE, FL
Mrs. Zeldy Caroline
Chabad of Key Biscayne
305.725.8758
avremel.caroline@gmail.com

LAKE WORTH, FL
Mrs. Leah Rosenfeld
Chabad Lake Worth
561.649.8468
Chabadlakeworth@gmail.com

LAKELAND, FL
Mrs. Libby Lazaros
Chabad of Lakeland
863.510.5968
mendel@chabadlakeland.org

LONGWOOD, FL
Mrs. Chanshy Majesky
Chabad-Lubavitch of North Orlando
407.636.5994
chanshy@JewishNorthOrlando.com

MAITLAND, FL
Mrs. Leah Dubov
Chabad of Orlando
407.644.2500
devorahleah@aol.com

MANALAPAN, FL
Mrs. Shaina Stolik
Chabad of South Palm Beach
561.889.3499
chabadspb@gmail.com

MIAMI, FL
Mrs. Chana Gopin
Chabad at Midtown
305.573.9995
info@maormiami.org

MIAMI, FL
Mrs. Gutal Fellig
Chabad of Miami
305.445.5444
info@chabadmiami.com

MIAMI BEACH, FL
Mrs. Chani Katz
Chabad House in Miami Beach
305.505.9065
rabbi@mbjewish.com

MIAMI BEACH, FL
Mrs. Tzippy Mann
Chabad of Venetian & Sunset Islands
305.674.8400
tzippymann@gmail.com

MIAMI BEACH, FL
Mrs. Devory Khazanovich
Chabad in South Beach
786.514.9593
rabbimann@gmail.com

MIAMI BEACH, FL
Mrs. Sara Lezak
Chabad of Bayshore
347.457.0441
sara@jewishbayshore.com

PALM BEACH, FL
Mrs. Hindel Levitin
Chabad of Northern Palm Beach Island
561.659.3884
hindelle@gmail.com

PALM BEACH GARDENS, FL
Mrs. Chana Vigler
Chabad of Palm Beach Gardens
561.624.2223
chana@jewishgardens.com

PALM COAST, FL
Mrs. Tzivie Ezagui
Chabad of Palm Coast
386.225.4941
Tzivie@chabadpalmcoast.com

PALM HARBOR, FL
Mrs. Mushky Adler
Chabad of Pinellas County
248.305.0462
mushky@yichabad.com

PALMETTO BAY, FL
Mrs. Chani Gansburg
Chabad of Palmetto Bay
786.282.0413
chabadpalmettobay@gmail.com

PLANTATION, FL
Mrs. Chanie Posner
Chabad of Plantation
954.600.7772
chanie@chabadplantation.com

PUNTA GORDA, FL
Mrs. Sheina Jacobson
Chabad of Charlotte County
941.833.3381
Chabadpg@gmail.com

ROYAL PALM BEACH, FL
Mrs. Leah Schtroks
Chabad of Royal Palm Beach
561.795.1534
rabbizevis@gmail.com

S. JOHNS, FL
Mrs. Dini Sharfstein
Chabad of S. Johns County
904.701.4422
Dini@JewishSJohnsCounty.com

S. PETERSBURG, FL
Mrs. Chaya Korf
Chabad Jewish Center
727.344.4900
Chaya@ChabadSP.com

SARASOTA, FL
Mrs. Sara Steinmetz
Chabad of Sarasota
941.925.0770
Sara@ChabadofSarasota.com

SUNNY ISLES BEACH, FL
Mrs. Chanie Kaller
Chabad Russian Center
305.803.5315
Rabbi@chabadrc.org

SURFSIDE, FL
Mrs. Chani Lipskar
The Shul of Bal Harbour
305.868.1411
info@theshul.org

SURFSIDE, FL
Mrs. Chaya Rochel Estrin
Aleph Institute - Military Division
206.371.3055
cestrin@aleph-institute.org

TAMPA, FL
Mrs. Sulha Dubrowski
Chabad of Tampa Bay
813.963.2317
lamplightersd@gmail.com

TRINITY, FL
Mrs. Dina Eber
Chabad of West Pasco
727.376.3366
lubavitcher@gmail.com

VALRICO, FL
Mrs. Tzippy Rubashkin
Chabad of Brandon
813.571.8100
tzipsor@gmail.com

WESLEY CHAPEL, FL
Mrs. Chanie Yarmush
Chabad of East Pasco & New Tampa
813.642.3244
chanie@ChabadatWiregrass.com

WEST DAVIE, FL
Mrs. Mushky Spalter
Chabad Lubavitch of West Davie
954.952.9785
mushky@chabadofwestdavie.com

WEST PALM BEACH, FL
Mrs. Chaya Gancz
Chabad of West Palm Beach
561.659.7770
Chaya@jewishwpb.com

WESTON, FL
Mrs. Leah Spalter
Chabad Lubavitch of Weston
954.349.6565
amychabadofweston@gmail.com

ALPHARETTA, GA
Mrs. Devora Leah Minkowitz
Chabad of North Fulton
770.410.9000
devoraleah@chabadnf.org

ATLANTA, GA
Mrs. Dassie New
Mrs. Leah Sollish
Chabad of Georgia
404.843.2464, ext. 102
office@chabadga.com

ATLANTA - INTOWN, GA
Mrs. Dena Schusterman
Intown Jewish Academy
404.898.0434
ija@chabadintown.org

CUMMING, GA
Mrs. Chaish Mentz
Congregation Beth Israel
470.253.7111
office@jewishforsyth.org

KENNESAW, GA
Mrs. Nechami Charytan
Chabad Jewish Center
678.460.7702
info@jewishwestcobb.com

PEACHTREE CORNERS, GA
Mrs. Esther Lerman
Chabad of Gwinnett
678.595.0196
esther@chabadofgwinnett.org

KAPA'A, HI
Mrs. Zisel Goldman
Chabad Kauai
808.647.4293
jewishkauai@gmail.com

DAVENPORT, IA
Mrs. Chana Cadaner
Chabad Lubavitch of the Quad Cities
563.355.1065
Chana@Chabadquadcities.com

IOWA CITY, IA
Mrs. Chaya Blesofsky
Chabad Lubavitch of Iowa City
319.358.1323
chabadiowa@msn.com

BOISE, ID
Mrs. Esther M. Lifshitz
Chabad Lubavitch of Idaho
208.841.9927
esther@jewishidaho.com

CHICAGO, IL
Mrs. Chaya Epstein
Women to Women
773.875.9147
w2wchaya@gmail.com

CHICAGO, IL
Mrs. Devorah Leah Kotlarsky
Chabad East Lakeview
773.495.7127
devlay@gmail.com

CHICAGO, IL
Mrs. Dinie Cohen
Jewish Women's Group
773.262.1381
ndcohen@sbcglobal.net

GLENVIEW, IL
Mrs. Sara Benjaminson
Rohr Chabad Center of Glenview
847.998.0770
Chabad@ChabadofGlenview.com

HIGHLAND PARK, IL
Mrs. Michla Schanowitz
North Suburban Chabad
847.433.1567
yschanow@sbcglobal.net

NORTHBROOK, IL
Mrs. Esther Rochel Moscowitz
Lubavitch Chabad of Northbrook
847.564.8770
info@chabadnorthbrook.com

OAK PARK, IL
Mrs. Nechama Dina Bergstein
Chabad Jewish Center of Oak Park
708.872.7771
info@oakparkjewish.org

RIVERWOODS, IL
Mrs. Sarale Notik
Chabad Riverwoods Initiative
224.415.4896
saralepruss@gmail.com

SKOKIE, IL
Mrs. Elka Wolf
Seymour J. Abrams Cheder Lubavitch Hebrew Day School
847.675.6777
elkiewolf@gmail.com

WILMETTE, IL
Mrs. Rivka Flinkenstein
Chabad of Wilmette
847.251.7707
JLI@chaicenter.com

LAWRENCE, KS
Mrs. Nechama Tiechtel
Chabad at KU & the Capital District
785.832.8672
info@jewishku.com

OVERLAND PARK, KS
Mrs. Blumah Wineberg
Neshei Chabad of KC
913.649.4852
nesheichabad@gmail.com

LEXINGTON, KY
Mrs. Shoshi Litvin
Chabad of the Bluegrass
502.576.0392
chabadofthebluegrass@gmail.com

BATON ROUGE, LA
Mrs. Mushka Kazen
Chabad of Baton Rouge
225.267.7047
Rabbi@chabadbr.com

METAIRIE, LA
Mrs. Chanie Nemes
Chabad Jewish Center
504.957.4987
chanienemes@gmail.com

ANNAPOLIS, MD
Mrs. Hindy Light
Chabad of Anne Arundel County
443.321.9859
hindy@chabadaac.com

BALTIMORE, MD
Mrs. Rochel Kaplan, OBM
Aleph Learning Institute

BALTIMORE, MD
Mrs. Chana Kaplan
Mikvah Mei Menachem
443.454.9589
Ckaplan@chabadsobo.com

BEL AIR, MD
Mrs. Fraida Malka Schusterman
Chabad of Harford County
443.353.9718
Chabad@HarfordJewish.com

COLUMBIA, MD
Mrs. Chaya Sufrin
Lubavitch Center of Howard County
443.474.0340
rabbi@chabadclarksville.org

GAITHERSBURG, MD
Mrs. Chana Raichik
Chabad Upper Montgomery County
301.537.0068
chana@ourshul.org

OLNEY, MD
Mrs. Devorah Stolik
Chabad of Olney
301.660.6770
info@jewisholney.com

OWINGS MILLS, MD
Mrs. Chanie Katsenelenbogen
Mrs. Chana Slavaticki
Chabad Owings Mills
410.356.5156
chanie@chabadom.com

POTOMAC, MD
Mrs. Sarale Bluming
Chabad of Potomac
240.621.0770
sara@chabadpotomac.com

POTOMAC VILLAGE, MD
Mrs. Chana Kaplan
Chabad of Potomac Village
240.543.4596
chana@fcmd.org

SILVER SPRING, MD
Mrs. Chaya Wolvovsky
Chabad of Silver Spring
301.593.1117
chayawolvovsky@gmail.com

SYKESVILLE, MD
Mrs. Feigie Cohen
Chabad of Carroll County
347.768.4885
Feigiet@gmail.com

ANDOVER, MA
Mrs. Faigy Bronstein
Chabad Lubavitch Jewish Center of Merrimack Valley
978.470.2288
Bronstein08@gmail.com

CHESTNUT HILL, MA
Mrs. Grunie Uminer
Chabad at Chestnut Hill
617.738.9770
grunie@chabadch.com

MANSFIELD, MA
Mrs. Tzivia Kivman
Chabad of Mansfield
508.339.8767
tzivikivman@gmail.com

MILFORD, MA
Mrs. Rochy Kivman
Chabad Lubavitch of Greater Milford
508.473.9724
rochykivman@gmail.com

NATICK, MA
Mrs. Chanie Fogelman
Chabad Center of Natick
508.202.2283
education@chabadnatick.com

NEWTON, MA
Mrs. Nechama Prus
Beth Menachem Chabad of Newton
617.244-1200
nechamaprus@gmail.com

PEABODY, MA
Mrs. Raizel Schusterman
Chabad of Peabody
978.977.9111
raizel@jewishpeabody.com

SHARON, MA
Mrs. Chanie Minkowitz
Congregation Menachem The Friendship Circle of Sharon
781.363.7053
Chanie@SharonFriends.com

STOUGHTON, MA
Mrs. Chana Gurkow
Shaloh House
781.344.6334
rabbi@shalohhouse.com

SUDBURY, MA
Mrs. Shayna Freeman
Chabad Center of Sudbury
978.443.0110
info@chabadsudbury.com

WELLESLEY, MA
Mrs. Geni Bleich
Wellesley Weston Chabad House
781.239.1076
JewishWomenRgr8@aol.com

WORCESTER, MA
Mrs. Sarah Fogelman
Chabad of UMASS Medical School
518.947.1165
sarahcohen97@gmail.com

BLOOMFIELD HILLS, MI
Mrs. Mushky Dubov
Chabad Jewish Center of Bloomfield Hills
248.949.6210
mushky@bloomfieldhillschabad.org

COMMERCE, MI
Mrs. Estie Greenberg
Chabad Jewish Center of Commerce
248.363.3644
estie@jewishcommerce.org

SOUTHFIELD, MI
Mrs. Tzippy Misholovin
FREE of Michigan
248.569.8514
free.michigan@yahoo.com

WEST BLOOMFIELD, MI
Mrs. Itty Shemtov
The Shul
248.788.4000
itty@theshul.net

WEST BLOOMFIELD, MI
Mrs. Zeesy Silberberg
Bais Chabad Torah Center
248.943.4172
Zeesy@baischabad.com

MINNEAPOLIS, MN
Mrs. Mushky Brook
CYP Minneapolis
612.405.6967
rabbi@cypminneapolis.com

MINNETONKA, MN
Mrs. Rivkie Grossbaum
Chabad Minneapolis
952.929.9922
rivka@ChabadMinneapolis.com

S. PAUL, MN
Mrs. Nechama Bendet
Chabad Lubavitch of Greater S. Paul
651.998.9298
jewishspaul@gmail.com

CHESTERFIELD, MO
Mrs. Chanala Rubenfeld
Chabad of Chesterfield
636.778.4000
chanala@chabadofchesterfield.com

KANSAS CITY, MO
Mrs. Chana'le Itkin
Chabad on the Plaza
816.645.6610
chana@plazachabad.com

S. LOUIS, MO
Mrs. Shiffy Landa
Chabad of Greater St. Louis
314.725.0400
Shiffylanda@gmail.com

BOZEMAN, MT
Mrs. Chavie Bruk
Chabad-Lubavitch of Montana
406.585.8770
chavs84@yahoo.com

MISSOULA, MT
Mrs. Shayna Nash
Chabad Lubavitch of Missoula
406.529.3196
berrynash@gmail.com

ASHEVILLE, NC
Mrs. Chana Susskind
Chabad-Lubavitch, WNC
828.505.0746
chana@chabadasheville.org

OMAHA, NE
Mrs. Mushka Tenenbaum
Chabad of Nebraska
402.330.1800
Mushka@ochabad.com

MANCHESTER, NH
Mrs. Shternie Krinsky
Chabad Center For Jewish Living
603.647.0204
Info@chabadofnh.com

BASKING RIDGE, NJ
Mrs. Chaya Shemtov
Chabad Somerset County
908.448.3226
chayas@chabadcentral.org

BOONTON, NJ
Mrs. Rivky Dubinsky
Chabad of Mountain Lakes
347.967.7720
rivkydubinsky@gmail.com

CHERRY HILL, NJ
Mrs. Dinie Mangel
Chabad Lubavitch in Cherry Hill
856.874.1500
Dinie@TheChabadCenter.org

ENGLEWOOD, NJ
Mrs. Dina Konikov
Chabad of Englewood
201.519.7343
chabadenglewood@gmail.com

FAIR LAWN, NJ
Mrs. Rivkah Bergstein
Anshei Lubavitch Outreach Center
201.794.3770
rivky@flchabad.com

FORT LEE, NJ
Mrs. Lieba Konikov
Chabad of Fort Lee
201.886.1238
Rabbi@chabadfortlee.com

FRANKLIN LAKES, NJ
Mrs. Mimi Kaplan
Chabad of NW Bergen County - Franklin Lakes
201.848.0449
Mimi@chabadplace.org

FREEHOLD, NJ
Mrs. Zisi Bernstein
Chabad of Freehold
732.972.3687
zisinj@gmail.com

HOBOKEN, NJ
Mrs. Shaindel Schapiro
Chabad Hoboken
201.386.5222
chabadhoboken@gmail.com

LEBANON, NJ
Mrs. Rachel Kornfeld
Chabad of Hunterdon County
908.238.9002
rachel@jewishhunterdon.com

MONTVILLE, NJ
Mrs. Chaya Schera Spalter
Chabad of Montville Township
973.216.1549
Chayasspalter@gmail.com

MORRISTOWN, NJ
Mrs. Chaya Gurevitz
Chabad Young Morristown
973.216.8077
mushkie@cypmorristown.com

MORRISTOWN, NJ
Mrs. Gani Goodman
Morristown RCA
917.860.0146
jdomber@gmail.com

MT. OLIVE, NJ
Mrs. Fraida Shusterman
Chabad Jewish Center of Mt. Olive
973.933.6011
fraida@mychabadcenter.com

RANDOLPH, NJ
Mrs. Chava Bekhor
Chabad of Randolph
973.895.3070
chava@ccfjl.com

SCOTCH PLAINS, NJ
Mrs. Malky Blesofsky
Chabad of Union County
908.790.0008
malky@chabaduc.com

TEANECK, NJ
Mrs. Nechamy Simon
Friends of Lubavitch of Bergen County
201-907-0686
nechamys@gmail.com

TOMS RIVER, NJ
Mrs. Chanie Gourarie
Chabad Toms River
732.349.4199
chanie@chabadtomsriver.com

VINELAND, NJ
Mrs. Nechama Rapoport
Chabad of Cumberland County
856.207.3797
yohama1@verizon.net

WANAQUE, NJ
Mrs. Esty Gurkov
Chabad Center for Jewish Life
718.501.2162
esty@JewishHighlands.org

WEST ORANGE, NJ
Mrs. Altie Kasowitz
Chabad of West Orange
973.486.2362
altiekas@yahoo.com

WEST WINDSOR, NJ
Mrs. Aliza Leverton
Chabad of the Windsors
609.638.2935
alileverton@gmail.com

WOODCLIFF LAKE, NJ
Mrs. Hindy Drizin
Valley Chabad
201.476.0157
hindy@valleychabad.org

LAS CRUCES, NM
Mrs. Chenchie Schmukler
Chabad of Las Cruces
575.524.1330
chenchie@ymail.com

LAS VEGAS, NV
Mrs. Binie Rivkin
Chabad of Red Rock
702.217.2170
binie@chabadredrock.com

BAYSIDE, NY
Mrs. Chany Pinson
Chabad of Northeast Queens
718.877.9389
Cfuterfas@gmail.com

BEDFORD HILLS, NY
Mrs. Sara Wolf
Chabad of Bedford & Pound Ridge Towns
914.666.6065
sara@chabadbedford.com

BRIARCLIFF MANOR, NY
Mrs. Miriam Labkowski
Chabad of Briarcliff-Ossining
914.923.2522
miriamlabkowski@gmail.com

BRONX, NY
Mrs. Sorah Shemtov
Chabad of Riverdale / Bronx
718.549.1100
sorahshmtv@gmail.com

BROOKLYN, NY
Mrs. Chana'le Levin
Chabad of Ditmas Park
347.850.2255
ChabadofDitmasPark@gmail.com

BROOKLYN, NY
Mrs. Chanel Lipskier
Mrs. Dvora Lakein
CH Women's Circle
718.778.6712
info@chwomenscircle.com

BROOKLYN, NY
Mrs. Devorah Marosov
Chabad of Midwood
718.338.3324
dmarsow@gmail.com

BROOKLYN, NY
Mrs. Elisheva Kirschenbaum
Osher Society
718.913.7900
oshersociety@gmail.com

BROOKLYN, NY
Mrs. Esther Abramowitz
Chabad-Lubavitch of Clinton Hill
718.974.9472
esther@greenechabad.com

BROOKLYN, NY
Mrs. Esther Winner
Chabad Neshama
718.207.8392
estherwinner@gmail.com

BROOKLYN, NY
Mrs. Hadassah Stroh
Chabad of Bay Ridge
718.974.6366
hadassahstroh@gmail.com

BROOKLYN, NY
Mrs. Sarah Hecht
Chabad of Park Slope
718.965.9836
shconquer@aol.com

BROOKLYN, NY
Mrs. Tzippy Vigler
Mayan Yisroel Chassidus Center
718.677.0030
tv@mayanyisroel.net

BROOKLYN, NY
Mrs. Riky Raichik
Chabad at BC
323.3605.480
rabbi@chabadatbc.com

DELMAR, NY
Mrs. Chanie Simon
Bethlehem Chabad
518.439.3310
chanie@bethlehemchabad.com

DOBBS FERRY, NY
Mrs. Hinda Silverman
Chabad of the River Towns
914.693.6100
office@chabadrt.org

EASTCHESTER, NY
Mrs. Mushka Deitsch
Chabad Jewish Center
914.458.2441
Mushka@ChabadJewishCenter.com

EAST NORWICH, NY
Mrs. Chana Shain
Chabad of Oyster Bay and Jericho
203.901.7206
chabadmn@gmail.com

FIVE TOWNS, NY
Mrs. Chana Wolowik
Chabad of the Five Towns
516.295.2478
chanie@chabad5towns.com

FLUSHING, NY
Mrs. Chanie Zalmanov
Chabad of Eastern Queens
718.464.0778
chaniezalmanov@gmail.com

FOREST HILLS, NY
Mrs. Mushky Mendelson
Congregation Machane Chodosh
917.754.3006
Mushkymendelson@gmail.com

GREAT NECK, NY
Mrs. Chanie Geisinsky
Chabad of Great Neck
516.528.6033
cgeisinsky@gmail.com

JERICHO, NY
Mrs. Devorah Brownstein
Chabad of Oyster Bay and Jericho
516.410.2658
devorahbrownstein@gmail.com

LONG BEACH, NY
Mrs. Baila Goodman
Chabad of the Beaches
516.897.2473
chabadofthebeaches@gmail.com

MAMARONECK, NY
Mrs. Chana Silberstein
Jewish Women's Circle
914.834.8000
chana@jewishlarchmont.com

MATTITUCK, NY
Mrs. Mushky Hurwitz
Chabad of North Fork
347.416.1299
mushky@chabadofnorthfork.org

MERRICK, NY
Mrs. Chanie Kramer
Chabad of Merrick-Bellmore-Wantagh
516.833.3057
chanie@chabadjewishlife.org

NEW ROCHELLE, NY
Mrs. Rochel Butman
Chabad of Westchester County
914.712.8332
chabadwestchester@gmail.com

NEW YORK, NY
Mrs. Chana Paris
Chabad of Tribeca
212.566.6764
info@chabadoftribeca.com

NEW YORK, NY
Mrs. Chanie Krasnianski
Chabad Upper East Side
212.717.4613
ckrasnianski@gmail.com

NEW YORK, NY
Mrs. Devora Wilhelm
Chabad Young Professionals UES
347.451.4375
chabadyp@gmail.com

NEW YORK, NY
Mrs. Frumie Weitman
Chabad Jewish Latin Center
646.678.3569
jewishlatincenternyc@gmail.com

NEW YORK, NY
Mrs. Gillie Shanowitz
New York Hebrew
646.573.6773
gillie@nychebrewschool.org

NEW YORK, NY
Mrs. Mushka Zaklos
Chabad of Battery Park
646.770.3636
jewishbpc@gmail.com

NEW YORK, NY
Mrs. Rachel Benchimol
Aleph Learning
646.827.9181
info@alephlearning.org

NEW YORK, NY
Mrs. Raizy Metzger
Upper Midtown Chabad
212.758.3770
raizymetzger@yahoo.com

NEW YORK, NY
Mrs. Sarah Alevsky
Chabad of the West Side
212.864.5010
sarah@chabadwestside.org

PORT WASHINGTON , NY
Mrs. Esti Paltiel
Chabad of Port Washington
516.767.8672
esti@chabadpw.org

POUGHKEEPSIE, NY
Mrs. Dalia Sanoff
Chabad on Fulton
845.214.6286
dalia@chabadonfulton.org

ROCHESTER, NY
Mrs. Chany Mochkin
Chabad Lubavitch of Rochester
585.981.0477
chanymo@yahoo.com

STONY BROOK, NY
Mrs. Chanie Cohen
Neshei Chabad Woman's Club
631.585.0521
chanie@chabadsb.com

STONY BROOK, NY
Mrs. Chaya Grossbaum
Chabad Stony Brook
631.585.0521
Chaya@ChabadSB.com

WOODBURY - SYOSSET, NY
Mrs. Rochel Leah Lipszyc
Town of Oyster Bay Chabad
917.655.0027
Rochelleah@jewishtob.org

SUFFERN, NY
Mrs. Devorah Gancz
Chabad Jewish Center of Suffern
845.368.1889
Devorah@JewishSuffern.com

SUFFERN, NY
Mrs. Esty Weber
NCFJE
443.418.4336
Estherweber7@gmail.com

YONKERS, NY
Mrs. Chanie Hurwitz
Chabad of Yonkers
718.679.3614
rabbi@jewishyonkers.com

BEACHWOOD, OH
Mrs. Rivky Gancz
Jewish Learning Institute
216.402.1328
Rivkyganсz@gmail.com

CINCINNATI, OH
Mrs. Chana Mangel
Chabad Jewish Center
513.793.5200
office@chabadba.com

COLUMBUS, OH
Mrs. Sarah Deitsch
Chabad at OSU
614.294.3296
osuchabad@gmail.com

DAYTON, OH
Mrs. Devorah Leah Mangel
Chabad of Greater Dayton
937.643.0770
chabad@chabaddayton.com

NEW ALBANY, OH
Mrs. Esther Kaltmann
Chabad of Columbus
614.610.4293
esther.kaltmann@sbcglobal.net

TOLEDO, OH
Mrs. Raizel Shemtov
Chabad of Toledo
419.270.3548
morahraizel@gmail.com

OKLAHOMA CITY, OK
Mrs. Nechoma Goldman
Chabad of Oklahoma City
405.286.0900
nechoma@jewishokc.com

HILLSBORO, OR
Mrs. Chaya Rivkin
Chabad of Hillsbro
503.747.5363
chaikyr@gmail.com

PORTLAND, OR
Mrs. Mimi Wilhelm
Chabad Lubavitch of Oregon
503.977.9830
chabador@hotmail.com

PORTLAND, OR
Mrs. Mushka Wilhelm
Chabad of Northeast Portland
971.402.9395
mushkawilhelm@gmail.com

SALEM, OR
Mrs. Fruma Perlstein
Chabad Jewish Center of Salem
503.383.9569
Fruma@chabadsalem.com

ALLENTOWN, PA
Mrs. Devorah Halperin
Chabad of the Lehigh Valley
610.351.6511
Rabbi@chabadlehighvalley.com

BROOMALL, PA
Mrs. Rikki Altein
Chabad of Delaware County
347.864.1693
rikkialtein@gmail.com

FORT WASHINGTON, PA
Mrs. Devorah L Deitsch
Lubavitch of Montgomery County
215.591.9310
devorah@jewishmc.com

LAFAYETTE HILL, PA
Mrs. Chaya Kotlarsky
Chabad of Lafayette Hill
484.681.1085
chayakotlarsky@gmail.com

MERION STATION, PA
Mrs. Michal Sherman
Chabad of the Main Line
610.660.9900
michal@chabadmainline.org

NEWTOWN, PA
Mrs. Rosie Weinstein
Lubavitch of Bucks County
215.497.9925
rosie@jewishcenter.info

PHILADELPHIA, PA
Mrs. Reuvena Grodnitzky
Chabad Young Philly
856.308.9930
rlgrod36@gmail.com

PHILADELPHIA, PA
Mrs. Shevy Lowenstein
Jewish Center Northern Liberties
610.203.0996
shevy.lowenstein@gmail.com

PITTSBURGH, PA
Mrs. Batya Rosenblum
Chabad of the South Hill
412.344.2424
batya812@gmail.com

PITTSBURGH, PA
Mrs. Chani Altein
Chabad of Pittsburgh
412.421.3561
jli@chabadpgh.com

PITTSBURGH, PA
Mrs. Chasi Rothstein
Chabad at Pitt
443.525.4212
chasirothstein@gmail.com

RYDAL, PA
Mrs. Dini Gurevitz
Chabad Lubavitch Jewish Center
267.536.5757
Dini@JewishAbington.com

STATE COLLEGE, PA
Mrs. Miri Gourarie
Chabad of the Undergrad
814.409.8130
mirigourarie@gmail.com

STATE COLLEGE, PA
Mrs. Sarah Meretsky
Chabad of Penn State
814.861.8063
sarahitameretsky@comcast.net

YARDLEY, PA
Mrs. Chaya Blecher
Lubavitch of Yardley
215.666.0698
rabbi@jewishyardley.com

CAROLINA, PR
Mrs. Rochi Zarchi
Chabad of Puerto Rico
787.501.4825
rachel@jewishpuertorico.com

COLUMBIA, SC
Mrs. Devorah Leah Marrus
The Chabad-Alef House
803.237.6084
devorahld@gmail.com

GREENVILLE, SC
Mrs. Musie Kesselman
Chabad of Greenville
864.256.1770
musie@chabadgreenville.com

MYRTLE BEACH, SC
Mrs. Leah Aizenman
Chabad of Myrtle Beach
843.448.0035
laizenman@gmail.com

KNOXVILLE, TN
Mrs. Miriam Esther Wilhelm
Chabad of Knoxville
865.588.8584
me@kjds.org

MEMPHIS, TN
Mrs. Rivky Klein
Chabad Lubavitch of Tennessee
901.754.0404
Rivky@JewishMemphis.com

NASHVILLE, TN
Mrs. Esther Tiechtel
Chabad of Nashville
615.646.5750
rabbi@chabadnashville.com

ARLINGTON, TX
Mrs. Risha Gurevitch
Chabad of Arlington
817.451.1171
rishi@arlingtonchabad.org

AUSTIN, TX
Mrs. Mussy Levertov
Chabad Young Professionals
512.905.2778
Mendyaustin@gmail.com

BELLAIRE, TX
Mrs. Esty Zaklikofsky
The Shul of Bellaire
713.484.9887
estyzak@gmail.com

DALLAS, TX
Mrs. Michal Shapiro
Chabad of Dallas
972.818.0770
moshenaparstek@gmail.com

DALLAS, TX
Mrs. Rivka Goldschmidt
Chabad of Dallas
972.818.0770
shikoon@aol.com

DALLAS, TX
Mrs. Yael Lewin
Maayan Chai
214.562.0807
yaellewin@yahoo.com

FORT WORTH, TX
Mrs. Chana Tovah Mandel
Chabad of Fort Worth
817.263.7701
Cgi@chabadfortworth.com

FRISCO, TX
Mrs. Mushkie Kesselman
Chabad of Frisco
214.460.7773
mushkiekesselman@gmail.com

HOUSTON, TX
Mrs. Shoshana Traxler
Chabad Lubavitch Outreach of Houston
713.774.0300
rabbi.traxler@ChabadOutreach.org

HOUSTON, TX
Mrs. Leah Marinovsky
Chabad Lubavitch
713.541.1774
leahfeige2@aim.com

HOUSTON, TX
Mrs. Rochel Lazaroff
Chabad at Rice
713.522.2004
Rochel@aishelhouse.org

MISSOURI CITY, TX
Mrs. Chaya Feigenson
Chabad of Sugar Land
832.758.0685
cbfeigenson@gmail.com

PLANO, TX
Mrs. Rivka Block
Chabad of Plano & Collin County
972.596.8270
connect@chabadplano.org

PLANO, TX
Mrs. Sara Block
Chabad at Legacy West
214.620.4083
chabadlw@gmail.com

S. ANTONIO, TX
Mrs. Rivkie Block
Chabad Lubavitch
210.492.1085
chabadsa@sbcglobal.net

SOUTHLAKE, TX
Mrs. Rishi Gurevitch
Chabad of Southlake
817.451.1171
rishi@arlingtonchabad.org

SALT LAKE CITY, UT
Mrs. Sheina Zippel
Chabad Lubavitch of Utah
801.414.3377
sheina@jewishutah.com

ARLINGTON, VA
Mrs. Yehudis Newman
Chabad Lubavitch of Alexandria-Arlington
703.820.2770
yehudisnewman@gmail.com

FAIRFAX, VA
Mrs. Nechamie Fajnland
Chabad Lubavitch of Northern Virginia
703.426.1980
nfajnland@yahoo.com

FAIRFAX, VA
Mrs. Raizel Deitch
Chabad of George Mason University
571.279.2587
raizelg@gmail.com

NORFOLK, VA
Mrs. Rashi Brashevitzky
Chabad of Tidewater
757.616.0770
Rabbilevi@chabadoftidewater.com

BURLINGTON, VT
Mrs. Draizy Junik
Chabad of Vermont
802.658.5770
chabad@chabadvt.org

BELLINGHAM, WA
Mrs. Noa-Miriam Truxton
Rohr Center for Jewish Life
360.393.3845
rabbi@jewishbellingham.com

ISSAQUAH, WA
Mrs. Nechama Farkash
Chabad of the Central Cascades
425.427.1654
nsfarkash@gmail.com

MERCER ISLAND, WA
Mrs. Devorah Kornfeld
Chabad of Mercer Island
206.679.9117
y-kornfeld2@yahoo.com

SEATTLE, WA
Mrs. Chana Levitin
Chabad of the Pacific Northwest
206.931.4100
chanielevitin@gmail.com

SPOKANE, WA
Mrs. Chaya Sarah Hahn
Chabad of Spokane
509.443.0770
rabbihahn@gmail.com

VANCOUVER, WA
Mrs. Tzivie Greenberg
Chabad Jewish Center
360.326.5923
info@jewishclarkcounty.com

BAYSIDE, WI
Mrs. Chava Edelman
The Shul Center
414.439.4041
Chava@chabadwi.org

KENOSHA, WI
Mrs. Rivkie Wilschanski
Chabad of Kenosha
262.359.0770
rabbitzali@jewishkenosha.com

MADISON, WI
Mrs. Henya Matusof
Rohr Chabad House at University of Wisconsin-Madison
608.257.1757
Info@jewishuwmadison.com

MEQUON, WI
Mrs. Dinie Rapoport
Center for Jewish Life
262.242.2235
dinie@chabadmequon.com

AUSTRALIA

SYDNEY, NSW
Mrs. Dina Koncepolski
Cremorne Synagogue
+61.4.1084.0009
rabbi@cremornessynagogue.com

SYDNEY, NSW
Mrs. Esther Feldman
Beis Menachem Chabad - Dover Heights Shule
+61.2.9731.8682
esterke_f@hotmail.com

SYDNEY, NSW
Mrs. Henya Milecki
South Head Synagogue
+61.4.2361.3770
henyam@me.com

SYDNEY, NSW
Mrs. Sara-Tova Yaffe
CBD Chabad
+61.4.2247.0655
saratova613@gmail.com

LAUNCESTON, TAS
Mrs. Rochel Gordon
Chabad of Tasmania
+61.363.449.129
rochel@chabadtas.com

CARNEGIE, VIC
Mrs. Mushky Raskin
Chabad Carnegie
+61.4.3369.5698
mushka@chabadcarnegie.com

ELSTERNWICK, VIC
Mrs. Dina Liberow
Hamerkaz
+61.4.1705.4171
dina@lamdeni.org

MELBOURNE, VIC
Mrs. Rivki Nathanson
Jewish Melbourne
+61.3.9636.3321
jewishmelbourne@gmail.com

MELBOURNE, VIC
Mrs. Sara Rosenfeld
Beis Chabad Ohel Devorah
+61.3.9525.9014
rivkah.groner@gmail.com

AUSTRIA

VIENNA
Mrs. Sivan Boas
Chabad of Döbling
+43.67.683.181.700
boas.sivan@gmail.com

BELGIUM

ANTWERPEN
Mrs. Debbie Rabenou
JLI Antwerp
+32.4.7770.0538
debbie@rabenou.com

BRUSSELS
Mrs. Nehama Tawil
EJCC
+32.2.231.1770
ntawil@ejcc.eu

BRUSSELS
Mrs. Shulamit Pinson
Chabad of Brussels
+32.47.621.7445
shulamitpinson@gmail.com

EDEGEM, ANTWERPEN
Mrs. Chaya Hertz
Chai Center
+32.3.288.7970
chajah@gmail.com

BRAZIL

MANAUS
Mrs. Dvorah Lea Raichman
Chabad-Lubavitch of Manaus
+55.92.3088.3302
Zagudeby@hotmail.com

S. PAULO
Mrs. Rivka Rosenfeld
Sinagoga Beit Menachem
+55.11.3816.6216
rivkyrosenfeld@hotmail.com

S. PAULO
Mrs. Sarah Steinmetz
Beit Chabad Central
+55.11.3081.3081
sarah.a.steinmetz@gmail.com

CANADA

RICHMOND, BC
Mrs. Chanie Baitelman
Chabad of Richmond
604.277.6427
admin@chabadrichmond.com

VANCOUVER, BC
Mrs. Chaya Rosenfeld
Lubavitch of British Columbia
604.266.1313
esti@lubavitchbc.com

VANCOUVER, BC
Mrs. Malky Bitton
Chabad of Downtown
778.688.1273
malky@chabadcitycentre.com

WINNIPEG, MB
Mrs. Adina Altein
Chabad-Lubavitch of Winnipeg
204.339.8737
adina@chabadwinnipeg.org

S. JOHNS, NL
Mrs. Tuba Chernitsky
Chabad of Newfoundland
709.341.8770
tubes770@gmail.com

HAMILTON, ON
Mrs. Shaina Rosenfeld
Chabad Lubavitch Hamilton
905.529.7458
shaina@chabadhamilton.com

KINGSTON, ON
Mrs. Esti Simon
Chabad Student Centre of Kingston
613.877.9880
estisimon@gmail.com

LONDON, ON
Mrs. Basie Gurkow
Congregation Beth Tefilah
226.234.5022
bgurkow@gmail.com

MAPLE, ON
Mrs. Toby Bernstein
Chabad Romano Centre
905.303.1880
chabad@chabadrc.org

OTTAWA, ON
Mrs. Devora Caytak
Jewish Youth Library of Ottawa
613.729.1619
Dev18@sympatico.ca

S. CATHARINES, ON
Mrs. Perla Zaltzman
Chabad at Brock
905.401.6281
perla@Jewishniagara.com

THORNHILL, ON
Mrs. Chanah Leah Beckerman
Chabad at York
905.771.6359
bekermans@gmail.com

THORNHILL, ON
Mrs. Chanie Hildeshaim
Chabad Russian Center of Thornhill Woods
905.326.9258
chanie@jewishthornhillwoods.org

THORNHILL, ON
Mrs. Faygie Kaplan
Chabad @ Flamingo
905.763.4040
faygie@chabadflamingo.com

THORNHILL, ON
Mrs. Goldie Plotkin
Chabad Lubavitch of Markham
905.886.0420
rabbi@chabadmarkham.org

TORONTO, ON
Bais Chomesh High School
416.631.0585
baischomesh@gmail.com

TORONTO, ON
Mrs. Chana Gansburg
Chabad on the Avenue
416.546.8770
chana@chabadavenue.com

TORONTO, ON
Mrs. Chanie Zaltzman
JRCC of East Thornhill
416.222.7812
Chanie.zaltzman@jrcc.org

TORONTO, ON
Mrs. Mushky Blau
JRCC South Thornhill
647.709.5770
Mushka.Blau@jrcc.org

TORONTO, ON
Mrs. Nechama Dina Jacobson
JRCC West Thornhill
416.902.9254
ndjacobson@rogers.com

TORONTO, ON
Mrs. Rivka Gansburg
Chabad on Bayview
416.551.9391
rivky@chabadbayview.com

TORONTO, ON
Mrs. Yehudis Steiner
Uptown Chabad
416.635.9696
yehudissteiner@gmail.com

WATERLOO, ON
Mrs. Rivky Goldman
Chabad Lubavitch of the Waterloo Region
519.725.4289
rivky@jewishwaterloo.com

WHITBY, ON
Mrs. Chana Borenstein
Chabad Jewish Centre of Durham Region
905.493.9007
info@jewishdurham.com

CÔTE S.-LUC, QC
Mrs. Chaya Naparstek
Beth Chabad CSL
438.409.6770
sos@chabadcsl.com

LASALLE, QC
Mrs. Chanie Brand
Chabad LaSalle
514.889.8565
chanieb@gmail.com

MONTREAL, QC
Mrs. Chanie Gansbourg
Chabad of Old Montreal
514.800.6966
Chanie@chabadoldmontreal.com

MONTREAL, QC
Mrs. Rashi Weiss
Chabad Student Centre
514.845.4443
rashi@chabadmcgill.com

MONTREAL, QC
Mrs. Simcha Fine
Chabad Zichron Kedoshim
514.738.3434
simchafine@gmail.com

MONTREAL, QC
Mrs. Shaina Markowitz
The Family Store Young Leadership
514.928.7770
getzy@themtc.com

MONTREAL, QC
Mrs. Zeldie Treitel
Montreal Torah Center
514.739.0770
zeldie@themtc.com

MONTREAL WEST, QC
Mrs. Chaya Marlow
Chabad Westminster
514.746.9649
chayamarlow@gmail.com

VILLE S.-LAURENT, QC
Mrs. Leah Silberstein
Chabad VsL & Bois Franc
514.747.1199
leah@chabadvsl.com

SASKATOON, SK
Mrs. Sarah Kats
Chabad Lubavitch of Saskatoon
306.384.4370
sarahkats770@gmail.com

CAYMAN ISLANDS

GRAND CAYMAN
Mrs. Rikal Pewzner
Chabad Cayman
717.798.1040
rikal@jewishcayman.com

CHINA

PUDONG
Mrs. Nechama Greenberg
Chabad of Pudong
+86.21.1780.0791
nechamieg@gmail.com

DENMARK

COPENHAGEN
Mrs. Rochel Loewenthal
ChabaDanmark
+45.3316.1850
Info@chabad.dk

FRANCE

ANNEMASSE-AMBILLY
Mrs. Rahel Szmul
Habad Annemasse
+336.59.44.70.10
rachel.info770@gmail.com

ANTIBES JUAN-LES-PINS
Mrs. Hanna Sebag
Habad Loubavitch d'Antibes Juan-les-Pins
+336.37.72.14.18
habadantibes@gmail.com

ARCUEIL
Mrs. Haya Goldberg
Beth Loubavitch d'Arcueil
+336.95.39.84.55
haya.mouchka@gmail.com

ATHIS-MONS
Mrs. Hanna Journo
Beth Habad Athis Mons
+336.36.98.20.61
hannajourno@gmail.com

AUBERVILLIERS
Mrs. Rivky Belinow
Beth Habad S. Denis
+336.09.49.23.87
rivky-belinow@hotmail.fr

BOBIGNY
Mrs. Hinda Esther Teichtal
Beth Habad Bobigny
+336.52.07.36.36
hindouche14@gmail.com

BOIS-COLOMBES
Mrs. Hanna Gershovitz
Beth Loubavitch Bois-Colombes
+336.30.46.94.05
sgershovitz@gmail.com

BOULOGNE
Mrs. Deborah Sojcher
Beth Habad De Boulogne
+336.20.440.763
debosoj@hotmail.fr

BORDEAUX
Mrs. Rachel Cohen
Beth habad
+336.60.494.994
celrac770@hotmail.com

BRY SUR MARNE
Mrs. Rahel Rotsztein
Beth Habad Bry sur Marne
+336.29.173.452
rahelsamama@gmail.com

CANNES
Mrs. Mushka Matusof
Habad Cannes
+336.79.22.58.36
hmmatusof@gmail.com

CERGY-PONTOISE
Mrs. Nehama Dawidowicz
Beth Loubavitch de Cergy Pontoise, S. Ouen L'aumône
+336.95.06.04.64
nehama770@hotmail.com

DRANCY
Mrs. Mushka Nisilevitch
Habad de drancy
+336.58.836.095
Mushkanis8@gmail.com

ECOLE SINAI
Mrs. Haya Piekarski
Ecole Sinaï
+336.51.501.787
mukelep@gmail.com

GRENOBLE
Mrs. Dina Attal
Beth Habad Grenoble
+337.81.45.75.99
cteen38@gmail.com

JOINVILLE
Mrs. Yordana Moaty
Loubavitch Joinville
+336.21.69.65.04
yordana53@hotmail.com

LA GARENNE COLOMBES
Mrs. Moussia Taieb
+337.69.77.20.85
moussiataieb@gmail.com

LA VARENNE S. HILAIRE
Mrs. Haya Benelbaz
Beth Habad La Varenne S. Hilaire
+336.28.53.53.17
mbenelbaz@gmail.com

LEVALLOIS
Mrs. Shterna Azoulay El Baze
Beth Habad ACJL
+336.02.237.647
bhacjl@gmail.com

LYON
Mrs. Aida Nemanow
Beth Habad
+336.06.536.763
anemanow@gmail.com

LYON
Mrs. Devorah Gurewitz
Beth Habad Centre Ville
+336.14.52.27.03
dl.gurewitz@gmail.com

MARSEILLE
Mrs. Mouchka Assouline
Habad 9 sud
+336.03.226.840
hayasseraf@gmail.com

MARSEILLE 5ÈME
Mrs. Sarah Bard
Beth Habad Marseille 5ème
+336.20.32.71.52
habadmarseille5@gmail.com

MARSEILLE 8ÈME
Mrs. Rivka Altabé
Beth Habad Marseille 8ème
+336.25.47.37.66
vivialtabe@gmail.com

NICE
Mrs. Dvora Nidam
Habad Loubavitch Nice Côte d'Azur
+336.13.12.89.88
adnidam@gmail.com

PANTIN
Mrs. Rivka Balouka
Beth Loubavitch Pantin
+336.13.32.55.49
activiteblp@gmail.com

PARIS 7ÈME
Mrs. Sarah Mergui
Beth Loubavitch Paris 7ème
+336.27.47.34.45
yymergui@gmail.com

PARIS 9ÈME
Mrs. Cheina Asseraf
Beth Loubavitch Paris 9ème
+336.03.36.35.86
cheina@asseraf.net

PARIS 11ÈME
Mrs. Beila Arnauve
Chabad Bastille
+336.50.025.955
glitsit@gmail.com

PARIS 17ÈME
Mrs. Haya Elbaz
Habad Loubavitch Batignolles–DCJB
+336.50.07.01.40
yacovielbaz@gmail.com

PARIS LUCO
Mrs. Yeoudith Apelbaum
Jeunesse loubavitch du Luco
+336.65.515.338
yudnis@gmail.com

PARIS BERCY 13
Mrs. Mushky Lachkar
Habad Bercy 13
+33.6.63.025.430
mushky92@gmail.com

PARIS 18
Mrs. Noemie Touboul
Bêth Loubavitch 18 e
+336.69.37.90.83
naomitouboul@gmail.com

SINAI, PARIS 17
Mrs. Chani Pevzner
Sinai, Paris 17
+336.99.64.07.70
abp770@gmail.com

PARIS 19N
Mrs. Dvorah Ouaki
Beth Loubavitch Paris 19N
+337.53.610.585
israelouaki@loubavitch.fr

PAU
Mrs. Shayna Matusof
Habad des Pyrenees-Atlantiques
+33.6.22.107.549
habadpyrenees@gmail.com

PERPIGNAN
Mrs. Rachel Pevzner
Loubavitch Pyré-Terranée
+334.68.50.54.86
rdpevzner@gmail.com

PIERREFITTE-SUR-SEINE
Mrs. Hanna Lumbroso
Aip
+336.25.498.945
Lumbrosobenjamin@gmail.com

S. MAURICE
Mrs. Myriam Basange
Beth Habad S.Maurice Plateau
+336.44.880.752
mio770@gmail.com

SEVRES
Mrs. Rahel Fraenkel
Beth Habad sevres
+336.13.497.279
rfraenkel@hotmail.com

STRASBOURG
Mrs. Tehila Samama
Beth Habad Strasbourg
+336.64.86.99.20
tehilasamama@gmail.com

TOULON
Mrs. Dvora Bitton
Chabad Toulon
+336.68.647.901
Leam770@hotmail.com

VILLENEUVE LOUBET
Mrs. Venezia Barbiera
Beth Habad Villeneuve Loubet
+337.69.69.38.65
ven.houri@gmail.com

VILLEURBANNE
Mrs. Rahel Zekri
Beth Habad Charpennes
+336.24.068.868
Rahel.770@hotmail.fr

GUATEMALA

GUATEMALA CITY
Mrs. Yael Pelman
Chabad of Guatemala
718.504.7344
yaell@hotmail.com

INDIA

MUMBAI
Mrs. Chaya Kozlovsky
Chabad of India
+9188.79.73.39.29
chayber88@gmail.com

ISRAEL

BAT YAM
Mrs. Rachel Meimoun
Chabad Francophone Bat Yam
+972.58.600.8980
Rahel.batyam@gmail.com

JERUSALEM
Mrs. Chana Canterman
Chabad Center of Talbiya
+972.54.682.3737
chabadtalbiya@gmail.com

TZFAT
Mrs. Chaya Bracha Leiter
Ascent
+972.52.677.0142
cb@ascent.co.il

ITALY

FIRENZE
Mrs. Sonia Wolvovsky
Chabad of Tuscany
+39.38.9595.2034
jewishtuscany@gmail.com

MEXICO

CANCUN
Mrs. Rachel Druk
Chabad of Cancun
718.362.5444
racheldruk@gmail.com

S. MIGUEL DE ALLENDE
Mrs. Raizel Huebner
Chabad of SMA
+52.425.181.8091
raizel@chabadsma.com

NIGERIA

ABUJA
Mrs. Mazal Sternbach
Chabad Nigeria
234.81.6651.7796
mazal@Chabadaid.org

PERU

LIMA
Mrs. Sara Blumenfeld
Chabad Peru
+51.987.648.916
jabadperu@gmail.com

PORTUGAL

LISBON
Mrs. Raizel Rosenfeld
Chabad Lubavitch of Portugal
+35.191.034.5639
raizel@chabadportugal.com

RUSSIAN FEDERATION

MOSCOW
Mrs. Rivky Wilansky
Chabad of Moscow
+7.495.645.5000
doamitzvah@gmail.com

SOUTH AFRICA

JOHANNESBURG
Mrs. Ita Hazdan
Johannesburg Torah Institute
+27.84.344.2684
info@thejti.org

SEA POINT, CAPE TOWN
Mrs. Avigail Popack
Chabad Center of Cape Town
+27.21.434.3740
avipopack@gmail.com

SWEDEN

MALMÖ
Mrs. Reizel Kesselman
Chabad Malmo
+46737088446
chabadmalmo@gmail.com

SWITZERLAND

LUGANO
Mrs. Yuti Kantor
Chabad Lugano
+41.91.921.3720
Yuti@jewishlugano.com

LUZERN
Mrs. Rivky Drukman
Chabad of Central Switzerland
+41.41.361.1770
Info@ChabadLuzern.com

UNITED KINGDOM

BIRMINGHAM, ENGLAND
Mrs. Rivky Cheruff
Chabad on Campus Birmingham
+44.78.0509.2236
dercheruff@gmail.com

BUCKHURST HILL, ESSEX, ENGLAND
Mrs. Henny Brandman
Chabad Buckhurst Hill
+44.20.8926.2376
Henny@chabadonthehill.co.uk

EDGWARE, MIDDX., ENGLAND
Mrs. Sarah Jacobs
Lubavitch of Edgware
+44.20.8905.4141
sarahjacobs@loe.org.uk

EDGWARE, MIDDX., ENGLAND
Mrs. Shterna Sudak
Lubavitch Foundation
+44.20.8800.0022
Shternasudak@yahoo.com

ILFORD, ESSEX, ENGLAND
Mrs. Devorah Sufrin
Chabad Lubavitch Centres Essex
+44.20.8554.1624
mrssufrin@chabadilford.co.uk

LEEDS, ENGLAND
Mrs. Dabrushy Pink
Chabad Lubavitch of Leeds
+44.11.3266.3311
jwc@judaismlive.com

LONDON, ENGLAND
Mrs. Chai Cohen
Chabad St. John's Wood
+44.77.7261.2661
cohenchai@gmail.com

LONDON, ENGLAND
Mrs. Sara Carlebach
Chabad of Greenwich and Docklands
+44.74.7225.5283
sara@jewishdocklands.com

LONDON, ENGLAND
Mrs. Rahel Davidoff
Chabad Francophone Maida Vale
+44.79.6620.7938
raheldavidoff@gmail.com

LONDON, ENGLAND
Mrs. Sarah Dubov
Chabad of South London
+44.7985.757.517
sarahdubov@gmail.com

LONDON, ENGLAND
Mrs. Devora Lew
Chabad of Bloomsbury - Central London
+44.20.7060.9770
info@bloomsburychabad.org

LONDON, ENGLAND
Mrs. Chanie Simon
Chabad of Golders Green
+44.20.8458.0416
office@chabadgg.com

LONDON, ENGLAND
Mrs. Devorah Leah Weisz
Chabad of Hampstead Village
+44.79.7652.2807
Shulinhampstead@gmail.com

LONDON, ENGLAND
Mrs. Hadasa Korer
Chabad Lubavitch of Islington
+44.20.7688.0169
mkorer@gmail.com

LONDON, ENGLAND
Mrs. Kezi Levin
Brondesbury Park Synagogue
+44.20.8451.0091
kezi@bark.org

LONDON, ENGLAND
Mrs. Roizy Gancz
Chabad of Finchley
+44.20.3719.2231
roizygancz@gmail.com

LONDON, ENGLAND
Mrs. Shira Lebhar
Chabad of West Hampstead
+44.78.6874.1235
shiramail2@gmail.com

MANCHESTER, ENGLAND
Mrs. Shaina Cohen
Lchaim Chabad Manchester
+44.16.1792.6335
Shaina@Lchaim.org.uk

SHEFFIELD, ENGLAND
Mrs. Faiga Rochel Golomb
Chabad of Sheffield
+44.11.4281.7459
rabbijgolomb@blueyonder.co.uk

WESTMINSTER, LONDON, ENGLAND
Mrs. Chana Kalmenson
Chabad of Belgravia
+44.75.8592.0195
jewishbelgravia@gmail.com

URUGUAY

MONTEVIDEO
Mrs. Musya Shemtov
Beit Jabad Uruguay
+598.2709.3444
rmusyashemtov@gmail.com

VENEZUELA

CARACAS
Mrs. Chani Rosenblum
Hogar Jabad Lubavitch
+58.212.264.7011
chaniros1@gmail.com

The Jewish Learning Multiplex

Brought to you by the Rohr Jewish Learning Institute

In fulfillment of the mandate of the Lubavitcher Rebbe, of blessed memory, whose leadership guides every step of our work, the mission of the Rohr Jewish Learning Institute is to transform Jewish life and the greater community through the study of Torah, connecting each Jew to our shared heritage of Jewish learning.

While our flagship program remains the cornerstone of our organization, JLI is proud to feature additional divisions catering to specific populations, in order to meet a wide array of educational needs.

THE ROHR JEWISH LEARNING INSTITUTE

A subsidiary of Merkos L'Inyonei Chinuch,
the adult education arm of the Chabad-Lubavitch movement

Torah Studies provides a rich and nuanced encounter with the weekly Torah reading.

Jewish teens forge their identity as they engage in Torah study, social interaction, and serious fun.

The Rosh Chodesh Society gathers Jewish women together once a month for intensive textual study.

TorahCafe.com provides an exclusive selection of top-rated Jewish educational videos.

Participants delve into our nation's past while exploring the Holy Land's relevance and meaning today.

This yearly event rejuvenates mind, body, and spirit with a powerful synthesis of Jewish learning and community.

Equips youth-facing adults with education and resources to address youth mental health.

Select affiliates are invited to partner with peers and noted professionals, as leaders of innovation and excellence.

MyShiur courses are designed to assist students in developing the skills needed to study Talmud independently.

This rigorous fellowship program invites select college students to explore the fundamentals of Judaism.

A crash course that teaches adults to read Hebrew in just five sessions.

Machon Shmuel is an institute providing Torah research in the service of educators worldwide.

NOTES

NOTES

NOTES

NOTES

NOTES

NOTES

NOTES

NOTES